P9-CBZ-965

SPICES & SEASONS

SPICES & SEASONS
Simple, Sustainable Indian Flavors

Rinku Bhattacharya

foreword by Suvir Saran

LIBRARY
NSCC, AKERLEY CAMPUS
21 WOODLAWN RD.
DARTMOUTH, NS B2W 2R7 CANADA

Hippocrene Books, Inc.
New York

Also by Rinku Bhattacharya:

The Bengali Five Spice Chronicles

☞

Copyright © 2014 Rinku Bhattacharya.

All rights reserved.

Color photographs by Rinku Bhattacharya.
Book and jacket design by Brittany Hince and K & P Publishing.

For more information, address:
HIPPOCRENE BOOKS, INC.
171 Madison Avenue
New York, NY 10016
www.hippocrenebooks.com

Library of Congress Cataloging-in-Publication Data

Bhattacharya, Rinku, author.
 Spices & seasons : simple, sustainable Indian home flavors / by Rinku Bhattacharya.
     pages cm
 Includes index.
 ISBN 978-0-7818-1331-0 (hardcover) -- ISBN 0-7818-1331-X (hardcover)
 1. Cooking, India. 2. Spices. I. Title. II. Title: Spices and seasons.
 TX724.5.I4B4994 2014
 641.6'383--dc23

                                        2014001640

Printed in the United States of America.

Dedicated to the people who add spice to the seasons of my life

My big boy – Khokon

My daughter – Deepta

My little boy – Aadi

Contents

Foreword by Suvir Saran

"This is indeed India . . . the cradle of the human race, the birthplace of human speech, the mother of history, the grandmother of legend, and the great grandmother of tradition . . . Our most valuable and most instructive materials in the history of man are treasured up in India only."
—Mark Twain

Twain's words are never far from my mind as I live my life as a resident of the USA. What this beloved son of America saw in India is what I grew up taking for granted: India can inform and educate, delight and comfort, and provide hope. In Rinku Bhattacharya, I found a great salesman for India. A scholar, really. A voice calm and strong, yet pure and comforting. Her words are chosen with care, and recipes created with respect for her homeland and her adopted land. The flavors are at once bright and addictive, and never too far from being practical and doable. Rinku and I met on Facebook, but it was our mutual love for the simple and pure that solidified our friendship. In Rinku I found a kindred spirit who seeks to share and teach, learn and grow, give and take, but most of all, always be present and observant.

Rinku's goal is to help readers understand the essentials of cooking with Indian spices, whilst still maintaining a sense of simplicity and a sustainable approach to life. She beautifully combines the time-tested traditions of the Indian kitchen with a practical, modern approach to educate those of us ready to cook alongside her. The instructions are easy, and the ingredients just as easy to find online or with a visit to a spice market. We are left with no excuses for not cooking food that is as delicious and fresh as possible.

Almost anyone who has grown up in India can attest to the natural affinity of spices and seasons. Indian cuisine seems rather modern when one realizes the masterful way in which ingredients are celebrated and paired together. Poverty can be the mother of invention and this is quite true in the Indian context. Nowhere does the notion of "less is more" shine with greater joy than in the world of Indian cuisine. With a few ingredients, humble spices and inexpensive aromatics—and of course the will to cook and share—your creations take on the aura of a meal with pageantry. If you feel pressed for time, if you are hurting from the economic downturn and you want delicious meals without a significant tear in your wallet, look no further. These recipes will bring the timeless wisdom of India to your own kitchen repertoire.

Rinku's recipes speak of a global village where nuances come together in a mosaic that is exceptional and vibrant when looked at as a whole. There is no identity crisis in this book. One can find recipes to suit all tastes and personalities. Recipes run the gamut from celebratory to everyday and from vegetarian to meat-based. You will look at the plant-based diet with new respect. If you are like me, you already know that vegetables can give you all the protein you need and then some. But if you ever doubted that, cook from these pages and you will find yourself enjoying new dishes that are delicious, comforting, and nutritionally sound.

From India one can learn the essence of living with full attention given to the moment. In the moment, India shines, captivates, and seduces. Even as their land was pillaged and plundered, Indians were busy fusing what was being brought in by the invaders and marrying it to their own traditions. The spirit of India is one of resilience and sustainability. India has seized opportunities and influences and in turn refashioned them into new inventions that seem classic and time-tested. This is also true for the recipes in this book— they are new yet connected to an ancient past. With Rinku as your guide, new dishes will seem exciting and exotic, but never too strange, tedious, or challenging. Such is the comfort that comes when cooking with a connection to the past and with respect for the future. Nothing more sustainable exists in the world of cooking and entertaining.

Having now met Rinku, her husband, and two kids, I am not surprised to discover a family that is living what it means to be one with the seasons, flavors, spices, foods, and habits that make for a sustainable today and a sustained tomorrow. A tomorrow we will be able to share with loved ones only if we are attuned to all that is expected of us today. Rinku and her family plant their garden early on in spring to ensure the season is sustained through logical planning and plantings. They eat from the garden all summer long and into the fall. While her husband Anshul gardens and gathers, Rinku cooks and creates.

In India we often say that what grows together should be savored together, and luckily these pages give us many opportunities to celebrate that age-old dictate. These recipes and stories take you to a place where seasons, spices, flavors, conversations, mindfulness, and magic all walk side by side.

Suvir Saran
Chef, Speaker, Educator, Hobby Farmer
Author of "Indian Home Cooking" and "Masala Farm"
www.suvir.com

Introduction

"Spring passes and one remembers one's innocence.
Summer passes and one remembers one's exuberance.
Autumn passes and one remembers one's reverence.
Winter passes and one remembers one's perseverance."
—Yoko Ono

The backdrop for this book is a fast-paced household with two energetic children, a foodie cat, an avid gardener, and an enthusiastic cook. In case you have not guessed, I am the cook and my husband is the gardener. My family also includes my daughter, age 10, and my son, age 8, both children at an interesting stage where they love to experiment with food and absorb the wonders of nature. I cannot exclude my cat from this equation, since Benji does his share of digging and scaring the raccoons in the garden, and of sampling certain food appropriately.

It is to ensure that my children do not get short-changed good nutrition in the busy and fast-paced daily grind that I take the time to cook healthy, nutritious food on most days of the week. Living away from India, the country of my birth, there are new traditions learned and old traditions retained, but the Indian home flavors that nurtured me continue to nurture my household. The act of cooking itself carries tradition and history from one generation to the next. Like me, my daughter loves to smell the cumin toasting, listen to the mustard seeds crackling in oil, and delight in the amazing fragrance of tiny cardamom seeds when they are freshly shelled from their sage green pods.

In this book, I've sought to marry the spices of my childhood with the four seasons of my New York kitchen to offer you a collection of recipes that are comforting, accessible, and well-loved in my home.

I am convinced that in order to get children to make healthy dining choices and lead a life of consciousness, it is essential to include them in sourcing and cooking the food. Simple things like taking a trip to a local farmers market, watching a cooking demonstration together, and even just having them sit around while you cook—all form a part of this connection for them. Connecting with the seasons of the year and developing a consciousness of the environment has been very educational for my young children. They see the benefits of composting and watch the bees and butterflies at work in their natural environment. The best part is that cooking together helps us connect around an everyday activity that is needed to keep the household churning. It is not very different from my own childhood, where I sat with my grandmother in her kitchen listening to both kitchen lore and folk lore, learning and understanding the connection between nature, nurture, and food.

I often refer to our tiny suburban backyard as the "little backyard that could," since this small plot of land offers us delight and self-sufficiency for over seven months of the year. It helps us reduce our food footprint just a little bit and it has taught me that you do not have to move into the wilderness to stay in touch with nature. I am not suggesting that everyone start growing their own produce (although I promise you that it is a very engaging process), but I do encourage you to get a little closer to the source of your food so you will taste and feel the difference. Here and there throughout the book I have thrown in "green tips" that I hope you will find useful and motivating.

My approach to a sustainable lifestyle is practical and flexible. I feel that it really is the little drops that make an ocean. I am blessed to have a home in Hudson Valley, a beautiful part of New York State, where we enjoy the bounty and beauty of each of the four seasons, with several artisan products, such as fruit wines and an abundance of cheese and dairy, all made close to home by our local farmers. This allows me to introduce local American accents to traditional, seasonal Indian cooking. I have also been afforded the opportunity to travel extensively since my childhood, so some of the best of the global flavors I have enjoyed make their way into my recipes as well.

Compared to some proponents of sustainability, I might be almost lax. I tend to eat fish and some meat in moderate proportions. I feel that this is part of conscious sustainability, since during the winter months the diversity of produce is limited and needs supplementation from non-plant sources. Since I cook Indian and Indian-inspired dishes, my pantry is not strictly local because some of our spices are sourced internationally. And I forgive myself if I forget my reusable bags in the grocery store and remind myself to do a better job next time. I think it is important not to let cooking lose its spontaneous quality. If I see a new ingredient in the market, such as an unknown fruit or vegetable, I would rather satisfy my curiosity and bring it home rather than obsess over whether it is organic, even though I do usually try to stick to organic or garden fresh options. Even a small degree of consciousness goes a long way towards a simple and greener lifestyle.

In *Spices & Seasons* I want to introduce you to the cooking of today's India—a cuisine that is innovative, inspired, and full of possibilities. Built on tradition and embellished with global influences, modern Indian cuisine is nutritious, simple, and seasonal, with a commitment to sustainability. Sometimes the notion of natural ingredients and homegrown vegetables can conjure images of hours of leisurely cooking. While there is certainly a place for that, rest assured that on most days my recipes are for busy people on the go. It is not about fuss or gimmicks but rather about fresh and well-seasoned simplicity.

I use short cuts and practical tools such as the pressure cooker and the slow cooker when appropriate. The slow cooker is essential to me on weekends as I tend to run around doing errands. But in a world where we have realized that good food is important for good health, I encourage a core return to the basics of simple and unprocessed foods. An investment of forty-five minutes in the kitchen can be worth its weight in gold for your future health.

Mainstream Indian restaurant fare here in America might have fostered the idea that Indian food is about hours of constant cooking and loads of chilies and dollops of cream. In truth, however, Indian cooking is more about flavors, freshness, and love. My grandmother's favorite adage sums it up: "When the flour is freshly milled and the ghee is pure, it is impossible for the *parathas* (flatbreads) to turn out bad."

In India, markets with the daily catch of fresh fish and seasonal vegetables are the norm rather than a novelty. Close your eyes and picture the bustling markets in India, a landscape where fresh spices are bought in small quantities and daily produce is dependent on the season and weather. A wet summer often means more greens, but a hot dry summer offers you vegetables like tomatoes and peppers in abundance. Smell the fragrant green limes and bask in the flowery scent of cilantro. When my mind travels back to India, I visualize the produce offerings in sync

Photo by Kenneth Marion

Green Tip: The journey to fresh produce often starts with small steps. I like to suggest growing your own herbs as the first step. Cilantro and mint, the two most-often used herbs in Indian cooking, are easy to grow in small pots. Growing your own reduces packaging (notably plastic clamshells) and saves money. And don't forget convenience—an herb garden puts fresh flavor at your fingertips!

with the time of the year—in winter, reddish-pink carrots, sweet white radishes, and fresh date palm jaggery nudged by delicate heads of snowy white cauliflower; in summer and early autumn, tender greens and squash with heady, sensuous mangoes; in autumn, fragrant juicy pomegranates; and in spring, tender turnips and lighter fruits.

The seasons also bring with them festivals and holidays, and the Indian table naturally reflects a culinary heritage deeply influenced by celebrations. India's diverse cultural and religious heritage allows us to enjoy a wide variety of festive holidays that find their way into the culinary landscape—celebrations of harvest, monsoons, summer, and autumn intersperse with religious festivals across the year. The seasons here in New York are different in some ways but still full of promise, variety, and bounty. I feel that it defeats the purpose to try to search for Indian produce grown miles away rather than adapt local bounty for Indian uses. It is also one of the reasons that I have not organized the recipes in this book by the seasons. I know that certain items are available in different parts of the world at different times of the year, and I do not want the order of the recipes to limit the possibilities of the book.

I am thrilled to see the popularity of farmers markets in the United States these days. I have always loved picking up vegetables, eggs, free-range chicken, and artisan breads at the market, sometimes along with a quick breakfast. I have to confess, however, on some Sundays after a busy week of work, getting up early to get to the market can be a challenge. To insulate myself against such days, I've taken the easy way out—I married a talented gardener who tends to our small backyard with care and attention, often surprising me with colorful and prolific produce.

And patterned after my own union, I've learned how to marry spices with the bounty of the garden to create simple, delicious Indian meals. Once you taste the difference between a fresh, tender autumn carrot from the garden and one that is procured commercially any time of the year, you will learn the value of cooking with the seasons. To this end, I cook with the everyday red radish rather than hunting for the harder to find daikon varieties, and prefer seasonal everyday greens and zucchini instead of imported opo squash. But we do have some fun growing ornamental varieties of vegetables, such as purple kohlrabi and red okra that add color and delight for the children in a natural way.

This recipe collection will bring you several rewards, but at the top of the list is the assurance of happy, well-fed friends and family. My goal is to help you understand the essentials of Indian spices and incorporate them into the fabric of a busy lifestyle in a simple, sustainable manner. My recipes have been teased out until they've reached their simplest variation. They are recipes for people who want to do something different with Brussels sprouts; or who want to find ways to include kale or radish greens into their diet; and for those looking for quick, flavorful methods to cook fish and meat as well. This collection of recipes captures the essence of Indian cooking in a simplified manner.

I began "playing" around in the kitchen fairly early in life, but did not necessarily make a lot of time for practical cooking. After graduate school, when I began working long days, I missed the simple pleasure of a home-cooked meal. While New York City provided me with a bountiful culinary landscape, I missed good home-made Indian food—simple wholesome flavors, bursting with the natural goodness of fresh ingredients. Unfortunately most Indian takeout was loaded with an unhealthy amount of cream and butter and did not taste anything like the food that I was missing.

I eventually realized that if I wanted home-cooked food, I needed to start cooking it myself! My culinary muses are my mother and grandmothers, who have over the years inspired my cooking through many anecdotes, meals, and lessons. From my paternal grandmother (who had a fairly large garden), I learned that fresh produce does not need much to make it shine. As she would say, "Cooking is all about love and common sense." After considerable time dabbling with both seasonings and seasonal produce, I learned unequivocally that "fresh" is more, and settled towards a minimalist approach to using spices.

To understand spices and how they are essential to the preparation of a flavorful, nuanced meal, think of them like the colors in an artist's paint box. I think we underestimate the importance of successfully matching and pairing spices. Along with spice guides, throughout this book you'll find additional guides for cooking legumes and lentils using your pressure cooker, and various other tips and tricks, like creating an addictive finger food from kale; combining quinoa and lentils to make a deceptively rich-tasting hearty one-dish meal; and turning Brussels sprouts into a delectable topping for homemade pizza.

A lot of people who enjoy my cooking are like me—busy working parents trying to put a good meal on the table for their families with a limited amount of time. Several of my recipes have emerged to cope with what I call "the 6:30 p.m. struggle," when you want to serve a nutritious, sustainable, appealing meal but are short on time. The uniqueness of Indian cuisine lies in its ability to adapt and evolve. Cooking is essentially creating a work of art, and some masterpieces are smaller than others, in the same way some meals are quicker and simpler than others. These meals can still be natural and spontaneous in their compact creation. *Spices*

& Seasons strives to dispel the notion that you can't make good Indian food at home as an everyday meal. I am occasionally asked whether my cooking is truly traditional. I think it is probably as traditional as any complex and evolving cuisine and culture can be.

I do not usually time my cooking, so while a lot of these recipes fall into the magic "30 minutes or less" category, I request that you do not get stuck on this mantra. Good food, much like the proverbial watched pot, takes time, and those extra ten minutes is sometimes the difference between good food and great food. Nonetheless these recipes are created by a working mother of two young children, who bring to our lives all the hustle and bustle of school, sports, and musical activities. My recipes are practical, not very lengthy, and fit into a busy lifestyle.

Indian cuisine is inherently very flexible and accommodates a lot of dietary restrictions, mostly due to the fact that the Indian table is all about balance. This is not a strictly vegetarian, vegan, or gluten-free cookbook. However, several of the recipes naturally fall into those categories and for ease of use and out of regard for various dietary needs, I classified them into distinct categories: **Vegan (VE), Vegetarian (V), Gluten-Free (GF), Fish and Seafood (F&S), and Meat and Poultry (M&P).** These categories should assist with some quick weeknight decision-making for spontaneous, flavorful, and satisfying meals for your table.

I hope that my passion for cooking and working with seasonal, local foods will be infectious, and that as you leaf through *Spices & Seasons*, you will learn to love nature's bounty the Indian way.

Sustainability in the Indian kitchen

My earliest food memories take me back to my grandmother's kitchen—a practical, functional space built upon concepts like energy efficiency and sustainability that we are now trying to recapture. Her pots and pans were made of copper, some of them handed down to her by her mother. Her culinary tools used a minimal amount of electricity, and instead of paper towels, she had an assortment of kitchen linens that were washed and kept scrupulously clean. Nothing was squandered—even tender tips and bits of vegetables were all thrown together into lovely stir-fries.

My grandmother also cooked in well-proportioned small quantities that did not leave room for waste. In my first cookbook, *The Bengali Five Spice Chronicles*, I share some of my grandmother's practical recipes. Her spices and supplies were set up and stored in tins, saved and re-used from other products. Most of her grains were sourced close to the original seller, allowing for freshness and minimal packaging. Years later, when I entered my mother-in-law's kitchen in Northern India, I found a very similar set-up and approach, making me feel quite at home in her North Indian kitchen even though she wasn't cooking Bengali food. Affinity for local products, minimal waste, and simple organization are common qualities in all traditional Indian kitchens.

In some ways, my own kitchen is not really revolutionary or trendy, but traditional in a "back-to-basics" way. I have gone back to re-using an assortment of glass jars and containers, and favor lunch boxes over brown paper bags. I use cloth kitchen towels more often than paper towels; I carry a reusable coffee mug rather than paper cups, and have a collection of water bottles for my children so we can avoid disposable ones.

Indian cooking features tender shoots and greens, and many times, I use leftover pieces in lentils or curries to add some nutrition and avoid waste. They can be simmered in nutty coconut milk with ginger and then pureed to create hearty soups; they can be finely diced and incorporated with chickpeas or potatoes; they can be tossed with whole spices to form stir-fries; small stalks and stems can be tossed into rice with a few aromatics to create unusual pilafs—and the list goes on.

In the traditional Indian kitchen, where not even the smallest items are overlooked for their potential usefulness, the philosophy of "waste not, want not" is perfected! The ideas and recipes in this book bring you close to this tradition of simple sustainability that is good for you and the world at large.

Learning the Essentials
An Approach to Indian Cooking

I began teaching Indian cooking because I loved to talk about spices and wanted to share how they were used in the Indian home kitchen. In time I realized that many people seemed daunted by the cuisine, often associating it with complexity and lengthy lists of unknown, exotic ingredients. It has served chefs and restaurateurs well to foster this concept—and indeed, I think when dining out, one should look for something offbeat and elaborate—but Indian home cooking is simple, practical, and built with everyday ingredients that reflect the preferences of each household.

In this book, I offer a simple, everyday approach to Indian food prepared with readily found ingredients. Along the way, I share my ways of organizing and simplifying the Indian pantry, with make-ahead spice rubs, essential spice kits, and a selection of simple spice blends that can easily and affordably be made at home. I always cook with what the season offers, so I assure you that authentic Indian cooking is adaptable. Working with spices is much like pairing wine with food: there are rules, but at the end of the day, it is about taste preferences.

I would love to tell you that the simple approach is something I created, but it is as ageless as the cuisine itself. It is the way my grandmothers cooked, it is the way my mother and mother-in-law cook. The Indian home cook, like anyone else, has countless demands on his or her time. He or she cannot pause everyday preparations in search of unusual ingredients. Where the Indian cook has an advantage, however, is that there are a multitude of flavors that enable innovation and flexibility. With its vegetarian basis and healthful spices, Indian cuisine also offers an inherent solution to health and lifestyle quandaries. I suggest that you learn to work with flavors, and if you want to play and have fun along the way, do not restrict yourself.

In this chapter, I outline an essential spice kit of seven ingredients that are the base of several of the recipes in this book. You will find that these ingredients are commonly known and readily available in most U.S. stores. Most of the techniques in this book are very practical, with several of my dishes baking unattended in the oven, and some even finished in the slow cooker. This is how I get food to friends and family, with minimal attention but still a strong emphasis on freshness and flavor.

I am very conscious of planning ahead and organizing (hey, my core academic training is accounting!), so those concepts are built into this book and my culinary pantry. If a sauce is essential and versatile, I offer a recipe to make it in bulk; if something lends itself to premixing, I have identified it.

This is where the last chapter of this book, "My Spices & Seasons Tool Chest," comes in handy. With the marinades, two essential curry sauces, and some help from the condiment chapter, there really is no reason not to cook healthy, simple, and flavorful Indian food without tears, fuss, and loads of time.

Benefits of spices

Indian cuisine offers us a practical way to use spices with multiple benefits. Beyond taste, the benefits and the practical uses of these spices are often rooted in the tradition of Ayurveda (Indian holistic medicine). The ayurvedic tradition of cooking comes from a 14th-century ancient Indian text or veda, that is the prescription or base of Indian cuisine. Some examples:

- Turmeric is a natural antiseptic, known to have cancer preventing qualities. It also has anti-inflammatory effects and can be mixed into a poultice to treat sprains and swelling. Turmeric is also often sprinkled on food before cooking to increase shelf life.
- Asafetida aids in digestion and has a tendency to reduce flatulence, therefore it is often used in cooking beans and lentils.
- Lemon is high in Vitamin C and citric acid and is often used in marinades as a natural meat tenderizer.
- Herbs such as cilantro and mint are high in minerals and tend to be sprinkled liberally on many Indian foods to make them a natural part of the culinary balance.

Sources and supplies

Most classes or talks that I give on Indian cooking lead to the inevitable question: Where do I get my supplies?

Living in the greater New York area, I have a fair selection of ethnic grocers, but this is not the case everywhere. My cooking style and the recipes in this book tend to use a small number of everyday spices, and fortunately a lot of the basic supplies used in Indian cooking are available in well-stocked grocery stores and organic markets such as Whole Foods Market or Trader Joe's. If your local supermarket has an international section, supplies such as beans, cumin seeds, coriander seeds, and basmati rice might also be available there.

Another supply resource available to people irrespective of where they live is the Internet and online Indian grocers. I would encourage you to explore the Internet on your own since sites are popping up every day.

I am fond of using fresh ingredients like ginger, garlic, and herbs rather than an excessive amount of spices to season my food. The staple ingredients in my cooking are fresh ginger and garlic and loads of chopped cilantro, lemon, cumin seeds, and black pepper. Do not try my recipes with pre-powdered variations of these essentials—they will not taste the same.

In terms of Indian brands for products and spice blends, there are several good options. I personally tend to favor MTR Foods Private Limited Spices or Everest Spices for spices. While Swad brand, manufactured by Raja Foods in Skokie, IL, offers a comprehensive array of products.

Storing and saving your spices

Indian spices conjure up the image of the *masala dani* (Indian spice box), usually a round container holding five or six smaller containers, designed to store your most essential spices. These essentials vary from house to house and chef to chef. However, the spice box takes care of two key needs: accessibility and air-free and moisture-free storage. The most essential thing to ensure that spices are stored properly is to keep them in airtight containers.

Green Tip:

Buying and grinding your own spices has so many advantages:

- The spices taste better and fresher.
- You save money because larger quantities of whole spices cost less than ground.
- Smaller quantities of pre-mixed or ground spices use a lot of packaging materials. You can avoid excess plastic packaging by grinding your own spices and storing them in reusable glass jars.

I keep ground spices no longer than six months and whole spices up to a year. The dates need to be applied with some common sense and instinct, but if you are more punctilious, then you can easily date your spices with labels. You may be able to get away with slightly longer storage times if you refrigerate your spices. I have friends who bring back essential spice mixtures made by their mothers in India. They like to refrigerate them to keep them as long as possible.

To gauge freshness, use your senses. Your spices should greet you with a clean fresh fragrance. The whole spices should be dry and loose to touch without clumping. Try to buy what you'll need for six months so you are not left with spices lingering too long. My spice closet is a well-stocked cupboard of mismatched containers, since I tend to reuse airtight glass jars from relishes, jams, and anything similar that I can find.

Larger quantities of spices do work out to be cheaper, but it is important to buy them in larger quantities only if you finish them quickly. For example, I use a lot of cumin and coriander and so I buy large packages of these spices. I buy medium-size amounts of cardamom, cinnamon, and cloves, and small amounts of spices such as allspice and asafetida.

I might as well tell you now, since you will hear this sentiment expressed in other parts of the book: I am not a fan of pre-ground spices since I feel that their flavor diminishes significantly. This being said, I do keep some pre-mixes handy, such as tandoori masala (my recipe is on page 349) and chaat masala (page 348), and I tend to buy or make these in small quantities because this way I replenish them within three to six months.

Buying the right quantities is something that I have worked through trial and error. So with experience you'll eventually be able to decide how much of the spices you would like to keep on hand.

Essential spices and herbs – The starter kit

This "starter kit" of spices is what I would begin with when setting up an Indian kitchen. Most people are rather surprised to see how common these spices are. It is important to note that how the spices are used is what makes the difference and shapes a cuisine. There are several recipes in this book that use just these essential spices. I think that we would shortchange the magic of Indian cooking, however, if I started limiting my recipes to just a few spices, so where appropriate I have offered options. This is not unlike the basic steps to a dance or the first steps in playing an instrument. Spices are called *masala* in Hindi and the concept of *masala* includes fresh aromatics, herbs, and seeds. I am partial to fresh ingredients such as ginger and garlic and use them more frequently than seeds and powders. Following is a list of the core essential spices in my kitchen.

Cilantro: Cilantro (coriander) leaves are a very versatile herb (sometimes also called Chinese parsley). It is the herb of choice in the Indian kitchen, with mint being a close second. My joke is that we use cilantro as a green vegetable in our house. A perennial plant that grows 1 to 2 feet and features dark green, cilantro has hairless soft leaves that are variable in shape. The leaves and stems have a light citrus flavor. It packs a strong dose of antioxidants, minerals, and vitamins, and is, of course, low in calories. Be aware, however, that there are a host of people to whom cilantro tastes like soap.

Coriander (*Coriandrum sativum*): These small brown seeds, used either whole or crushed, are native to Europe and North Africa and belong to the coriander plant. Coriander is the word used to describe both the seeds and the herb in most places. In the U.S. we use the Spanish word "cilantro" for the herb. I personally like the distinction; however this difference in names often masks the fact that the two ingredients are related. Coriander seeds are rarely used as a sole flavoring. Coriander is most commonly used to complement and round off the flavors of other spices, most commonly cumin. I use it for spice rubs and crusts where it holds center stage. Coriander has a softer flavor that rounds off the tastes of stronger spices such as cumin and black pepper.

Cumin seeds (*Cuminum cyminum*): Cumin is native to Middle Eastern and Mediterranean regions. It was grown in ancient Egypt where the seeds were used in rituals and to season food. There is mention of this spice in the Old and New Testaments of the Bible where it is spelled "*cummin.*" Cumin seeds have been found at the site of an excavation dating to the 2nd millennium BC, so this spice is at least 4,000 years old. Cumin belongs to the parsley family and is the seed of a flowering plant. It comes in varieties of white, brown, and black. There are differences in taste depending on the color and type of cumin used. In my kitchen, I typically use the brown variety. Cumin is also used in powdered form. The recipes in this book are made with freshly ground cumin seeds and coriander seeds, which make a much stronger spice than the pre-made commercial varieties.

Red cayenne pepper powder (*Capsicum annuum*): Cayenne peppers are the chilies most commonly used in Indian kitchens. These long slender chilies, named after the town of Cayenne in French Guyana, are usually ripened until red and then dried and ground into what is known as red chili powder or red cayenne powder. Its heat makes an Indian dish complete. Cayenne pepper powder is portable and convenient to keep around since it does not spoil. Chilies and chili peppers come in a multitude of varieties and are used in various ways in Indian cooking. In fact, this is why I find it difficult to believe that red chilies are native to the Americas and were actually introduced to India by way of trade by the Portuguese in the 16th century.

Garlic (*Allium sativum*): Garlic is a species in the onion family. Its close relatives include the onion, shallot, leek, and chives. Dating back over 6,000 years, garlic is native to central Asia and has long been a staple in the Mediterranean region, as well as a frequent seasoning in Asia, Africa, and Europe. Garlic can be ground with ginger in equal portions to create a **ginger-garlic paste**. Fresh ginger-garlic paste will keep in the refrigerator for up to two weeks, and it can also be stored in the freezer almost indefinitely.

Ginger (*Zinggiber officianale*): Fresh ginger is really a rhizome that is often referred to as a root. This rhizome belongs to the ginger plant. The brown skin is peeled to reveal a pale yellow inside. The sharp, fragrant root is usually grated or ground into a paste. I find that the sharpness of ginger offers a nice contrast and complement to fruity sauces (such as the Blueberry Ginger Sauce for scallops on page 201). Ginger also works as a twin spice with garlic. Ginger paste can be made in large amounts in the blender and then frozen in small amounts (try using an ice cube tray) to be used as needed.

Turmeric (*Curcuma longa*): Turmeric is a rhizome, not unlike ginger. It is popularly used in Indian cooking in a dried and powdered form. I like to call it "trendy" turmeric as it seems to be the happening spice these days because of all its health benefits. Indeed, it is an anti-inflammatory spice that is supposed to prevent cancer, offer the skin a glow, and of course, add flavor and color to your food.

Oils and cooking mediums

Here I outline the fats and oils that are suitable for use in my recipes. If you are vegan, the clarified butter called for in some of my vegetarian recipes can be substituted with one of these oils.

Grapeseed oil: This light-tasting oil is found in most stores in the U.S. these days and is almost always available in Mediterranean stores. I tend to use this for shallow frying and anything that needs higher temperatures, since it has a higher smoking point than olive oil. I use this more often than canola or olive oil, since it is healthier than canola oil and its milder taste works better with some of the dishes. The best variety of grapeseed oil has a clean finish and a pale green color.

Extra virgin olive oil: Though this might be considered a controversial choice for Indian kitchen "purists," I tend to use olive oil quite frequently. Some people argue that EVOO has too much flavor for everyday cooking. Since I tend to cook my vegetables and fish with a lighter touch, I find it works rather well for my stir-fries and sautéed dishes. But do not fry food with EVOO as you will get very smoky and unsuitable results.

Canola oil: Canola oil is the workhorse of most Indian kitchens. Its neutral taste, high smoking point, and lack of saturated fat make it a practical choice for everyday cooking. Depending on your preference, this oil can be effectively used for most of the recipes in this book. There has been some concern lately that canola oil might be being made from GMO seeds, if this is of concern to you, grapeseed oil is a good substitute.

Mustard oil: Because of the supposed toxicity of erucic acid that is found in mustard oil, it has become a controversial ingredient for cooking in the United States, and tends to be sold in its purest form and labeled "for external use only." But since erucic acid is also found in canola oil (just in smaller doses), and mustard oil has been used in Indian cooking for centuries without any detrimental effects, I still use it. There are some recipes where I like and crave the distinct, sharp taste of this oil. I am comfortable with using pure mustard oil, and in fact, I grew up eating food cooked in this oil. If you are troubled by the labeling, however, there are mustard oil blends (like the one made by SWAD) that offer most of the flavor of pure mustard oil. There are recipes in this book where I offer extra virgin olive oil as a substitute for mustard oil, and while these oils could not be further apart in taste, they are both dense, rich-tasting, and offer a nice depth of flavor to the food.

Ghee: Clarified butter with the water and milk solids drained out is a concentrated form of butter called ghee. It is used in Indian cooking as well as Middle-Eastern cuisine in lieu of butter. I use it in moderation as a little goes a long way to add a nutty rich flavor or finish.

Note on dairy substitutions: If you want to substitute dairy items in a recipe, soy yogurt is a good alternative to yogurt, and coconut milk is a good alternative to cream.

Tools of the trade

We all have kitchen tools that we consider indispensable and most of us love to browse kitchen stores and pick up new gadgets. For my recipes you don't need any special tools, but I do recommend some equipment I've found very helpful:

Non-stick or coated pots and pans: Most Indian kitchens tend to use hard anodized non-stick cookware. These pots require less oil and significantly simplify cooking. Most of these recipes have been tested with non-stick pans, so they may need a little more oil if using cast-iron or steel cookware. It is important to replace non-stick pans as soon as they scratch. An alternative to non-stick cookware is coated cast-iron cookware that I also find handy and useful when cooking stews and curries.

Strainers and colanders: Since there is a lot of rinsing and chopping of herbs and vegetables involved in Indian cooking, I find it helpful to have an assortment of small strainers and colanders available. They seem to be more useful than prep bowls. I chop the vegetables and herbs directly into the colanders, wash them, and keep them ready to be tossed into the cooking dish.

Microplane grater: This is one of the most useful tools in my kitchen, particularly for grinding ginger and garlic in small quantities. It offers the right texture without much fuss.

Spice or coffee grinder: A powerful coffee grinder kept for grinding spices is one of the few essentials in my kitchen. They are very hardy—I have had my coffee grinder for over a decade, use it every day, and it works wonders!

Mortar and pestle: I like to have a small mortar and pestle handy for coarsely grinding nuts and fragrant spices such as cardamom, which should be done in small quantities. A mortar and pestle is also very helpful for bruising or coarsely grinding spices to extract their flavor.

Small chopper or small food processor: These little machines make a huge difference in prep time. I use my mini food processor extensively for chopping onions, tomatoes, ginger, and garlic, and mixing Indian bread dough. It makes life a lot easier. The preferred size for everyday Indian cooking is the 5-cup small food processor.

Blender: It is good to invest in a powerful blender. My industrial strength blender doesn't complain when I grind seeds into a paste and easily blends deliciously smooth sauces.

Pressure cooker: A pressure cooker is one of the few tools that have survived as a kitchen essential through generations. Indian kitchens are incomplete without one. Most people picture a large unwieldy device, but pressure cooker manufacturers, or for that matter the Indian cookware industry, have come a long way in developing attractive cookers of all shapes and sizes. Pressure cookers also come in non-stick and hard anodized varieties and are available in all conceivable sizes. The most common one that I use is about the size of a 1½-quart saucepan and very effectively cuts down cooking time for beans, lentils, and potatoes. I still meet people who are daunted by this kitchen device, so I have included my "Pressure Cooker 101 Guide" (page 89) to make it all clear and easy.

Slow cooker: This is an all-American classic that fits wonderfully into my life and kitchen. It is good for cooking beans and lentils, does a good job with more complex curries, and keeps saucy foods hot when you have a large number of guests.

Rice cooker: I love *birayanis*, the wonderful saffron-scented rice casseroles that layer the meat and rice to produce a multi-hued dish of fragrant perfection. Several of the pilafs in this book can be finished off in the rice cooker after the addition of ingredients. The rice cooker is also great to keep rice warm, if I am not around or when I have company. But I will emphasize that for regular everyday rice, the stovetop method is best.

Chapter One

A Flavorful Prelude:
Appetizers & Small Plates

Twinkling fairytale lights, pretty glasses of multi-colored drinks, clinking bangles and sparkling saris, a hub of animated people filling the room, and a seductive assortment of palate tingling pleasers—this makes an evening event in India complete! When I think of starters in the Indian context, the image is very different from what one typically thinks of as a first course in the U.S. An Indian starter or appetizer is separate and distinct from the meal, and very special—much like a prelude to a kiss. It stimulates and sets the stage for the main meal.

The rest of the Indian meal is usually served family-style rather than in courses, which is all the more reason for the appetizers to shine on their own. An interesting component of the Indian meal structure is teatime, arguably a meal in itself that keeps people satisfied until dinner, which tends to be late in the evening. Teatime is often where several of these snacks and starters are served.

Appetizers have their place at the start of an event to break the ice and get the conversation going. These crisp anytime snacks can also warm you on a rainy day, when you want something to eat while you cuddle up and read *Pride and Prejudice* for the tenth time. They can warm and stimulate conversation with favorite friends and they are also what you expect when you visit your grandmother's house.

Nowadays adapting small plates for events and festivities, to allow the diners to sample more variety, is commonplace. This seems to be an emerging trend in the ever-popular Sunday brunch buffet in the U.S, where the star attraction seems to be a well-stocked appetizer table. I've embraced this trend because it allows me flexibility when entertaining and also allows a forum for my guests to mingle with each other without the constraints of a formal seating arrangement.

I start you here with a small collection of appetizers that are more in the genre of small munchies and starters. Please mix and match these as you see fit.

Radish and Scallion Fritters
(VE, GF)

Indian fritters (*pakoras*) are as wonderful and simple as a basic appetizer can get. Crisp, flavorful, and easy to make, these delectable, chickpea batter-coated delights work well for all gatherings. This variation is made with spring radishes and scallions, but you can use any vegetable of your choice. Radishes usually ring in the growing season for us with their early spring presence. I finish these *pakoras* off by dusting them with Kashmiri red chili powder or chaat masala. The light taste of the fritters showcases the mildly sweet flavors of the pepper well. I make them any time we need a pick-me-up, and my family loves to eat them as I fry them. In fact, very few of these actually make it to the table because I too join the fun as I cook.

Prep Time: 15 minutes | Cook Time: 25 minutes | Serves: 4

Ingredients

¾ cup besan or chickpea flour

1 tablespoon cornstarch

½ teaspoon cayenne pepper powder

½ teaspoon turmeric

1 teaspoon salt or to taste

½ teaspoon cumin seeds

15 red radishes, thinly sliced

½ cup scallions, finely chopped

2 cups or more oil for frying

Kashmiri red chili powder or chaat masala for dusting (optional; see page 348)

Preparation

1. Place the chickpea flour, cornstarch, cayenne pepper powder, turmeric, salt, and cumin seeds in a mixing bowl and mix well with a wire whisk (this is done to separate the lumps and ensure a smooth batter).

2. Gradually add enough water (about 1 cup) to make a smooth paste.

3. Stir in the radishes and scallions

4. Pour oil in a frying skillet or wok that is at least 6 inches deep and heat on medium-high heat for about 2 minutes. Test the temperature of the oil with a drop of the batter, the mixture should puff up and rise to the top.

5. When the oil is hot enough, drop the batter into the oil by the tablespoonful. Add about 3 or 4 fritters at a time, depending on the size of the wok. Leave adequate room for the fritters to move comfortably in the oil. Fry them for about 2 to 3 minutes and then turn the fritters and cook on the other side for the same time. It is important to make sure that the temperature of the oil remains constant and not too hot. The fritters should cook to a uniform golden brown on both sides.

6. Remove the fritters carefully with a slotted spoon and drain on paper towels. Dust with the chili powder or chaat masala and serve immediately while hot.

Tips and Tricks

The pakora batter can be prepared a couple of days ahead and brought out of the refrigerator 15 minutes before cooking.

Any vegetable of your choice can be substituted for the radish. If you have picky children, these fritters are a great way to get them started with Indian food as well as disguise any unwanted vegetable.

The texture of the batter is important for these fritters; you need batter the consistency of pancake batter, otherwise you will not end up with light-tasting, crisp fritters.

Pineapple and Citrus Chicken Wing Kebabs
(M&P, GF)

This recipe offers an unusual variation for chicken wings that marries sweetness with tang. I favor a touch of sweetness in my cooking because it is natural to the cuisine of Eastern India, where my early taste buds were formed. The citrus and fruity notes make it a refreshing starter for spring or summer. These wings can be threaded on skewers and cooked outdoors on a grill or simply baked in an oven.

Prep Time: 2 hours (mostly to marinate) | Cook Time: 8 to 10 minutes on grill • 20 to 25 minutes in oven |
Serves: 4 to 6

Ingredients

1 lemon or lime

2 oranges

1-inch piece ginger, peeled

3 cloves garlic

1 teaspoon cayenne pepper powder

¾ teaspoon turmeric

1 teaspoon brown sugar

1 teaspoon salt or to taste

2 pounds chicken drumettes (could be skinless), tips removed

2 cups fresh or canned pineapple chunks

Bamboo skewers for threading

Non-stick cooking spray

For the Garnish

1 tablespoon cilantro or chives, finely chopped

Extra lemon for serving

Preparation

1. Cut the lemon or lime and oranges in half and squeeze their juice into the bowl of a blender. Add the ginger, garlic, cayenne pepper powder, turmeric, brown sugar, and salt and blend until smooth.

2. Optional: To prepare the wings, remove as much skin as possible, cut the meat at the base and push all the way up to essentially "French" the drumettes. (This makes them easier to eat.)

3. Place the chicken wings in a mixing bowl and pour in the marinade and mix well. Marinate the chicken wings at room temperature (up to 70 degrees) for 2 hours, adding the pineapple chunks to the marinade during the last 15 minutes.

4. While the wings are marinating, soak the skewers in water. Start the grill or pre-heat the oven to 375°F.

5. Thread the chicken wings and the pineapple chunks onto the skewers. You want a couple of pineapple pieces before and after each wing on the skewers.

6. Grilling: Spray with cooking spray and grill for about 8 to 10 minutes on each side. Baking in oven: place the skewers on a large baking sheet and spray well with cooking spray. Bake for 20 to 25 minutes and finish off by broiling the chicken wings on low for a few minutes.

7. Remove the kebabs from the grill or oven and arrange on a serving dish and garnish with the cilantro or chives before serving.

Tips and Tricks

The chicken can be placed in the marinade and refrigerated the night before.

For a vegetarian option, use Indian paneer cheese in place of the chicken wings, or for a vegan version, use seitan.

This recipe also works well with peaches and other stone fruits such as nectarines substituted for the pineapple.

Stuffed Roasted Tomatoes
(V, GF)

Translating recipes from another language can be difficult. My husband tells me of a home-style food stall around the UM campus in Minneapolis, MN (my husband completed his graduate education in this chilly state and savors very fond memories of the place). The owner of this stall served authentic Indian food. His translation of these recipes was without embellishment and thus the tomato-based potato curry dish was simply "potato-tomato." This stuffed tomato recipe is often jokingly referred to in our house as "potato-tomato," homage to the man whose comforting food nourished my husband on many a cold Minnesota day. This pretty and satisfying appetizer also appeals to the youngsters. It is a beautiful summer dish, when both tomatoes and basil are available in abundance. I prefer to use the small tomatoes that are popularly sold as Campari tomatoes, but any smaller-size tomatoes would work.

Prep Time: 10 minutes | Cook Time: 10 minutes | Serves: 4 to 6

Ingredients

20 medium Campari tomatoes (with stems if possible)

3 tablespoons olive oil

2 teaspoons minced garlic

1 medium potato, boiled and peeled

⅓ cup cooked quinoa or rice

2 tablespoons finely chopped walnuts

3 tablespoons crumbled feta cheese

½ teaspoon freshly ground black pepper

½ cup finely chopped basil leaves

Preparation

1. Preheat the oven to 350°F.

2. Carefully cut the tops off the tomatoes and save them for presentation purposes. Carefully scoop out the pulp without cutting through the tomato and reserve in a bowl.

3. Heat the oil in a small skillet and add the garlic and sauté lightly until fragrant and pale toffee color. Add to the tomato pulp. Add the boiled potato and quinoa or rice and mash well.

4. Mix in the walnuts, feta cheese, pepper, basil leaves, and salt to taste.

5. Stuff the tomatoes with the potato mixture and place on a greased baking sheet.

6. Bake for 10 minutes and then remove immediately. The objective of this is to heat the tomatoes, but not cook them.

7. Cover with the saved tomato tops and serve.

Tips and Tricks

For a light lunch, these can be served with a side of cucumber *raita* (page 59).

You can use other tomatoes if you wish, but try to avoid very large ones.

Split Pea and Red Onion Fritters
(VE, GF)

The turn of the 21st century brought with it a huge influx of immigrants from India who came to pursue the dot-com dream. One such person who followed her husband to this country was Nive (Nivedita Shivraj), a talented musician who worked as an accountant to pay the bills. Well, clearly she was a talented cook too, since this recipe for the traditional South Indian snack called *masala vada* is from her repertoire, with some modifications along the way. These fritters work well with roasted bell pepper chutney (page 71) and are a favorite in our house.

Prep Time: 10 minutes after soaking lentils overnight | Cook Time: 25 to 30 minutes | Serves: 8 to 10

Ingredients

1 cup dried yellow Bengal gram lentils (sold as cholar dal, channa dal, or split chickpeas)

10 to 15 curry leaves

4 to 6 green chilies

1 teaspoon salt or to taste

2 medium red onions, finely chopped

1 tablespoon ginger paste

3 tablespoons chickpea flour (besan)

4 tablespoons finely chopped cilantro

Oil for frying

Preparation

1. Soak the lentils overnight in plenty of water.

2. Drain the lentils, rinse them and place in the bowl of a food processor. Add the curry leaves, green chilies, and salt and process until coarsely ground and mixed. The mixture might have a couple of pieces of whole lentils here and there which is okay.

3. Put the mixture in a mixing bowl and stir in the onions, ginger paste, chickpea flour, and cilantro until a coarse crumbly mixture. (Note: The mixture remains loose, but once immersed into the oil, it holds together instantly. It is just a matter of getting used to the concept.)

4. Place about 4 inches of oil in a large wok or skillet and heat. Shape the lentil mixture into round 2 to 3-inch oval patties and carefully immerse some into the hot oil. Add as many as the wok or skillet will hold without overcrowding.

5. Cook on medium-low heat for about 3 minutes on each side (resist the need to keep poking and shifting the fritters, let them cook to dark golden perfection and turn only once or twice in the process). Remove with a slotted spoon and drain on paper towels.

Tips and Tricks

While these fritters taste best hot, they also work well when transported somewhere and reheated to an acceptable temperature in a microwave.

Roasted Spice-Rubbed Cauliflower Wedges
(VE, GF)

We love the flavors of this recipe so much that my family started asking me to make a double batch of this easy-to-prepare baked cauliflower dish. Depending on our mood and hunger level, we sometimes finish the entire double batch. I like to finish this with some sage, which adds an unusual nuance, however this is optional. My sage bush is on the way to the kitchen, so sometimes it is just difficult for me to resist picking some off to use.

Prep Time: 40 minutes (includes 30 minutes for marinating) | Cook Time: 40 minutes (mostly unattended) | Serves: 6

Ingredients

1 medium head cauliflower (about 1½ pounds), cut into large florettes

3 tablespoons fenugreek and black pepper rub (page 35)

¾ teaspoon turmeric

4 tablespoons oil (canola or mustard)

15 to 20 sage leaves (optional)

For Garnish

1 large lime, halved, plus additional lime slices

1 tablespoon chopped cilantro

Thinly sliced red onion (optional)

Preparation

1. Mix the cauliflower with the fenugreek and black pepper rub, turmeric, and oil and set aside for about 25 to 30 minutes. Meanwhile pre-heat the oven to 375°F degrees.

2. Lay the cauliflower on a baking sheet or in a casserole and bake undisturbed for about 20 minutes. Open the oven and stir the mixture once to allow the spices to coat evenly. Scatter with the sage leaves, if using. Bake for another 20 minutes, until the cauliflower is nice and well done with well-crisped spots.

3. To serve, arrange on a serving dish, sprinkle with lime juice, cilantro, and the thinly sliced red onion. Serve with small serving plates, plenty of forks, and some fruity white wine.

Tips and Tricks

If you wish, you can thread the cauliflower wedges onto skewers and then place on the baking sheet. Or this recipe can also be made as a whole baked cauliflower and served as a main dish with impressive results.

How to spice things up? Let me count the ways!

Chilies were brought to India by the Portuguese by way of the spice trade. Indians wasted no time in placing their own stamp on the chili pepper, and today India produces the largest crop of chili peppers in the world. Heat is introduced to Indian cooking in various ways through different types of chilies as well as through peppercorns, which impart a potent heat and flavor quite distinct from chili peppers. We can classify heat options into the following broad categories:

Green Chili Peppers: The small green chili is sold in many varieties: in Asian supermarkets, small green chilies are sold as Vietnamese chilies; then there is the unripe, green fruit of the cayenne tree, the cayenne pepper; and then the family of American peppers including the Serrano, jalapeno, and habanero. For the recipes in this book—other than not substituting green chilies with red ones—I usually leave it up to you what type of green chili you use depending on how much heat you want.

Dried Whole or Powdered Red Cayenne Pepper: Dried whole red chilies are mostly used for flavor and sometimes even appearance since they do not offer a lot of heat when added as a whole spice to recipes. For more heat, the dried red chili is also crushed and made into red chili powder (in Indian groceries) or red cayenne pepper powder that is part of my starter kit of spices (see page 12). The mixture found in mainstream U.S. stores labeled chili powder is a spice blend distinct and different from what I describe here. I also enjoy using dried red pepper flakes, often as a garnish to offer a rougher distribution of heat.

Paprika or Sweet Chili Peppers: There is a whole assortment of ground Indian peppers that range from a gentle heat to an almost sweet taste. The most common of these is sold as *deghi mirch*. I often use ground ancho peppers or sweet paprika as a substitute. My favorite are the wrinkled chilies from Southern India, sold as *byadagi*; if you find them, try using them freshly ground. You will love the combination of fresh fragrance and mild heat. The other Indian contender is the vividly red Kashmiri red chili pepper, which has a dazzling, vibrant red color with just a hint of sweetness. But while each of the sweeter pepper varieties do have their unique flavors, in most cases they are being added for color and I feel that any readily available sweet pepper powder such as paprika can be used as a substitute.

Bell Peppers: Now while I do use bell peppers mostly as a vegetable, the fresh green variety can be added to a dish to complement the use of chilies. Green bell peppers are called capsicum in India, and have a significantly strong fresh chili or true capsicum flavor (without the heat). This distinct fresh, juicy flavor is the hallmark of a beautiful green bell pepper. As for the colored ones (the red one being my favorite), they all offer complements of the same amazing fragrance, usually fruitier and sweeter in taste than the green bell pepper.

Peppercorns: The black peppercorn is the fruit of a flowering vine that is native to Southern India and Sri Lanka. The assorted colors of the peppercorn—white, green, and black—are really different degrees of ripeness and result in varying degrees of heat. Black pepper powder is the ground-up version of black peppercorns and is one of the most commonly used spices in the world. A peppermill is worth its weight in flavor, so it is very important to have one around for introducing the spark of freshly ground black pepper to food.

SOME TIPS:

- Do not be intimidated or constrained by the number of chilies in a recipe. The preference for heat is much like that for salt, and can be modified to suit the individual palate. If you like it spicy, notch it up and if you like it mild tone it down.

- Spice tolerance seems to be much like temperature preference between couples. I never fail to have pairs in my class where one likes their food spicier than the other. In my household, my children cannot handle the heat, and my husband likes it really hot, so almost all these recipes have been tested with both extremes and the measurements I've given offer a comfortable middle ground.

- In case you haven't noticed, I am trying to dispel the common myth that Indian food is too spicy and that a high level of heat is a hallmark of good Indian food. For the spices to work in harmony, they need to work like an orchestra. Thus the chili pepper is something like the cello or flute section that must blend in rather than dominate.

Lemon Herb Chicken Kebabs
(M&P, GF)

These kebabs or mini chicken patties capture the essence of fresh summer herbs and get a nice touch of spice from the mustard oil, garlic, and black pepper. This recipe uses my magic trinity masala that consists of ginger, garlic, and onions), fresh jalapenos, and gets an interesting tang from both crushed pomegranate seeds and lemon juice. The marinated chicken mixture can be premixed, shaped, and frozen as well.

Prep Time: 4½ hours (mostly to marinate) | Cook Time: 20 to 25 minutes | Serves: 4 to 6

Ingredients

1½ pounds ground chicken

6 tablespoons magic trinity masala (page 355)

2 jalapenos, seeded and very finely chopped

2 teaspoons coriander seeds

2 teaspoons dried pomegranate seeds

1½ teaspoons black peppercorns

1 teaspoon salt

2 tablespoons chopped cilantro

1 teaspoon chopped fresh thyme (optional)

2 tablespoons minced fresh mint

1 lemon, halved and seeded

1 egg, beaten

3 tablespoons oil (I like mustard oil)

For Garnish

Lemon slices

Thinly sliced red onion rings

Preparation

1. Place the ground chicken in a mixing bowl and mix in the magic trinity masala and minced jalapeno.

2. In a small skillet, lightly toast the coriander seeds, pomegranate seeds, and peppercorns until fragrant. Grind to a powder and mix into the chicken along with the salt.

3. Mix in the cilantro, thyme (if using), and mint. Squeeze in the lemon juice and stir. Let the mixture marinate in the refrigerator for at least 4 hours.

4. When ready to cook, remove the chicken mixture from the refrigerator, mix in the egg and shape into 2-inch patties.

5. Heat a skillet and spread with about 1½ tablespoons of the oil. Add some of the patties in a single layer and cook for about 2 minutes and then turn and cook on the other side for another 2 to 3 minutes, pressing the patties down so they cook evenly and release any excess fat. The cooked patties should no longer be pink and should be covered with uniform darker brown spots.

6. Continue cooking in batches until all the chicken mixture is used. Serve hot garnished with lemon and onion slices.

Tips and Tricks

The chicken can be marinated in the refrigerator for up to 3 days. It can also be prepared without the fresh herbs, cooked, and then frozen and reheated and then garnished with the herbs.

These can also be made into larger patties and served as chicken burgers.

Mango and Goat Cheese Mini Crisps
(V)

Director Mira Nair has called her movie *Monsoon Wedding* a love poem to her beloved Delhi, and brought the colors, intensity, and complexity of Indian culture to our homes and consciousness. The vivid colors and beautiful marigolds that were so plentiful in the movie still move me. The colors and flavors of this dish remind me of an Indian wedding—intense, light, ethereal, and bursting with flavors—and like my own wedding, it is topped with a little western influence to complete the flavors.

Prep Time: 15 minutes | Cook Time: 25 minutes | Makes: 35 diamond-shaped puffs

Ingredients

1 package frozen puff pastry (I use Pepperidge Farm or Trader Joe's)

Cooking spray

1 recipe Monsoon Mango Salsa (see page 73)

2 ounces chevre goat cheese, crumbled

1 tablespoon finely chopped fresh basil (optional)

Preparation

1. Preheat the oven to 375°F. Spray a baking sheet with cooking spray.

2. Spread the puff pastry sheets and cut them into small squares (about 3 inches) and then into triangles.

3. Place the pastry triangles on the baking sheet. Put about 1½ teaspoons of the mango salsa on each triangle. Top with a small amount of the goat cheese.

4. Bake in the oven for 25 minutes, until the pastry has risen and is crisp.

5. Sprinkle with the basil, if using, and serve.

Short-cut Vegetable Samosas
(V)

Almost everyone associates Indian food with samosas, the classic potato-and-green-pea-based turnovers encased in flaky, fried pastry. So I couldn't leave samosas out of this book, but in this version, I use pre-made empanada wrappers, usually found in the frozen Goya section of my grocery store—if not, wonton wrappers also work. For a touch of novelty, I offer a potato, cauliflower, and green pea filling that is wonderful if made with spring chives and fresh green peas. I sometimes add grated carrots, depending on the season.

Prep Time: 15 minutes | Cook Time: 35 to 40 minutes | Serves: 10 to 12

Ingredients

2 tablespoons oil

1 teaspoon cumin seeds

1 tablespoon freshly grated ginger

4 medium potatoes (about 1½ pounds), boiled, peeled, and cubed

1 cup cauliflower florets, cut into very small pieces

¾ cup fresh or frozen green peas

1 teaspoon salt or to taste

½ teaspoon sugar

¾ teaspoon red cayenne pepper powder

1 teaspoon amchoor (dried mango powder) or 2 tablespoons lemon juice

3 tablespoons chopped chives

1½ tablespoons chopped cilantro

1 package empanada wrappers (from a brand such as Goya), thawed and ready to use

Oil for frying

Preparation

1. Heat the oil on medium-high heat. Add the cumin seeds and let them sizzle for about 30 seconds. Add the ginger and mix well.

2. Add the potatoes, cauliflower, and green peas and stir well.

3. Stir in the salt, sugar, red cayenne pepper, and mango powder or lemon juice. Stir the mixture well. Cover and cook on low heat for 7 to 8 minutes, until the vegetables are soft.

4. Coarsely mash the mixture with the back of a wooden spoon and stir in the chives and cilantro. Let the mixture cool.

5. Cut the empanada wrappers in half and shape into cones (if using wonton wrappers, cut them in half diagonally and continue the process).

6. Place about 3 teaspoons of the filling into a cone and press down to form a pyramid-like shape and carefully seal the edges. It is important to stuff until nice and plump and also to have well-sealed edges. Continue this process until all the samosas are assembled.

7. Heat about 1½ cups of oil in a large skillet or wok. Gently deep fry about 2 or 3 of the samosas at a time for a couple of minutes. The samosas should be crisp and golden. The number of samosas fried at one time depends on the size of the wok, the key is not to overcrowd them. Drain them on paper towels and serve.

Chicken Tikka Kebabs
(M&P, GF)

These chicken tikka kebabs are an easy-to-make crowd pleaser. Most people, including my children, love them. You can make this with chicken on the bone as well. I like to make the boneless variety, and I usually make a double batch that I can later convert into Chicken Tikka in a Tomato Cream Sauce (page 235).

Prep Time: 5 to 10 minutes plus 4 hours marinating | Cook Time: 25 minutes | Serves: 6

Ingredients

1 tablespoon ginger-garlic paste (page 14)

2 tablespoons tandoori masala (page 349)

1 cup plain yogurt

1 teaspoon salt or to taste

1 teaspoon cayenne pepper powder

2 pounds skinless boneless chicken thighs

Oil or cooking spray

Skewers

For Garnish

Onion rings

Lime or lemon wedges

Preparation

1. Stir the ginger-garlic paste, tandoori masala, yogurt, salt, and cayenne powder into a smooth paste. Cut the chicken thighs into smaller pieces and marinate in the prepared mixture for 3 to 4 hours.

2. Pre-heat the oven to 350°F.

3. Thread the chicken pieces on skewers and place on a baking sheet and brush with oil or spray with cooking spray. Bake for about 15 to 20 minutes.

4. Broil on low for another 6 to 7 minutes to let the chicken crisp a little and get a slightly smoky taste. Serve immediately with onion slices and lime or lemon wedges.

Working with herbs in the Indian kitchen

In India, the use of and preference for herbs tends to vary based on region. Cilantro is universally popular as a garnish, but other herbs, such as dill, mint, curry leaves, fenugreek, and basil, are used as recipes call for them. I have thrown in parsley, thyme, and rosemary for good measure to round out this segment (also see the herbs included in my "Starter Kit" on page 12). Fresh herbs are relatively easy to find in most grocery stores and also fun to grow, so I tend to use a lot of them in my cooking. In fact, this herb usage is the area of cooking where I have improvised the most. I have combined lovely herbs like thyme and sage with the already well-rounded flavors of common Indian herbs such as cilantro and mint, to add a touch of playfulness and fun to my cooking. Like spices, most herbs have benefits beyond just taste.

Basil (*Ocimum basilicum*): Indian basil is referred to as "holy basil" and the holy basil tree is considered auspicious, especially in Hindu or Tulsi households. Borrowing from Thai cuisine, I comfortably incorporate basil into my cooking. At first, I would go out of my way to get holy basil, but I have now settled for the regular sweet basil or the purple Thai basil. Most people do not realize what herb flavors some of my popular recipes such as my basil and green chili chicken or garlic basil *tandoori* breads. This is another herb that is relatively effortless to grow and lasts all through summer and longer if you keep a pot on your windowsill. Thai basil is different from the regular sweet basil but for the recipes in this book either can be used.

Curry leaves (*Murraya koenigii*): These addictive and strong-smelling leaves of the kari or curry leaf tree are probably the only single item in the Indian kitchen named "curry" despite the belief that all Indian spices are curry. The small curry leaf tree grows a few feet tall with a trunk up to 40 cm in diameter. The leaves are pinnate and highly aromatic. Curry leaves freeze well and impart an unmistakable fragrance to both stews and stir-fries. They add a nice touch of flavor, especially in creamy coconut-based sauces. Try bruising a leaf to inhale the luscious aroma. Potted curry leaf trees thrive indoors in warm, sunny corners.

Dill (*Anethum graveolens*): This herb, also known as dill weed, originated in the area around the Mediterranean and the south of Russia. Dill has green fernlike leaves and is similar to coriander in that its seeds and leaves are both edible. In Indian cooking, dill is well-liked for its cooling and anti-inflammatory properties and is used for flavoring rice and lentils. I use it for marinades and chutneys and feel that it offers a pleasant and unusual fragrance to these dishes.

Fenugreek leaves (*Trigonella foenum-graecum*): Both the seeds and leaves of the fenugreek plant have culinary uses. A winter staple in India, fresh fenugreek greens are very nutritious. I've found that fresh fenugreek greens in the U.S. do not have the characteristic faintly maple flavor of their Indian counterparts. However, dried fenugreek leaves called *Kasuri methi* are readily available and more reliable in terms of flavor. This is one of the exceptions in my kitchen where I tend to use the dried leaves more often than fresh ones, however they cannot always be used interchangeably. The dried leaves are used in curry sauces and tandoori marinades, including the rather popular Chicken Tikka in a Tomato Cream Sauce (page 235). Fenugreek is what gives commercial curry powder mixes their characteristic "curry" flavor.

Mint (*Mentha piperita*): Mint is the most popular herb in Indian cooking after cilantro, particularly in northern India. I often recommend it as a substitute for cilantro in recipes for a variation but mint has a strong taste and should be used in smaller amounts than cilantro. It is most popularly used in marinades, smooth pesto-like chutneys, and flatbreads. In a bind, powdered mint can be used; I like dried varieties from Middle-Eastern stores the best.

Parsley (*Petroselinum crispum*): Though it is native to the Mediterranean region, I first encountered parsley in India during my early experimental cooking days. I tried parsley in a few select dishes and forgot about it. Later, when I found markets did not always stock cilantro, I bought parsley—more for color since the flavor is different from cilantro. Along the way I discovered that the milder flavor of parsley sometimes works better to season a recipe or complement the other flavors of a dish.

Rosemary (*Rosmarinus officinalis*): When we bought our home thirteen years ago, the previous owners told us about many of the plants they had in their yard. One of the plants was rosemary. I soon learned to use the herb as a delicious addition to many Indian dishes and I have used it to great effect in soups and flatbreads among others. Rosemary seems to be coming of age with Indian chefs now as I see a lot of modern restaurants in India offering dishes using this herb.

Sage (*Salvia officinalis*): Sage is an evergreen that survives the winter much like thyme. It darkens a little in the cold but once the sun is out again it is back to pretty green leaves. The herb has a mild but distinct camphor-like odor. Sage leaves have a sharp, warm, and slightly bitter taste, which is a property of its volatile oil. For centuries sage was used for medical (aiding digestion) as well as culinary purposes, particularly in Italian and Mediterranean cooking. I love to use sage when I am roasting vegetables.

Thyme (*Thymus vulgaris*): Thyme is a highly aromatic herb that grows especially well in dry, sunny conditions. A Mediterranean herb, thyme holds its flavor in cooking and blends well with other flavors of that region, like garlic, olive oil, and tomatoes. Thyme is also considered to have antiseptic and preservative properties and has long been used medicinally, as well as to preserve meats. Though similar in flavor to the Indian spice ajowain or carom seeds, thyme is milder. My family prefers this milder flavor, so I use thyme a lot in my cooking. And of course it is helpful that thyme survives the cold New York winter and is therefore readily available in my backyard.

Hint of Spice Shrimp Cakes
(F&S, GF)

This is one of the first recipes I developed for my children, trying to get them to eat Indian food. They are much more adventurous with flavor today, but this recipe is something we still like because it showcases a multitude of sauces and condiments. These shrimp cakes make a good substitute for crab cakes, and in fact I discovered it's easier to find and work with wild-caught shrimp rather than crabmeat, and the chewier texture works better with spices.

Prep Time: 10 minutes | Cook Time: 30 minutes | Makes: 10 3-inch cakes

Ingredients
2 medium potatoes (about 1½ pounds)

1½ pounds shrimp, shelled and de-veined

1 tablespoon cumin powder

1 teaspoon salt

1 tablespoon freshly grated ginger

1 cup cilantro leaves, chopped

2 green chilies

2 tablespoons chickpea flour (besan)

1 egg, beaten

Oil for shallow frying

Preparation
1. Cut the potatoes into quarters and place in a pot of water and cover and cook until soft.

2. While the potatoes are cooking, place the shrimp, cumin powder, salt, ginger, cilantro, and green chilies in a food processor and pulse for 2 minutes until well mixed.

3. Cool and peel the potatoes. Place them in a mixing bowl and mash well. Add the processed shrimp mixture and mix well. Add the chickpea flour and egg and mix well.

4. Place a heavy-bottomed skillet on medium heat and add oil to a depth of ½ inch and heat for 3 minutes.

5. Shape the shrimp-potato mixture into 3-inch cakes and gently lower about 4 or 5 of the cakes into the oil. Cook for about 3 minutes on each side, until the cakes are golden and crisp on both sides. Drain on paper towels. Cook the remaining cakes in the same way.

6. Serve hot drizzled with tamarind mayonnaise.

Almond and Saffron Salmon Kebabs
(F&S, GF)

Our friend Vivek Kumar, who makes a tandoori version of fish kebabs, inspired these salmon kebabs. I love delicately grilled or baked fish morsels and decided to see if I could do more with the spicing. This recipe emerged. The spices in this recipe are designed to highlight and accentuate the saffron which leaves a delicate orange color against the natural pink of the rich-tasting salmon. Since I do not use additional cream, it is important to use whole milk Greek yogurt in this recipe.

Prep Time: 10 minutes plus 2 hours for marinating | Cook Time: 15 minutes | Serves: 4 to 6

Ingredients

½ cup whole milk Greek yogurt

½ cup blanched almonds or cashew nuts

1-inch piece fresh peeled ginger

2 green chilies

1 teaspoon saffron strands

¾ teaspoon salt or to taste

2 or 3 mace blades

⅛ teaspoon nutmeg

1½ pounds salmon fillets, cut into 1½-inch pieces

2 tablespoons oil

1 tablespoon chopped fresh dill to garnish (optional)

Preparation

1. Place the yogurt, almonds or cashews, ginger, green chilies, saffron, salt, mace blades, and nutmeg in a blender and grind until smooth. You will get a pretty saffron-colored thick sauce.

2. Place the salmon in a mixing bowl and gently toss with the yogurt mixture. Marinate for about 2 hours in the refrigerator.

3. Pre-heat oven to 350°F. Grease a baking dish with 1 tablespoon of oil.

4. Place the salmon pieces with the marinade on the baking dish about 1 inch apart to allow room to pick the cooked pieces up neatly (skewers are optional). Drizzle with the remaining tablespoon of oil.

5. Bake the salmon for about 10 minutes, then broil for 2 to 3 minutes to gently brown the top (the salmon should have a few golden brown specs, but it is important not to dry it out).

6. Serve immediately garnished with dill.

Kale and Potato Patties
(VE, GF)

Tikkis (fried Indian patties) are really addictive. Even my husband who swears by healthy food cannot resist them. They make great sliders, so a good way to enjoy them is on small whole wheat rolls topped with chutneys, sliced tomatoes, and onions. *Tikkis* are a hallmark of the northern state of Uttar Pradesh, although different iterations of vegetables cakes or patties are popular all across India. Once I made a batch of these before work and left them for a guest's breakfast. I came home to find they had not been offered to our guest. My husband claims he did not find them. This has always left me a little suspicious considering the enthusiastic picnic lunch later, enjoyed by the father and two children, in which these *tikkis* did make an appearance.

Prep Time: 40 minutes (mostly unattended) | Cook Time: 40 minutes | Makes: about 25

Ingredients

2 cups fresh kale or seasonal greens, finely chopped (about 12 ounces)

¼ cup blanched peanuts

2 large russet potatoes (about 1½ pounds), boiled and peeled

1 teaspoon cayenne pepper powder

1½ teaspoons cumin-coriander powder (page 353)

2 teaspoons amchur (dried mango powder) or about 2 tablespoons lemon or lime juice

¾ teaspoon salt or to taste

1 teaspoon fresh ginger paste

½ cup chopped cilantro

3 tablespoons chickpea flour (besan)

Oil for frying

Preparation

1. Place the kale in a large glass bowl and steam with minimal water for about 3 minutes (I do this by covering it and microwaving). Squeeze out any water.

2. Place the steamed kale in a food processor and process until finely chopped. Add the peanuts and pulse a few more times until the peanuts are evenly chopped through. Place in a mixing bowl.

3. Add the potatoes and mash the mixture until fairly smooth. (Because of the varying textures of these ingredients, I find that mashing this by hand is the best.)

4. Add the cayenne powder, cumin-coriander powder, dried mango powder, salt, ginger paste, and cilantro and mix well. Add the chickpea flour and mix well.

5. Shape into small patties and place them in the refrigerator for about 30 minutes. This helps the ingredients bind.

6. Heat the oil in a flat heavy-bottomed medium skillet for 2 minutes. Test the temperature with a breadcrumb. Add the patties in a single layer, 3 or 4 at a time and fry them for 3 to 4 minutes on each side. These patties are somewhat delicate and cook best if handled minimally during the frying process.

7. Remove carefully and drain on paper towels and serve with chutney.

Tips and Tricks

A good *tikki* uses a minimum amount of additional flour; in fact, when I make these with just potatoes I do not add any flour, as potatoes do not have the moisture that kale adds. In this recipe, if you substitute lemon or lime juice for the dried mango powder, increase the amount of chickpea flour to 4 tablespoons.

These patties can be assembled ahead of time and refrigerated until ready to eat; I often do this and then serve them for breakfast. They also taste pretty good warm instead of hot. Though a little crumbly with a somewhat rough finish, due to the texture of the peanuts and kale, they will hold together if your oil is hot and you do not disturb them too much while they are frying.

Spring — Season of Hope & Renewal

"If winter comes, can Spring be far behind?"—Percy Bysshe Shelley

Spring reminds me of the beginnings of a beautifully executed piece in Indian classical music (a *raag*). A *raag* begins with introductory notes (the *Alaap*) that gently foretell the sounds and potential of the music that will follow. This is much like the tiny sprouts and little shrubs that begin to make their appearance in Spring. We welcome Spring with the anticipation of warmth and freshness, after the soil has rested over winter. To herald this proverbial season of rejuvenation, my children eagerly await the groundhog's forecast and are convinced that his shadow is what makes the season come.

For my husband, early Spring is when the tiny saplings get started. And for me Spring is about the yellow colors of forsythia and the patch of daffodils that show up without fail near our mailbox. These were planted when my daughter was born and have diligently reappeared for the past nine years just a little after her birthday.

The daffodils arrive before the April showers, which actually begin in early Spring, adding much-needed moisture that gradually brings life to the trees and fills many of them with colorful flowers. Along with the daffodils, I also enjoy the beautiful irises, dogwoods, and cherry blossoms that all begin to take their place like characters in a well-rehearsed play. Before long our small yard is filled with color, bees, birds, and butterflies.

The bright yellow colors of the daffodils and forsythias connect me to Spring in India, which was heralded in my childhood with Saraswati Puja (the festival invoking the Goddess of Learning) and her symbolic color of yellow. She was also called Vasanti Devi (Spring Goddess) named after the Indian word *Basant* for Spring. Traditional offerings for Saraswati Puja include rice and lentil porridges along with an accompaniment of seasonal vegetables—light, comforting, and satisfying. Spring in India is also about new beginnings and the diversity of India allows us to celebrate the season in spiritual and symbolic ways with simple festivities. These festivals, irrespective of their symbolism, are at heart always about food. At the end of the day, it is food that nourishes us and completes our lives.

Other Indian festivals that mark new beginnings in early Spring include Ugadi, a New Year celebration in South India. Later in Spring is the mega celebration of Holi, a festival of colors. Holi is one of my favorite Indian Spring festivals, brought in with color and an assortment of sweets. Colorful Punjab in Northern India rings in their harvest festival *Baishaki* with a riot of colorful dances including the lively and boisterous *Bhangra* with its very infectious beat and the *Giddi*, a similar folk dance that is usually done by women. In eastern India around the same time, in Assam the community celebrates the three-day festival of *Bohag* or *Rongali Bihu*, symbolized by cow worship, cleaning, worship of idols, traditional sweet and savory foods, and lively folk songs and dances.

The milder weather offers an opportunity to enjoy a broader and more diverse assortment of food, ranging from heartier curries to crispy flaky treats. It is truly one of the most versatile culinary seasons. Spring brings with it a craving for fresh, crisp foods. I begin by growing fresh herbs. The herbs are my personal contribution to our homegrown collection (as the rest of the produce is grown by my husband). Mint, cilantro, and basil all start in my house for the season this time of the year. Tender red radishes follow with green onions, ramps, and wild garlic. The Spring radishes are lighter and sweeter than their autumn counterparts. The first time I saw an asparagus tree, I did not really believe that the bushy green leaves would tighten together to form the tender stalks of asparagus. Almost in keeping with the concept of freshness Spring vegetables tend to be of the lighter crisper variety that allow you to cook them with minimal fuss, so as to savor their flavors and taste while allowing yourself time to enjoy the beauty and bounty of the waking earth.

Chapter Two

Palate Cleansing Pleasers:
Salads, Condiments & Chutneys

In case you think your Indian food is lacking in flavor, condiments, salads, and relishes can come to the rescue. A typical meal usually has a couple of pickles or salads on the table to cater to the diversity of tastes and flavors.

Salads in the Indian meal fall into three categories: heavier North Indian creations called *chaats* (which tend to be an appetizer or light meal), lighter side dishes such as *raita* or yogurt-based salads, and citrusy side salads called *kachumbers* that work much like a salsa in a Mexican meal. Another Indian salad that uses raw fruits and vegetables is *koshumbir* which originated in western India where they generously add lemon and a sprinkling of crushed peanuts for good measure.

Indian salads—no matter how you slice, or for that matter dice, them—are refreshing, tangy, and full of freshness. The natural flavor of light vegetables such as tomatoes and red onions harmonize nicely with tangy citrus and other light spices. Balancing ingredients is at the heart of Indian cooking and the addition of nuts or legumes adds a dash of protein to the nutritious vegetables. I could go on at great length about the variations and names attributed to the salads of India, and would still fall short of describing them all. What is consistent is their use and purpose on the Indian table. Salads are meant to cool and cleanse the palate between courses.

A sweet and savory relish is typically offered at most meals. This is another built-in natural method of using the excess seasonal bounty. I usually do not make many traditional pickles, partly because of time constraints and weather. It is difficult to get the assurance of a week of hot sunshine here in New York, even in summer— something that traditional Indian pickles thrive on. Pickle recipes are like heirlooms: you learn them with all the frills and fuss that go along with intergenerational cooking. If, like me, you had to learn by instinct, supplemented with frantic calls to Mom, embellished with web and blog-based knowledge, you are batting low in the traditional pickle department.

I swap out oily sun-dried pickle recipes with an assortment of fresh chutneys and condiments in my everyday cooking. I make chutneys to use up the excess seasonal produce, such as the prolific quantities of green tomatoes at the end of the season. In general, Indian chutneys tend to come in two primary flavors: the fresh uncooked savory purees like mint chutney (these can on occasion be gently tempered with seasoned oil), and the sweet, tangy chutneys that are cooked, and if desired, stored and bottled. The latter tend to be more popular on the western table. You can use my chutney recipes as a guideline to make personal variations with seasonal fruits that work for your region and palate.

Spicing Indian condiments

Souring agents

The key flavor in most Indian salads is a predominantly sour taste.

Amchur: Amchur or dried mango powder is a souring agent essential to the cuisine of Northern India, and the key ingredient in the spice blend called *chaat masala* (see page 348). Green mangoes are sliced, dried, and then ground to result in this delicately fragrant and tart spice that is pale brown and powdery. It is great for spice rubs where you want a tang. In fact, it is most often used in recipes where a tart, dry taste is desired (such as my Crisped Okra with a Dry Spice Rub on page 167). In a pinch, lime or lemon juice can be substituted for amchur.

Lime or Lemon: Possibly following cilantro, lime is the next popular ingredient in my kitchen. I use lime and lemon interchangeably and I leave it up to you to decide which citrus fruit catches your fancy. Since these are more readily available, there are several recipes that I modified using lime juice instead of tamarind or amchur. In some cases, however, the substitutions do not necessarily work.

Dried Pomegranate Seeds: Dried pomegranate seeds are a deep reddish brown color and have a sweet-tart taste. They are typically used in the cuisine of Persia and India. People often think that they can be used interchangeably with fresh pomegranate seeds, but this usually yields rather unacceptable results. Dried seeds need to be ground before using. Dried pomegranate seeds are used in the Indian kitchen to finish off lentil or chickpea dishes, salads, and grilled meats and fish. I have often substituted the Mediterranean spice sumac for these ground seeds. Sumac has a milder tartness, but nonetheless a fruity flavor.

Tamarind: This dark sticky fruit is the fruit of the tamarind tree. In its natural form tamarind is used as a souring agent for cooking purposes. As a condiment, however, sweet and sour tamarind chutney is very popular and used as a dressing to complement other spicy chutneys. Particularly in the cuisine of Southern India, tamarind is the traditional souring agent. Currently tamarind is available in markets as a strained and prepared paste. This form offers freshness and convenience.

Yogurt: Plain natural yogurt is an essential cooking ingredient in the Indian kitchen. My personal preference is to use natural 2% yogurt. It is great to make your own natural yogurt at home, and I do this occasionally, but store-bought organic plain or Greek yogurt varieties work well. In the case of Greek yogurts, I find that the low-fat varieties do have a bit of an aftertaste. So I recommend using the whole milk varieties in my recipes. I have modified the fat content in my recipes to balance out the richness provided by this yogurt. In fact, in recipes requiring cream, whole yogurt can provide a nice and complex flavor.

To balance and round off the souring agents, we have two additional flavoring mixes that feature in the world of Indian salads. These are not souring agents but complement and enhance the flavor of souring agents:

Black Salt: Black salt is a special type of Indian mineral salt. It is actually pinkish grey rather than black and has a very distinctive sulfurous mineral taste (like hard-boiled egg yolks). It enhances tangy foods such as fruits and salads. In a simple salad, a basic combination of lime juice and black salt is used to add seasoning to the ingredients. In Indian cuisine, black salt is also sprinkled over green mangoes or sweet guava to balance out their flavors. Black salt is sold as *kala namak* and can be found in Indian stores.

Chaat Masala: This much-loved spice blend is popular for adding a tangy and spicy spark to salads and is also a finishing spice for grilled kebabs and other appetizers. It is one of my favorite spice mixtures. My own recipe for this spice blend is on page 348, but the quality of the store-bought, premixed version is quite good. My favorite brands are Swad and MDH.

Spicy Chickpea and Pomegranate Salad in Puris

(V)

I created this recipe as an adaptation of *pani puri*, a water-filled spicy appetizer usually served in these crispy cups. Despite its other cooling elements, I love to serve this dish during the late winter months. The recipe has a brightness of colors, and a light piquancy of flavors that promises you that spring is on its way. This chickpea salad is served in crispy round puffs or *puris* (also called *golgapas*) that are available in most Indian stores. If you absolutely cannot get the *puris*, serve the salad on crackers. Salads such as these are often topped with fine chickpea noodles called *sev* that are available in most Indian stores. Keep a package handy, they add some crunch to a salad not unlike croutons. If you want this dish to be gluten-free you can serve the salad over rice crackers.

Prep Time: 10 minutes | Chilling Time: 30 minutes | Serves: 6

Ingredients
1 cup cooked chickpeas
1 lime, halved
1 onion, finely chopped
2 to 3 tablespoons chopped cilantro
1 tablespoon chaat masala (page 348)
1 teaspoon salt or to taste
¾ cup fresh pomegranate seeds
½ cup plain whole milk yogurt
5 puris per person
1 to 2 tablespoons *sev* or chickpea
  noodles (sold in Indian stores)

Preparation
1. Squeeze the lime juice over the chickpeas.

2. Mix the chickpeas with the onion, cilantro, chaat masala, salt, pomegranate seeds, and yogurt and set aside for 30 minutes to let the flavors mix together.

3. Fill the puris and serve.

Well-Seasoned Potato and Mint Salad
(VE, GF)

Much as I like a heavier creamy potato salad, this recipe with loads of flavor and a light crisp citrusy finish will make you realize that you can enjoy a potato salad without guilt. This last summer, my mother got me hooked on grapefruit juice, so I like using it for this recipe but you can use lime juice if you prefer. With some imagination, this salad will remind you of the North Indian *alu chat,* . It works well with both western-style and Indian-style meals and pairs especially well with the pineapple chicken wings on page 23.

Prep Time: 30 minutes | Chilling time: 20 minutes | Serves: 4 people

Ingredients

3 tablespoons oil

1 teaspoon mustard seeds

3 cloves garlic, minced

½ teaspoon red pepper flakes

¾ teaspoon freshly ground black pepper

3 medium potatoes, boiled and cubed

1 small red onion, finely chopped

2 green chilies, minced

⅓ cup grapefruit juice or the juice of 1 lime

1 teaspoon black salt

2 tablespoons finely chopped fresh mint

Preparation

1. Heat the oil in a large skillet or wok and add the mustard seeds and wait till they pop. Add the garlic and gently cook for about 1 to 2 minutes until pale golden. Stir in the red pepper flakes and black pepper.

2. Add the potatoes and toss gently until they are coated and warmed through. Mixture should be very fragrant and the spices should be coating the potatoes with specs of golden brown.

3. Place in a mixing bowl and toss with the red onions, green chilies, grapefruit or lime juice, and black salt. Mix in the mint. Let the mixture chill for about 20 minutes before serving.

Cucumber, Carrot and Almond Salad with Yogurt

(V, GF)

This quintessential Indian salad is a more conventional variation of a *raita*, as simple and cooling as the cucumber used in it. We make two versions at our house: with and without carrots. In the really hot months of August I enjoy this as a morning snack.

My children love cucumber and bringing the slightly thorny, crisp, and tender cucumbers in from the garden is a summer highlight. Most often we simply slice them and enjoy with a pinch of black salt, but other times we make this salad. In fact, these days my daughter whips it together. The *raita* makes a wonderful side with Indian flatbreads, and also a refreshing cooler for spicy kebabs. It can also be swapped for mayonnaise in a sandwich.

Prep Time: 15 to 20 minutes | Serves: 6

Ingredients

2 medium cucumbers

1 medium carrot

2 tablespoons coarsely ground or sliced almonds

1 tablespoon minced fresh mint leaves (optional)

¾ cup low-fat plain yogurt

½ teaspoon salt or to taste

½ teaspoon sugar

Freshly ground black pepper

A sprinkle of red pepper flakes (optional)

Preparation

1. Peel the cucumber and grate into a mixing bowl discarding any whole seeds.

2. Peel the carrot and grate into the same bowl. Add the almonds and mint, if using.

3. In a separate bowl, beat the yogurt, salt, sugar, and black pepper until well mixed. Stir into the cucumber mixture.

4. Garnish with the red pepper flakes if using.

Tips and Tricks

The almonds add both texture and nutrition to this recipe. If you wish you can add pistachios instead of, or in addition to, the almonds for a more colorful effect.

Black-Eyed Pea Salad in Phyllo Cups
(VE)

This recipe is adapted from my mother-in-law's recipe for a hearty one-dish salad with black-eyed peas that is perfect for the summer in Northern India. She throws in boiled potatoes to make the dish heartier. I added some fresh summer corn and red onions for color and texture. You can add your choice of salad vegetables, such as radishes in autumn instead of the cucumber, and enjoy this simple colorful dish other times of the year when there are no cucumbers, and also for that matter no tomatoes. The real simplicity of this recipe comes from using premade phyllo cups instead of making the pastry shells yourself. This is a vegan salad and most phyllo cups usually are vegan as well, but this needs to be checked on the package.

Prep Time: 20 to 25 minutes (not including time to cook the peas) | Chill Time: 1 hour | Serves: 6

Ingredients

¾ cup cooked black-eyed peas

2 medium potatoes, boiled and diced (about ⅔ cup)

½ cup fresh or frozen (and defrosted) corn kernels

2 ripe tomatoes, chopped

½ cup diced cucumber

1 red onion, finely chopped

2 tablespoons extra virgin olive oil

1 or 2 limes (if your limes are juicy, you will not need more than one)

1½ teaspoons chaat masala (see page 348)

½ teaspoon red cayenne pepper powder

¾ teaspoon raw cane sugar

3 tablespoons finely chopped cilantro

10 to 12 mini phyllo cups (I use the Athens brand)

Chickpea flour noodles (sev) to garnish (optional)

Preparation

1. Put the black-eyed peas, chopped potatoes, and corn in a large mixing bowl and toss well.

2. Stir in the tomatoes, cucumbers, and red onions and toss well.

3. Add the olive oil. Cut the lime(s) and squeeze in the juice. Toss to coat the vegetables.

4. Sprinkle in the chaat masala, red cayenne pepper, raw sugar, and cilantro and toss to combine.

5. Chill salad for 1 hour.

6. To serve, put small amounts of the salad in the phyllo cups and top with the chickpea flour noodles (sev) before serving.

Black Bean, Corn, and Stone Fruit Salad
(VE, GF)

Not surprisingly, my kitchen has its share of global influences, from all the wonderful flavors that I have tasted through my life's journey. This Mexican-inspired salad with classic Indian seasonings works well on both Mexican and Indian tables and is something my family enjoys by the bowlful in summer, since the colorful balance of ingredients reminds them of a Mexican salsa. The magic to this salad is black beans cooked to the right level of softness and married to the tangy, tart combination of nectarines and plums. I try to stick to using our local summer fruit, but confess to often making this in winter or autumn with mangoes.

Prep Time: 20 minutes (not including cooking the black beans) | Serves: 4 to 6

Ingredients

1 cup cooked black beans

1 medium nectarine

1 large firm plum

1 cup fresh or frozen (and defrosted) corn kernels

1 medium red onion, finely chopped (about ½ cup)

2 tablespoons finely chopped cilantro

2 jalapeno chilies, seeded and very finely chopped

1½ teaspoons chaat masala (page 348)

½ teaspoon black salt

1 medium lime, halved and seeded

Preparation

1. Place the black beans in a mixing bowl.

2. Dice the nectarine and plum (discarding the stone but leaving the skin on) and add to the beans.

3. Add the corn, red onion, cilantro, and jalapeno and mix well.

4. Add the chaat masala and black salt and toss well to coat. Squeeze in the lime juice and mix.

5. Let the mixture rest for 10 to 15 minutes before serving to let the flavors marry.

Tips and Tricks

You can also use mangoes and peaches in this recipe.

Essential Indian Chopped Salad
(VE, GF)

Basic Indian salads tend to be fresh with lots of lime and black salt. This standard chopped salad is often referred to as *kachumber*. This colorful, zesty mixture is a lot like salsa, with a slightly greater hint of spice from the black pepper, and a little more delicate use of lemon.

Prep Time: 15 minutes | Chilling Time: 20 minutes | Serves: 4

Ingredients

1 medium cucumber, peeled and chopped

2 medium tomatoes, chopped, or 1 cup grape tomatoes, halved

1 red onion, chopped

2 green Serrano chilies, minced

¼-inch piece peeled ginger, minced

2 tablespoons cilantro, chopped

1 lime

½ teaspoon sugar

1 teaspoon black salt or to taste

1 teaspoon freshly ground black pepper

¼ teaspoon freshly ground cumin seeds

1 tablespoon crushed peanuts (optional)

Preparation

1. Place the cucumber, tomatoes, and onion in a large bowl.

2. Add the minced green Serrano chilies, ginger, and cilantro and toss.

3. Cut the lime in half and squeeze the lime juice over the tomato mixture. Mix in the sugar, black salt, black pepper, cumin, and crushed peanuts (if using).

4. Chill for at least 20 minutes prior to serving to let the flavors settle.

Tips and Tricks

If you want to make this a more formal creation, you can add tomatoes of different colors and garnish with peanuts and pistachios.

Bruised Tomato and Mint Salad
(VE, GF)

This salad is a favorite in my kitchen. I usually make it through the hot days of summer and early autumn, when the vine is blissfully laden with ripe, perfect tomatoes. Peanuts add an earthy crunch and texture to the fragrant mint-and-fresh-tomato medley that is wonderfully dressed with soothing natural yogurt.

Prep Time: 20 minutes | Cook Time: 7 to 8 minutes | Serves: 4

Ingredients

4 to 6 small fresh tomatoes, cut in half

1 teaspoon minced garlic

¼ cup olive oil

½ teaspoon red pepper flakes (optional)

2 tablespoons chopped fresh mint leaves

1 tablespoon chopped fresh oregano (optional)

½ cup low-fat plain yogurt

1 teaspoon salt or to taste

½ teaspoon sugar

½ cup lightly roasted coarsely ground peanuts

1 small red onion, halved and thinly sliced

Extra mint to garnish

Preparation

1. Toss the tomatoes with the garlic, olive oil, and red pepper flakes, if using, and set aside for 10 minutes.

2. Cook the tomatoes lightly on a grill for 3 to 4 minutes skin side down, till the skin of the tomato is barely bruised and lightly charred (reserve any leftover oil in bowl). Alternately, the tomatoes can be broiled for 6 to 7 minutes with the skin side up.

3. Place the tomatoes in a mixing bowl as they are done and pour any remaining oil marinade into the bowl over the tomatoes. Add the mint leaves and lightly toss.

4. In a separate small bowl, whip the yogurt with the salt and sugar and then pour over the tomatoes.

5. Lightly mix in the peanuts and garnish with the red onions and extra mint.

Tips and Tricks
This salad can be enjoyed as a light, balanced summer meal.
It can be served warm or chilled.

Warm Red Cabbage Slaw with Pecans
(V, GF)

This is a crisp, crunchy, gently spiced take on coleslaw. I like to call this a salad, however most people would call it a slaw. My husband grows colorful vegetables that he offers to me as a compromise for banning store-bought commercial cut flowers in our house. Hence, the choice of cabbage in this recipe is the red variety.

Prep Time: 15 minutes plus cooling time | Cook Time: 5 minutes | Serves: 6

Ingredients

1 tablespoon oil (mustard oil if you have it is great)

¾ teaspoon mustard seeds

1 tablespoon freshly grated ginger

2 cups grated red cabbage

½ teaspoon salt or black salt or to taste

3 tablespoons fresh lime juice (about 1 lime)

½ teaspoon honey

1 teaspoon red pepper flakes

2 tablespoons chopped cilantro

4 tablespoons coarsely crushed pecans

Preparation

1. Heat the oil in a large skillet or wok on medium heat for a minute until the oil is hot but not smoking.

2. Add the mustard seeds and wait for them to crackle. Add the ginger and sauté lightly.

3. Add the red cabbage and salt and toss well for 3 to 4 minutes until very slightly wilted.

4. Place the cabbage mixture in a mixing bowl. In a small bowl stir together the lime juice, honey, and pepper flakes and toss with the cabbage mixture along with the cilantro.

5. Cool the salad and place on a serving platter and serve topped with crushed pecans.

Roasted Bell Pepper Chutney
(VE, GF)

Once I tried roasting my first batch of fresh, straight-off-the-tree red bell peppers I was hooked. I love the mellow, well-rounded sweetness of this beautiful gift of early autumn. This chutney is great as a condiment, and as later recipes in this book attest, it offers a versatile and adaptable base for other dishes (see Shrimp in a Creamy Bell Pepper Sauce, page 209; Quick Fix Lovely Red Spinach Tofu, page 135). Its light, savory overtones enhance the innate sweetness of the red bell pepper.

Prep Time: 5 minutes | Cook Time: 40 minutes (mostly unattended) | Makes: about 1 cup

Ingredients

6 to 8 medium red bell peppers

4 garlic cloves, minced

¼ cup good quality olive oil or other flavorful vegetable oil

2 teaspoons coriander seeds

1 teaspoon mustard seeds

2 dried red chilies

15 curry leaves

1 teaspoon sugar

½ teaspoon salt or to taste

Preparation

1. Pre-heat the oven to 375°F.

2. Cut the bell peppers into quarters and remove the seeds and white center membranes. Place on a large baking sheet and toss with the garlic and all but 1 tablespoon of the oil. Bake for about 40 minutes.

3. In the meantime, heat the remaining 1 tablespoon of oil in a small skillet or wok and add the coriander seeds and wait till they darken. Add the mustard seeds and wait for them to crackle. Add the red chilies and curry leaves and turn off the heat.

4. When the peppers are done, cool slightly and place in the jar of a blender, add the seasoned oil and spices, sugar, and salt and blend to a smooth paste. Use as needed. This will keep in the refrigerator for about a week.

Tips and Tricks

This recipe works well with mustard oil or raw sesame oil, which are common in Indian pantries for pickling and savory relishes.

Quick Carrot Pickle
(VE, GF)

This recipe was created to cope with the indifferent sunshine that we get most of the time in the northeast United States. This almost instant pickle is close in taste to traditional sun-dried pickles, but is made in 10 minutes. It makes a lovely bright addition to any table.

Prep Time: 5 minutes | Cook Time: 10 minutes | Makes: 1 cup

Ingredients

2 tablespoons mustard oil

1 teaspoon mustard seeds

1 teaspoon fennel seeds

2 carrots, peeled and cut into thin sticks

1 teaspoon salt or to taste

1 teaspoon cayenne pepper powder

2 tablespoons vinegar

1 tablespoon sugar

Preparation

1. Heat the oil in a small pan or skillet. Add the mustard seeds and fennel seeds and cook for 30 seconds until the mustard seeds pop.

2. Add the carrots, salt, cayenne powder, vinegar, and sugar and cook for 5 to 7 minutes.

3. Cool and use as needed. This quick pickle will store in the refrigerator for up to 3 months.

Monsoon Mango Salsa
(V, GF)

This is a simple salsa that is very versatile, it can be used as a dip, and in recipes like my Mango and Goat Cheese Mini Crisps (page 35), and as a condiment for grilled fish, tofu, and shellfish. The colors of this simple medley remind me of the monsoon season in India—rich, bright, and vibrant.

Prep Time: 25 minutes (includes 15 minutes to let the flavors settle) | Makes: about 1 cup

Ingredients

2 ripe mangoes, peeled and diced

1 ripe tomato, chopped

1 medium red onion, finely chopped

2 tablespoons finely chopped cilantro

1 or 2 jalapeno peppers, seeded and chopped

1 medium lime, halved

1 teaspoon chaat masala (page 348)

Preparation

1. Place the mangoes, tomato, and onion in a non-reactive mixing bowl and toss together.

2. Add the cilantro and jalapeno peppers and mix well.

3. Squeeze in the lime juice and mix in the chaat masala.

4. Let the flavors rest for 15 minutes before serving.

Variation: Peach Salsa

If you want a local substitution for the mango, sweet summer peaches can be used.

The essentials of whole spices in Indian cooking

Whole spices are used in Indian cooking to infuse texture, color, and taste to the Indian table. Whole spices are usually added to hot oil to infuse it with flavor. Spice-infused oil is used for pickles and curries and is absolutely essential for finishing off lentils. The process of adding spicy oil to lentils or other dishes is called tempering or *tarka*. To achieve the best effect the oil must be hot before the spices are added, allowing the flavors of the spices to evolve and reach their full potential.

Cumin seeds: The most common whole spice (*see* Starter Spice Kit, page 13).

Nigella seeds: These shiny black seeds have a characteristic onion-like flavor. They are used for sautéing vegetables, finishing lentils, and for pressing into bread to offer some colorful contrast.

Mustard seeds: Common mustard seeds come in black and yellow varieties. The yellow mustard seed is better suited to someone who finds the taste of fresh ground mustard too strong. I use black mustard seeds for most of the recipes in this book. When added to oil, mustard seeds crackle and transform, the seeds turning darker and nutty.

Fennel seeds: Fennel seeds are a sweet-tasting anise-like spice. They are one of the few spices eaten raw as a mouth freshener. They are an essential spice for some pickle and chutney recipes, and I like to add them to some basic curries as well.

Panch Phoron or **Five Spice Mixture:** This is a mixture from Eastern India comprised of equal parts of fennel seeds, mustard seeds, fenugreek seeds, cumin seeds, and nigella seeds. It is available premixed in this form and is also a great spice for tempering and stir-frying dishes.

Pear Chutney with Roasted Fennel Seeds and Raisins
(VE, GF)

In the style of Bengali chutneys (from the Eastern region of India), this chutney is made with tart, seasonal fruit and is almost like a light curry that complements the other items in the meal. Fennel seeds, which are usually added in several layers by roasting and then crushing them and sprinkling over the top, give this chutney its characteristic taste. In autumn, when I often have a lot of colorful young green cayenne peppers that have not yet become hot, I finish off this chutney by adding a nice touch of chopped cayenne peppers.

Prep Time: 15 minutes | Cook Time: 15 minutes | Serves: 4 to 6

Ingredients

4 to 6 medium red pears, cored and diced (do not peel)

1 lime

1 tablespoon oil

1¼ teaspoons fennel seeds

½ teaspoon red pepper flakes

2 tablespoons finely grated ginger

2 tablespoons malt or cider vinegar

⅓ cup sugar or brown sugar

⅓ cup mixed raisins

1 to 2 tablespoons chopped dried sweetened cranberries (craisins)

2 long green chilies (young cayenne or long Italian peppers)

Preparation

1. Place the pears in a colander and squeeze the lime juice over them.

2. Heat the oil on medium heat for about 5 minutes. Add the fennel seeds and wait until the seeds sizzle and turn a few shades darker, this will take 20 to 30 seconds.

3. Add the red pepper flakes and stir lightly.

4. Mix in the pears, vinegar, sugar, raisins, and cranberries and stir well. Let the sugar dissolve and let the mixture come to a simmer, and then simmer for about 5 minutes, until the raisins are swollen and the pears are soft. Do not let the pears turn mushy.

5. Sprinkle with the minced green chilies before removing the mixture from the heat.

6. Store and use as needed; this mixture will keep in the refrigerator for 6 to 8 months.

Coconut and Almond Chutney
(VE, GF)

This traditional coconut chutney is a classic accompaniment to South Indian breakfast or snack dishes such as *Masala Vada* (Split Pea and Red Onion Fritters, page 27) and *Dosas* (page 311). I use sliced almonds in this recipe instead of the typical puffed gram as I tend to have almonds in my pantry. I use frozen grated coconut from Indian stores, so this chutney can be made in a cinch. My eight-year-old son has come to appreciate the magic of coconut and usually helps himself to a generous handful every time I make this chutney.

Prep Time: 15 to 20 minutes | Makes: 1 cup

Ingredients

1 cup grated unsweetened coconut (can be frozen)

2 green chilies

3 tablespoons chopped cilantro

1½ tablespoons freshly prepared tamarind paste or lime juice

⅓ cup sliced almonds

1 teaspoon salt or to taste

For tempering

1 teaspoon oil

⅛ teaspoon asafetida

1 teaspoon mustard seeds

10 curry leaves

2 to 3 red chilies (coarsely crushed)

Preparation

1. Place the coconut, green chilies, cilantro, tamarind paste or lime juice, sliced almonds, and salt in a grinder and grind into a paste. You may need a little water to get the blades moving, but do not use too much or the chutney will not have the right consistency. Put chutney in a serving bowl.

2. For tempering, heat the oil in a small pan and add the asafetida and mustard seeds and wait until the mustard seeds begin to pop. Add the curry leaves and red chilies and quickly pour the seasoned oil over the coconut mixture and lightly stir in. This chutney can be served immediately or stored in a glass non-reactive jar in the refrigerator for up to a week.

Tips and Tricks

For tempering the oil, have all the ingredients measured and beside the stove to make sure that you do not burn the spices as you have to work in fairly quick succession.

Classic Green Mint Chutney
(VE, GF)

Green mint chutney is a classic, popular staple, omnipresent next to snacks, particularly in the summer months. This recipe is a very simple free-form variation of the classic recipe. There are other creative variations using tomatoes, green mangoes, and the works, so I encourage you to create and innovate to suit your fancy. Mint by itself in this recipe can have a bitter aftertaste, so it is tempered with cilantro. You can mix and match other herbs as desired. This chutney can be used as a condiment or sandwich spread, or can be added to sauces.

Prep Time: 10 minutes | Makes: 2 cups

Ingredients

1 bunch cilantro leaves (about 3 cups of leaves; tender stems can also be used in this recipe)

2 bunches mint leaves (about 1½ cups)

2 green Serrano chilies

1 teaspoon cumin powder

½ teaspoon salt or to taste

1 teaspoon black salt

1 teaspoon sugar

2 teaspoons oil (such as mustard or canola)

2 tablespoons fresh lime juice

Preparation

1. Place the cilantro, mint, green Serrano chilies, cumin powder, salt, black salt, sugar, oil, and lime juice in the bowl of a blender.

2. Grind mixture until smooth. This chutney will keep for 3 to 4 days in the refrigerator, but the color will darken due to the lime.

Tips and Tricks

It is important to ensure that the mint leaves used for this chutney are tender or they tend to add a bitter taste to this condiment.

This chutney can be mellowed by adding 1½ tablespoons of yogurt or coconut milk as a vegan option. If adding yogurt you can skip the lime juice.

Another variation is to add some blanched peanuts or almonds.

Cranberry Conserve
(VE, GF)

On one of my trips to India, I was pleasantly surprised to discover the Indian cranberry. It is not quite as pretty as the cranberries we get in the United States but it makes a very good tart relish. This cranberry relish is a staple on my holiday table, a recipe adapted from one of my culinary inspirations, Liz Johnson.

Cook Time: 20 minutes | Makes: 1 cup

Ingredients

¾ cup port wine

1 cup sugar

6 clementines

1 tablespoon grated ginger

½ teaspoon red cayenne pepper powder

1 cup fresh cranberries

¾ cup raisins or currants

⅓ cup finely ground walnuts

Preparation

1. Put the port wine and sugar in a saucepan and bring the mixture to a simmer.

2. Cut the clementines in half and squeeze the juice and pulp into the port wine mixture.

3. Add the ginger, red cayenne pepper powder, and cranberries (reserving a handful for later) and bring back to a simmer.

4. Add the raisins or currants and continue simmering for about 10 minutes, until the cranberries pop.

5. Add the reserved cranberries and cook for another 5 minutes until the additional cranberries soften but are still whole.

6. Stir in the walnuts and remove from heat. This conserve can be served at room temperature or cold. It will keep in the refrigerator for 3 to 4 weeks.

Tamarind and Date Chutney
(VE, GF)

This traditional sweet-and-sour chutney can be used as a basic condiment, salad dressing, marinade—the possibilities are endless! My version is not very sweet. I use the tamarind paste that is available in jars, making this chutney very easy to put together. It is just a matter of simmering the ingredients into a thick puree.

Cook/Prep Time: 25 minutes | Makes: 1 cup chutney

Ingredients

1 jar tamarind paste (the Swad or Laxmi brands are good)*

1 cup chopped pitted dates

½ cup brown sugar or jaggery

½ teaspoon black salt

1 teaspoon fennel seeds

1 teaspoon cumin seeds

2 dried red chilies

Preparation

1. Place the tamarind paste, dates, brown sugar, black salt, and 2 cups water in a pot and bring to a boil. Reduce heat and simmer for 10 minutes. Cool slightly.

2. While this is simmering, place the fennel seeds and cumin seeds in a small heavy skillet and toast until the seeds darken and smell fragrant, about 20 to 30 seconds. Add the dried red chilies and toast for a few more seconds. Place in a spice grinder and grind until powdery.

3. Put the tamarind mixture in a blender and blend until smooth. Return to the pot and stir in the spice mixture and cook for another 5 minutes. Cool and store in air-tight jars in the refrigerator for up to 3 months.

Tips and Tricks

Raisins can be substituted for dates in this recipe with interesting results.

*It is important to note that tamarind paste is different from tamarind concentrate which is also sold in tubs and jars; the latter will not work in this recipe.

Variation: Tamarind Mayonnaise

Mix ¼ cup of commercial mayonnaise with 4 tablespoons of the Tamarind and Date Chutney and 1½ teaspoons of chaat masala (page 348) and use as needed.

Chapter Three

The Soulful Bowlful:
Soups & Lentils

Soups are common fare in most parts of India, particularly in the cooler hill regions. Indian soups vary from rich, creamy varieties to lighter broths. Included under the category of soups are Indian lentil soups and stews. The line between soups, soupy lentils, and the lentil curry we call *dal* is blurry. Of course, soups can be made with ingredients other than lentils, but most Indian tables favor lentil-based soups. I personally love my lentils and they feature in all their glory in our household.

Lentils are probably one of the most consistent elements of the Indian diet and every region of India has some variation of lentil soup. They are very important to the vegetarian Indian diet, since they provide protein. Lentils with rice or bread are to the Indian table what rice and beans are to the Latin table—essential, sustaining, and comforting all at once.

In Indian roadside stalls called *dhabas* you can find a simmering pot of lentils called *dhaba dal*; the creamy rich consistency of these lentils is hard to recreate. The closest I could come is the Slow-Simmered Creamy Lentils recipe (page 103), a gift from a friend who is a native of the Peshawar region in Pakistan.

While lentils are essential in all parts of India, they are handled differently depending on the region. In Northern India, lentils and beans are used interchangeably and there is a preference for heavier varieties, such as whole brown or green lentils and beans such as chickpeas and red kidney beans. Lighter lentil creations are hallmarks of eastern Indian cooking. South Indian lentils are stewed and mostly cooked with an assortment of healthy vegetables with a little rice.

If you are cooking lentils and beans every day, you probably value the importance of the reduced cooking time as well as the flavor that slow cookers and pressure cookers offer (see page 89). If you do not have either of these, you can cook lentils in a large pot on the stove top. While the lentils need a little more attention this way, they are still relatively easy to put together. There are also several varieties of split lentils that work perfectly for stovetop cooking without either of these devices. For these lentil recipes, I provide cooking times for using a regular pot and a slow cooker or pressure cooker.

For simple wholesome Indian meals, pick a good lentil stew, pair with a rice or bread recipe, and serve with a side of salad or a quick pickle. It will bring India straight to your table without much fuss.

Photo by Aadi Gupta Bhattacharya

Using a pressure cooker and slow cooker in Indian cooking

Though this may sound slightly oxymoronic, I am passionate about both my slow cooker and my pressure cooker. Both these simple devices go a long way with cooking lentils and beans and limit the time and attention needed to produce the creamy traditional consistency.

When I discuss these cooking tools with students, I find many people need an initiation to using the pressure cooker. Although the pressure cooker seems to be making a comeback, people tend to be less familiar with it. The slow cooker might be more familiar to people, but I think that it still underappreciated, and relegated to chilies and beans. So, I shall tackle these individually.

Pressure cooker

There are several varieties of pressure cookers on the market. If you do not have one, I would recommend starting with a smaller one. I have seen fewer small pressure cookers made by non-Indian manufacturers; however it is up to you to decide what brand and variety to buy. I do not have a preference in terms of functionality, however, I find more flexibility of models with Indian manufacturers since the Indian pressure cooker is almost as essential to the Indian home as the tea kettle for morning tea.

The pressure cooker is a pot with a tight-fitting lid, usually secured by a rubber lining. There is an extended steam release mechanism that is secured by a weight or pressure. Cooking under this pressure allows some intense temperature to build inside the cooking pot, thereby cooking the food significantly faster while preserving the nutrients.

Learn how to close the pressure cooker, being careful to follow the manufacturer's directions. Then let the pressure build. When the pressure builds up the pressure cooker essentially whistles. At this point it is important to turn down the heat and cook the food for the desired period of time I give in my recipes.

Slow cooker

The slow cooker allows food to cook for an extended period of time at a low temperature. It is close to the original Indian method of sealed pot slow cooking called *dum pukht*. Meats and lentils prepared in a slow cooker are surprisingly tender and often have a deeply flavorful texture. The advantage of a slow cooker is that the food can be left to cook with minimal attention. I do not use pressure cookers and slow cookers interchangeably except when cooking beans and lentils. My personal choice for a slow cooker is a programmable self-shutting-off variety. I have found brands such as Rival offer these features at relatively inexpensive prices. Most curries and stews can be adapted easily for the slow cooker—though you cannot skip the processes of browning the aromatics or adding in tempering where appropriate, but most of the cooking can indeed be done unsupervised.

Corn, Coconut and Bell Pepper Soup
(VE, GF)

It has taken me some time to get used to the concept of a cold soup, however after a visit to Spain I fell in love with the gazpacho, which led to further experimentation with different types of cold soups. This recipe is a late summer or early fall soup and can be enjoyed either cold or hot. It is perfect to make when the corn is sweet and colored bell peppers are just coming of age. The corn cobs are used to create a deep and flavorful stock. If desired this stock can be used in lieu of other vegetarian stock in any recipe of your choice.

Prep Time: 15 minutes, plus 2 hours to chill if serving cold | Cook Time: 1 hour (mostly unattended) |
Serves: 4

Ingredients

For the cornhusk stock

6 to 8 corncobs with the kernels
    removed and reserved

1 (2-inch) cinnamon stick

1 onion, coarsely chopped

Salt to taste

For the soup

3 tablespoons oil

1 white onion (such as a sweet Vidalia),
    chopped (about ¾ cup)

1 tablespoon grated fresh ginger

1½ cups fresh corn kernels (from the
    corncobs used in stock)

1 red bell pepper, diced

1 medium poblano pepper or mild
    green pepper, diced

Juice of 2 limes or lemons

½ cup fresh basil leaves

3 or 4 curry leaves

1½ cups coconut milk

Thinly sliced scallions to garnish
    (optional)

Preparation

1. For the stock, in a large pot, place the corncobs, cinnamon stick, onion, salt, and 6 cups of water and simmer for 20 minutes. Cool and strain the stock.

2. While the stock is cooking, heat the oil in a large saucepan on medium heat. Add the onion and cook slowly until soft and beginning to turn golden, about 7 to 8 minutes.

3. Add the ginger, corn, red pepper, and poblano pepper and cook for 5 minutes.

4. Stir in the corn stock and simmer for 15 minutes.

5. Let mixture cool and then squeeze in the lime or lemon juice and stir in the basil leaves and curry leaves.

6. Puree the mixture in a blender and then strain through a fine mesh sieve. Return to the saucepan.

7. Stir in the coconut milk and simmer for 10 minutes.

8. Serve hot or chill for at least 2 hours and serve cold. Garnish with thinly sliced scallions if desired.

Tips and Tricks

To add a rich finish, you can stir in 2 to 3 tablespoons of coconut milk prior to serving.

Split Pea Soup with Cilantro and Chorizo
(M&P, GF)

This simple soup can be left almost unattended in the slow cooker, and then finished off with the classic technique of spice-infused oil that we refer to as *tarka*. A good *tarka* adds the signature touch of flavor to most lentil dishes. Fresh spicy chorizo, which I often pick up from our local farmers market, adds an additional spark to this soup. The use of spicy sausages is not uncommon in the Indian kitchen particularly in regions of Goa and Kerala. Now, back to this wonderful soup—I think this will become a wintertime staple once you try it.

Prep Time: 5 minutes | Cook Time: 4 hours, mostly unattended in a slow cooker | Serves: 4 to 6

Ingredients

¾ cup yellow split peas (motor dal)

¼ pound chorizo, diced

1 red onion, finely chopped

2 tablespoons grated ginger

Salt to taste (*this depends on the saltiness of the chorizo*)

½ teaspoon turmeric

1 lime or lemon

2 tablespoons finely chopped cilantro

For tempering

2 tablespoons oil

1 teaspoon freshly ground cumin seeds (*I like to do this with a mortar and pestle to retain some texture*)

½ teaspoon red pepper flakes

Several grinds fresh black pepper

Preparation

1. Place the yellow split peas in a slow cooker and add 6 cups water and the chorizo, red onion, ginger. salt, and turmeric. Cook the soup for about 3½ hours on high heat, stirring occasionally. The soup should reach a creamy thick consistency at this point.

2. Stir the mixture well. Cut the lime in half and squeeze in the lime juice and add the cilantro. Taste for salt.

3. Assemble the ingredients for the tempering. Ladle the soup into serving bowls.

4. Heat the oil on medium-low heat in a small pan for about 1 minute. Working quickly add the ground cumin seeds and wait until it begins to sizzle. Add the red pepper flakes and black pepper and cook for a few seconds. Remove from heat.

5. Pour small quantities of the seasoned oil over the soup in each bowl and swirl in lightly before serving.

Lazy Mulligatawny Soup
(M&P, GF)

A comforting soup that hails from the heritage of Anglo-Indian cooking and meshes Indian spices with British inspirations. This soup gets its depth of flavor from an assortment of sweet and savory ingredients. The traditional variation is complex, but in this lazy version I have simplified it considerably. It is my families winter go-to soup, so I have learned to make this in less than half an hour with some help from the pressure cooker, or on more leisurely days, I let it softly simmer in the slow cooker. This soup is enriched with the gentle sweetness of fresh autumn apples and tends to be perfect for that time of the year as well.

Prep Time: 15 minutes | Cook Time: 30 minutes in a pressure cooker or 3 hours in a slow cooker | Serves: 6 to 8

Ingredients

4 tablespoons oil

1 large red onion, finely chopped (about ¾ cup)

⅓ cup chopped celery

1 tablespoon minced garlic

1½ teaspoons freshly grated ginger

2 boneless chicken thighs, diced (about ½ pound)

¾ teaspoon turmeric

1 teaspoon red cayenne pepper powder

1 teaspoon curry powder (page 354 or store-bought)

2 Granny Smith apples, peeled and chopped

1 medium sweet potato, peeled and chopped

2 carrots, peeled and chopped

¾ cup split red lentils (masoor dal)

2 cups chicken stock or water

½ cup brown rice or barley

1 cup coconut milk

2 to 3 tablespoons chopped cilantro

3 tablespoons lemon juice

Red pepper flakes and freshly ground black pepper for serving

Preparation

1. Place the oil at the base of a pressure cooker or large pot and heat for about 1 minute.

2. Add the onion, celery, garlic, and ginger and cook for about 8 minutes, until the onion is softly wilted and the color of toffee.

3. Add the chicken with the turmeric, cayenne pepper powder, and curry powder and cook for 2 to 3 minutes, until the chicken is no longer pink.

4. Add the apples, sweet potato, carrots, red lentils, and stock or water. If you are using water add some salt to taste.

5. Add the brown rice or barley and pressure cook for 10 minutes; or simmer on the stove top for 1 hour; or slow cook for about 3 hours.

6. Cool slightly and mix well. The mixture should be soft and almost a puree.

7. Stir in the coconut milk and some additional water or stock if needed (the soup should be the consistency of buttermilk) and simmer for 2 to 5 minutes.

8. Stir in the cilantro and lemon juice and garnish with red pepper flakes or black pepper to taste.

Tips and Tricks

If you want a vegetarian or vegan soup, skip the chicken and add 2 cups of diced mushrooms and use vegetable broth or water.

Sweet Potato Soup with Saffron, Sage and Nutmeg
(VE, GF)

This soup always makes me think of Halloween, when my brother visits from Seattle every year to join the kids. They love dressing up with their uncle to go trick-or-treating. I made this soup for them one year, its orange color fitting into the season nicely. The kids felt very excited and grown up when they realized that the soup had ginger in it, as they associate ginger with what they consider grown-up food. A sweet variety of onion such as Vidalia or cipollini also works well instead of the shallots, and of course this soup can be made with any variety of winter squash also. The flavors of saffron and sage add a lovely depth of flavor to the nutritious sweet potato. It is important to begin prepping the shallots or onions while the potatoes are baking.

Prep Time: 10 minutes | Cook Time: 60 minutes | Serves: 6

Ingredients

3 medium sweet potatoes (about 1½ pounds)

3 tablespoons oil plus 1 teaspoon

4 shallots, finely chopped (about ¾ cup)

1 tablespoon grated ginger

1 tablespoon minced garlic

2 teaspoons freshly ground coriander seeds

1½ teaspoons freshly ground fennel seeds

1½ teaspoons salt or to taste

1 teaspoon red cayenne pepper powder (this can be increased for a bolder flavor)

1 cup coconut milk

4 cups water or vegetable broth (if using broth please take a note of the salt and adjust accordingly)

2 teaspoons saffron strands

Freshly grated nutmeg

¼ cup fresh sage leaves

Preparation

1. Heat the oven to 350°F. Wrap the sweet potatoes in foil and place on a baking tray. Bake for about 40 minutes, until soft. Cool the potatoes slightly and then peel and chop coarsely.

2. While the sweet potatoes are baking, heat 3 tablespoons of oil on medium heat. Add the shallots and cook low and slow until they soften and begin to turn a pale toffee color, about 8 to 10 minutes.

3. Stir in the ginger and garlic and sauté for another 2 to 3 minutes, until the mixture is aromatic.

4. Add the coriander, fennel, salt, and cayenne pepper powder and stir well.

5. Stir in the coconut milk, 2 cups of the water or broth, and most of the saffron (reserve about ½ teaspoon for garnish) and bring to a simmer. Add the sweet potatoes and simmer for 8 to 10 minutes.

6. Cool mixture slightly and then blend to a puree with the remaining water or broth. Re-heat if needed.

7. Heat the remaining 1 teaspoon oil and add the sage leaves and fry lightly. Reserve a few to garnish and crush the rest and stir into the soup.

8. To serve, ladle the soup into bowls and sprinkle each with some nutmeg, a few strands of saffron, and some fried sage leaves and serve.

Know your beans and lentils

In Indian cooking, we eat beans and lentils in various shapes, sizes, and colors. This has been a source of confusion to some people. To demystify beans and lentils completely would take much longer than the couple of pages that I am allotting here, but I do think that I can get you started with some basics and offer you a clear directive on the beans and lentils being used in this book.

Beans and lentils usually come with a skin on and the un-husked and un-skinned variety is healthier. However, the un-husked variety does take longer to cook and is harder to digest. This brings us to the issue of soaking lentils. It is a good idea to soak dried beans and un-husked lentils for a few hours prior to cooking, if possible with a couple of changes of water. Soaking lentils softens them and allows them to cook quicker. The process also removes some of the insoluble starches that are harder to digest and tend to cause flatulence. The skinless varieties tend to have brighter colors and are usually surgically split to allow quick cooking.

Black-Eyed Peas (*Lobia*): The black-eyed pea plant was first domesticated in West Africa, and the legume pods are light beige in color with black middles or eyes. These are popular in several cultures as well as in India. In the southern United States, black-eyed peas are considered a lucky way to start the New Year. They cook quicker than red kidney beans or chickpeas and can be used in salads or as a substitute for the red kidney beans in recipes like my Slow-cooked Traditional Curried Kidney Beans (page 115).

Chickpeas / Garbanzo Beans (*Kabuli Chola*): These beige legumes are popular in North Indian and Middle Eastern cuisine. They are low maintenance since they grow with very little water and are therefore a boon to drier desert-like climates. Less common brown chickpeas have an interesting taste and can be used the same way as yellow chickpeas.

Red Kidney Beans (*Rajma*): Named because of their indented shape resembling a human kidney, these beans have a dark red color making them rich in both antioxidants and iron. They cook up to a nice comforting softness. White beans can be used as a substitute in the kidney bean recipes in this book.

Brown Lentils (*Sabut Masur Dal*): I like to call these whole brown lentils "lentil soup lentils" since they are most commonly used for lentils soups in American, Mediterranean, and various other cuisines. In Northern India, you'll find them in comforting lentil stews and served with rice or handmade flatbreads.

Black Lentils (*Sabut Urad Dal*): Small whole black lentils are the Indian version of black beans. They can be cooked the same way as in black bean recipes. Slow simmered for hours in North Indian kitchens, these lentils have a satisfying texture that works well in soups or stews.

Green Lentils (*Sabut Moong Dal*): Whole green lentils are usually cooked in dry preparations. They are my favorite lentil for sprouting and using in salads. They also work well in recipes for lentil pancakes and rice and lentil pilafs.

Orange/Red Split Lentils (*Masur Dal*): Orange/red split lentils are one of the most common lentils in my kitchen, due to their quick cooking time. They cook up to buttery softness and can be finished nicely with some light tempering or even just a touch of butter or ghee.

Yellow Split Lentils (*Dhuli Moong Dal*): These split lentils are the husked variety of green lentils. They cook up fairly quickly and tend to have a slightly stronger taste than orange lentils. I like to combine these lentils with vegetables.

Yellow Split Pigeon Peas (*Arhar/Toor Dal*): These lentils are similar to yellow Bengali gram lentils but have a slightly darker ochre-like color. These lentils have a very distinct, earthy taste. They work well with tart flavors and are usually cooked with a souring agent such as tamarind, lime, or green mango.

White Split Lentils (*Dhuli Urad Dal*): White split lentils are the husked counterpart of whole black lentils and are typically used to make batters for crepes and fritters since they grind up to a soft consistency. They can, of course, be cooked as a lentil stew as well.

To pressure cook and slow cook beans and lentils:

It is a good idea to soak the beans and unhusked lentils for a few hours and rinse several times before cooking.

Standard pressure cooker times are:

50 minutes for chickpeas (1 cup soaked chickpeas with 2 cups of water and salt to taste)

35 minutes for kidney beans, black-eyed peas, whole brown or black lentils (¾ cup soaked beans/peas/lentils with 1½ cups water and salt to taste)

25 minutes for split white lentils (½ cup lentils with 1½ cups water and salt to taste)

15 minutes for red or yellow split lentils (½ cup lentils with 1½ cups water and salt to taste)

Standard slow cooker times are:

4 hours on high for chickpeas (1 cup soaked chickpeas with 2 cups of water and salt to taste)

3½ hours on high for kidney beans, black-eyed peas, whole brown or black lentils (¾ cup soaked beans/peas/lentils with 1½ cups water and salt to taste)

3 hours on high for split white lentils, red lentils, and yellow split lentils (½ cup lentils with 1½ cups water and salt to taste)

Fragrant Brown Lentil Soup
(V, GF)

This soup is simple and comforting as well as really rich and creamy without the addition of any cream or coconut milk! When I was pregnant with my son Aadi, there was not a lot that I could keep down, so these wonderful lentils with steamed rice was one of my staple meals and interestingly enough, it is one of my son's favorite dishes. The simple richness of slow-simmered lentils is actually rather easy on the waistline. This lovely lentil soup does not really need anything more, but if you feel compelled, by all means finish it off with that tablespoon of butter!

Prep Time: 5 minutes | Cook Time: 15 minutes in pressure cooker • 4 hours in slow cooker • 1 hour on stovetop | Serves: 4 to 6

Ingredients

1 cup whole brown lentils (*masur dal*)

½ teaspoon turmeric

1 teaspoon salt

1 teaspoon red cayenne pepper powder

4 tomatoes, chopped

1 onion, finely chopped

2 cloves garlic, finely chopped

1½ teaspoons oil

2 teaspoons bruised cumin seeds

1 tablespoon butter (*optional*)

2 tablespoons cilantro, finely chopped

Preparation

1. Place the lentils, turmeric, salt, red cayenne pepper powder, tomatoes, onion, garlic, and 3 cups water in a pressure cooker. Cook on low under pressure for 15 minutes. The consistency of the lentils should be soft and creamy while retaining their shape. (Alternately place the ingredients in a slow cooker on high for 4 hours. Or to use the stove top, place in a heavy-bottomed pot and bring to a simmer, cover and cook on low heat for about 1 hour.)

2. Heat the oil in a small pan on medium heat. Add the cumin seeds and bring them to a quick sizzle. Pour over the lentils and stir well.

3. Stir in the butter, if using, and the cilantro. Serve either over rice or by itself as a soup.

Slow-Simmered Creamy Lentils
(V, GF)

The beauty of this bowl of lentils is their rich, dense taste. Elegant and satisfying at the same time, these lentils make a great dish for a party. There are many variations of this dish and this recipe that they call *Dal Peshawai* is from my friend Ashraf's family kitchen in Peshawar. It is a close cousin to the dish commonly known as *Dal Makhani*. I usually cook this in the slow cooker, but have provided stove top timing as well. It is actually a good recipe to make when you are doing other things in the kitchen, since you only need to stir occasionally between other tasks. You can serve this dish with salad and some bread for a hearty meal.

Prep Time: 5 minutes | Cook Time: 4 hours in slow cooker • 2½ hours on stovetop | Serves: 4 to 6

Ingredients

¾ cup whole black lentils (sabut urad dal)

½ cup red kidney beans (rajma)

4 to 6 tomatoes, chopped

2 or 3 cloves garlic, minced

1 tablespoon grated fresh ginger

1 onion, finely chopped

¾ teaspoon coriander powder

½ teaspoon cumin powder

2 green chilies, minced

1 teaspoon salt

2 tablespoons clarified butter

1 teaspoon cumin seeds

1 teaspoon red pepper flakes

1 tablespoon dried fenugreek leaves (*Kasuri methi*)

⅓ cup heavy cream (optional)

3 to 4 tablespoons chopped cilantro

Preparation

1. Put the black lentils, red kidney beans, tomatoes, garlic, ginger, onion, coriander powder, cumin powder, chilies, salt, and 4 cups water in a slow cooker and set on high for 3¼ hours. (Alternately, to cook on stovetop, place ingredients in a heavy-bottomed pot, bring to simmer and cover and cook for 2 hours, stirring occasionally.) During this time the lentils thicken and acquire a smooth silken consistency.

2. In a small pan, heat the clarified butter on medium heat for 1 minute. Add the cumin seeds and wait for them to sizzle. Stir in the red pepper flakes. Pour the seasoned oil over the lentils and stir well.

3. Add the fenugreek leaves. Mix in the cream (if using) and stir well. Continue to cook in slow cooker for another 45 minutes or simmer on the stovetop for another 30 minutes.

4. Garnish with the cilantro before serving.

Spicy Lentil Broth with Pineapple
(VE, GF)

Here is a simple and flavorful take on the South Indian lentil broth called *rasam*. *Rasams* are supposedly the inspiration for the famous Indian mulligatawny soup. I usually make this with pineapples, and when the season is right, I add Granny Smith apples as well. The key is to find a fruit that is mostly tart with a touch of sweetness. I have kept the spices simpler and lighter than a traditional *rasam*, adding just a finish of cumin and black pepper instead of a more complex *rasam masala*. The recipe is finished off with a light tempering with mustard seeds.

Prep Time: 10 minutes | Cook Time: 30 minutes in pressure cooker • 60 minutes on stovetop |
Serves: 4 to 6

Ingredients

¾ cup yellow split pigeon peas (*toor dal*)

½ teaspoon turmeric

1½ teaspoons fresh ginger paste

1 teaspoon salt

2 tomatoes, chopped

1 teaspoon cumin seeds

½ teaspoon black peppercorns

½ cup pureed fresh pineapple

½ cup diced fresh pineapple

1 lime or lemon

Cilantro to garnish

For tempering
1 teaspoon oil

⅛ teaspoon asafetida

½ teaspoon mustard seeds

2 dried red chilies

8 curry leaves (optional)

Preparation

1. Put the pigeon peas, turmeric, ginger paste, salt, and 3 cups water in a pressure cooker or large pot and stir. Add the chopped tomatoes.

2. In a small skillet, lightly dry roast the cumin seeds and black peppercorns until fragrant and slightly darkened and then grind to a powder. Add to the lentils.

3. Cover lentils and cook under pressure for 15 minutes. (Or simmer for 45 minutes on the stovetop. If you are doing this on the stovetop you may need to add more water, the cooked lentils should be fairly thin in consistency.)

4. Remove the cover and stir in the pureed and diced pineapples and simmer for 10 minutes.

5. Cut the lime in half and squeeze in the juice.

6. Heat the oil in a small pan on medium heat and add the asafetida and mustard seeds and wait until the mustard seeds begin to crackle. Add the dried red chilies and turn off the heat. Stir in the curry leaves and immediately pour the oil over the lentils. Garnish with cilantro and serve.

Red Lentils with Thyme and Caramelized Shallots
(VE, GF)

These quick-cooking and extremely satisfying red lentils are the mainstay of many of my family meals. A lot of people including my children are sometimes disappointed that red lentils tend to change their color to the pale yellow associated with all lentils; the distinction however is in their taste. Red lentils become meltingly soft, rich, and buttery in taste when cooked, called *mushoorir dal*, they are comfort food in eastern India. The thyme and lime in this recipe offer some interesting overtones that are almost Middle Eastern, a region that creates some lovely lentil soups.

Prep Time: 5 minutes | Cook Time: 20 minutes | Serves: 4

Ingredients

¾ cup red split lentils (*masur dal*)

¾ teaspoon turmeric

1 teaspoon salt

2 green chilies, slit halfway through lengthwise

1 tablespoon fresh thyme

2 tablespoons oil

3 shallots, very thinly sliced

1 lime

Preparation

1. Put the lentils, turmeric, salt, chilies, thyme, and 2 cups water in a cooking pot and bring to a boil. Turn down the heat and simmer for 20 minutes, stirring occasionally. The lentils become softer, change color, and then slowly melt into the water.

2. While the lentils are cooking, heat the oil in a medium skillet and add the shallots and cook on low heat, stirring frequently until they wilt, soften, and ultimately turn crisp and golden.

3. Pour the shallots with oil on the lentils and mix well.

4. Cut the lime in half and squeeze in the lime juice before serving.

Tips and Tricks

The shallots take about the same amount of time to brown as it takes to cook the lentils, so if you start them right after the lentils begin to cook the entire dish is done in about 20 minutes.

Stir-fried Whole Green Lentils with Onions and Tomatoes
(VE, GF)

This is a very simple, yet nourishing lentil preparation using the slow cooker. The lentils can also be cooked on the stovetop with plenty of water. The only thing to watch for with these beans is that they are cooked thoroughly without getting mushy. I like to cook the lentils ahead of time with 1 teaspoon of salt and then hold them aside for the rest of the preparation. The lentils used in this recipe are whole green moong lentils but you can make this with any bean or whole lentil of your choice.

Prep Time: 5 minutes | Cook Time: 3 hours in slow cooker plus 15 minutes on stovetop | Serves: 4

Ingredients

¾ cup whole green lentils (*sabut moong dal*)

2 tablespoons oil

1 teaspoon cumin seeds

1 onion, finely chopped

1 teaspoon grated fresh ginger

1 teaspoon coriander powder

1 tomato, chopped

2 green chilies, finely chopped

1 teaspoon salt or to taste

1 tablespoon dried sweet coconut (optional)

2 tablespoons chopped cilantro

1 lime, cut in half

Preparation

1. Put the lentils in a slow cooker with 3 cups water and cook on high for 3 hours. The lentils should be soft but retain their shape. Cool and drain any excess water.

2. Heat the oil in a medium skillet. Add the cumin seeds and wait for them to sizzle.

3. Add the onion and ginger and cook, stirring frequently, until the onions soften and turn slightly golden on the edges.

4. Add the coriander powder and tomatoes and cook for another 2 minutes until the tomatoes soften.

5. Add the chilies, cooked lentils, and salt and gently stir. Cook for about 1 minute until heated through.

6. Stir in the coconut and cilantro and squeeze in the lime juice.

Split Gram Lentils with Cabbage
(VE, GF)

Our household is often blessed with weeknight visitors who are en route to New York City. Balanced one-dish meals like this are perfect for such impromptu visitors. This wintertime lentil dish is best made with tender young cabbage. I like to serve this meal with a hearty bread such as the potato-filled flatbreads on page 297.

Prep Time: 5 minutes | Cook Time: 15 minutes in pressure cooker • 2 hours on stovetop | Serves: 4

Ingredients

¾ cup yellow Bengali gram lentils (*chana dal*)

1 teaspoon turmeric

1 tablespoon grated fresh ginger

4 cloves garlic, grated

1 teaspoon salt

2 tablespoons oil

1 teaspoon cumin seeds

¾ teaspoon mustard seeds

1 teaspoon cayenne pepper powder

¼ teaspoon asafetida

1 onion, chopped

1 cup finely chopped cabbage

1 tomato, chopped

2 tablespoons cilantro, finely chopped

Preparation

1. Put the lentils, turmeric, ginger, garlic, salt, and 1½ cups water in a pressure cooker and cook under pressure for 15 minutes. (Alternatively, to cook on stovetop put ingredients in a heavy-bottomed pot and cook on low heat for 2 hours, stirring occasionally.) The lentils needs to reach a soft texture, but not become completely mushy.

2. When the lentils are almost done cooking, heat the oil in a large skillet on medium heat for about 1 minute. Add the cumin seeds and mustard seeds and when the mustard seeds begin to pop add the cayenne pepper powder and asafetida, followed by the onion. Sauté the onion lightly for about 2 to 3 minutes, until softened and turning lightly translucent.

3. Add the cabbage and tomato and cook for another 5 minutes until the cabbage is cooked but still fairly crisp and tomatoes are softened.

4. Stir the cooked lentil mixture until fairly smooth and then pour into the cabbage mixture and simmer for another 3 to 4 minutes until the flavors are mixed. Check the seasonings for salt.

5. Stir in the cilantro and serve.

Tips and Tricks

I make this recipe with yellow lentils, also known as Bengali gram dal. If you are unable to find them in your store, you can use regular yellow split peas that are readily available in most stores.

Yellow Split Peas with Dill and Thyme
(VE, GF)

My first internship was a rather nerve-racking experience; I think I picked up my nail biting habit back then and never lost it. One consolation was the lovely and competent assistant to my supervisor. She was from the Sindhi community and originally came from the Mumbai region in India. I learned this lentil recipe from her, but have made it my own over time. The distinct taste she added to her lentils was the dill, a flavor not familiar in my mother's kitchen.

Prep Time: 5 to 7 minutes | Cook Time: 25 minutes using pressure cooker • 60 minutes on stovetop

Ingredients

¾ cup dried yellow split pigeon peas (*toor dal*)

½ teaspoon turmeric

1 teaspoon salt or to taste

½ teaspoon red cayenne pepper powder

1 tablespoon chopped fresh dill

1 tablespoon chopped fresh thyme

½ lime or lemon

For tempering

2 tablespoons canola oil

¾ teaspoon cumin seeds

¾ teaspoon mustard seeds

1½ teaspoons minced fresh ginger

1 large tomato, coarsely chopped

Preparation

1. Dry roast the split peas at the base of a pressure cooker or heavy-bottomed pot, stirring frequently until the mixture is fragrant and a few shades darker.

2. Add the turmeric, salt, cayenne powder, and 3⅓ cups water. Cook under pressure for 6 to 7 minutes; or on stovetop for 40 minutes, until soft and creamy, adding more water if needed. Cool slightly, remove the lid and stir well. Stir in the dill and thyme.

3. In a separate pan, heat the oil on medium heat for 1 minute. Add the cumin seeds and wait till they sizzle and then add the mustard seeds and wait till they crackle. Stir in the ginger and cook for about 1 minute. Stir in the tomato and cook for 2 minutes.

4. Pour the seasoned oil into the lentils and simmer for 15 minutes.

5. Squeeze in the lime or lemon juice and serve with steamed hot rice.

Slow-Cooked Traditional Kidney Beans
(VE, GF)

Rajma (made with red kidney beans) is a variation of rice and beans that most children in North India grow up eating. If you add in some chopped carrots, this dish is very reminiscent of a vegetarian chili. For most people from North India, a serving of *rajma* resonates with memories of home. This being said, as with all Indian cuisine, each family and region has its own variation and this recipe comes from my Punjabi friend Rajni.

Prep Time: 5 minutes | Cook Time: 4½ hours using slow cooker • 50 minutes using pressure cooker •
3 hours on stovetop | Serves: 4 to 6

Ingredients

¾ cup dried red kidney beans, soaked
   for 2 to 3 hours

2 teaspoons salt

3 tablespoons oil

1 teaspoon cumin seeds

1 onion, finely chopped

1 tablespoon grated fresh ginger

1 tablespoon finely chopped garlic

3 green chilies, finely chopped

1 teaspoon cumin powder

1 tablespoon turmeric

1 teaspoon sugar

4 tomatoes, coarsely chopped

3 tablespoons chopped cilantro

Preparation

1. Put the kidney beans, 1½ teaspoons of the salt, and 4 cups water in a slow cooker, pressure cooker, or heavy-bottomed pot. Cook for 4 hours on high in the slow cooker; or under pressure for 25 minutes; or simmer on stovetop for 2½ hours.

2. Cool the kidney beans slightly and reserve about ¾ cup of the cooking water.

3. Heat the oil in a medium pot. Add the cumin seeds and wait until they sizzle. Add the onion, ginger, and garlic and cook for 5 minutes, stirring occasionally, until the onion is soft and beginning to crisp at the edges.

4. Add the green chilies, cumin powder, turmeric, and sugar and stir well. Mix in the tomatoes and cook for 10 minutes, stirring frequently. The tomatoes should soften and then cook through until the oil begins to resurface.

5. Add the kidney beans with the ¾ cup reserved cooking water and the remaining ½ teaspoon salt and simmer for 10 minutes.

6. Check for seasonings and garnish with cilantro. Serve.

Tips and Tricks
This recipe can be very comfortably adapted to other beans, such as black beans or white beans. For a heartier variation, some ground chicken can be added while cooking the tomatoes.

Comforting Slow-Cooked Chickpeas with Tomatoes and Ginger
(VE, GF)

Chickpeas (or choley or channa masala) were one of the first dishes that I learned to make away from home. They are such a crowd pleaser I have learned to savor them in many different ways as can be seen from their proliferation in this book. This particular recipe is one of my signature recipes, and extremely simple since I make it in the slow cooker and it practically cooks unattended. It is also virtually fat free and loaded with nutrition and flavor. My husband loves raw red onions with this creation while other members of the family find them too sharp so I have compromised by using scallions.

Prep Time: 10 minutes | Cook Time: 8 hours in a slow cooker | Serves: 6

Ingredients

¾ cup dried chickpeas, rinsed several times

1 teaspoon salt

4 tablespoons oil

2 onions, diced

2 tablespoons grated fresh ginger

3 green chilies, minced

3 tomatoes, quartered

½ cup cilantro leaves

1½ teaspoons cumin powder

1 lime

½ cup chopped scallions

Preparation

1. Put the chickpeas, salt, and 3 cups water in a slow cooker.

2. Heat the oil in a medium skillet on medium heat for 1 minute. Add the onions and ginger and cook for about 7 to 8 minutes, until the onions wilt, soften, and turn pale golden. Add the onion mixture to the slow cooker and cook the chickpeas on low undisturbed for 6 hours.

3. Put the green chilies, tomatoes, cilantro, and cumin powder in a blender and blend until smooth.

4. Add this mixture to the chickpeas and let simmer for 2 more hours (you should then have a soft mass of chickpeas coated in a reddish orange sauce).

5. Cut the lime in half and squeeze in the lime juice. Garnish with the scallions and serve.

Chapter Four

Nature's Protein: Eggs, Paneer & Tofu

This section covers the vegetarian alternatives to meat and fish. In Indian cooking, these proteins are usually served in lieu of vegetables rather than as a vegetarian alternative to meat. The debate in Indian kitchens is about eggs—people are unsure whether to place them with the meats or as a meat-alternative. I chose to place them in this chapter.

The preferred Indian vegetarian protein is paneer, a rich cheese created by curdling milk and pressing the milk solids into a block. Paneer is readily available in most Indian grocery stores and while it can be easily made at home, I tend to use store-bought paneer more often than not.

I use tofu, which is even more accessible than paneer, in some of the recipes in this section as well. Tofu is not typically Indian, but it makes a great vegan substitute for paneer. I have seen tofu featured on more restaurant menus in India these days, possibly due to diet preferences. Tofu is usually available in mainstream grocery stores. For Indian cooking, I prefer to use extra-firm tofu, which I like to drain and press before using. These days you actually can find the pre-cubed variety of this tofu made by Nasoya, which is my commercial brand of choice.

Tofu is plain or flavorless on its own, but it absorbs flavors beautifully, making it a wonderful ingredient to add to Indian gravies. If you are also looking for vegan alternatives to these recipes, tofu is the way to go. Tofu is also lower in fat than most paneer varieties and if you use the extra-firm variety there is not a lot of difference in the taste.

Egg Curry with Shallots, Potatoes and Peas
(GF)

Today's fast-paced world is connected in a myriad of virtual ways. I was so pleased when this recipe caught the attention of fellow mommy blogger Dara. It is very satisfying to connect with people through my cooking. This recipe is an adaptation of my father's egg curry (*Dimer Dalna*), and his signature additions are the fennel seeds and crushed pepper finish.

Prep Time: 15 minutes | Cook Time: 30 minutes | Serves: 6

Ingredients

8 hard-boiled eggs, shelled

1½ teaspoons red cayenne pepper powder

½ teaspoon turmeric

2 teaspoons salt

⅓ cup oil

1 large potato

1 teaspoon cumin seeds

4 cloves garlic, grated

4 shallots, coarsely chopped

1 teaspoon freshly ground black pepper

2 teaspoons cumin-coriander powder (page 353)

1 tomato, quartered

⅓ cup plain yogurt

1 green chili, minced

½ cup frozen peas

For tempering
1 teaspoon oil
¾ teaspoon whole fennel seeds
½ teaspoon red pepper flakes

To garnish
2 tablespoons chopped cilantro

Preparation

1. Coat the eggs with half the cayenne pepper powder, half the turmeric, and half the salt and let them absorb the spices for 15 minutes. The eggs should be lightly rubbed with the spices and will have a colorful streaked appearance.

2. Heat half the oil in a shallow skillet and carefully add the eggs. Cook the eggs until lightly browned, about 3 to 4 minutes, stirring gently to allow them to get evenly cooked. The eggs might sputter a little during this process. Drain the eggs on paper towels and set aside.

3. Cover the potato with cling wrap and cook in the microwave on high for 2 minutes. Cool, peel, and cut the potato into cubes. (Alternately you can boil the potato in hot water for about 6 to 7 minutes and then cut.)

4. Add the remaining oil to the shallow skillet and heat. Add the cumin seeds and garlic and sauté until the mixture begins to turn light brown. Add the shallots and cook for another 2 minutes.

5. Add the potato cubes, the remaining 1 teaspoon salt, the remaining cayenne pepper powder, the remaining turmeric, the black pepper, and cumin-coriander powder and cook on medium heat stirring well for 10 minutes, until the potatoes are browned.

6. Put the tomato and yogurt in a blender and blend until smooth. Add to the potato mixture along with the green chili and peas. Cover and cook for another 10 minutes on low until the potatoes are very soft.

7. Stir in the eggs and let cook for 3 minutes.

8. Heat the tempering oil in a small pan and add the fennel seeds and red pepper flakes. When the fennel seeds begin to sizzle pour the hot oil over the curry.

9. Garnish with the cilantro just before serving.

Creamy Coconut Egg Curry
(GF)

This soothing and flavorful recipe for eggs is inspired by the cuisine of the coastal state of Kerala in Southern India. I have toned down the amount of coconut milk usually used to make this dish, because much as I love the rich taste of coconut milk, there is no denying that it is rather rich in saturated fat. I use a smaller amount of coconut cream with buttermilk to get the same taste. The egg curry is finished off with a delicate and very flavorful tempering of mustard seeds, curry leaves, and star anise. This curry makes a wonderful brunch dish, and is one of my favorite carry-away meals when I pack my weekday lunch.

Prep Time: 15 minutes | Cook Time: 25 to 30 minutes | Serves: 6

Ingredients

1 tablespoon coriander seeds

1 teaspoon black peppercorns

2 mild dried red chilies (such as kashmiri chilies)

⅓ cup magic trinity masala (page 355)

½ teaspoon turmeric

¾ teaspoon salt or to taste

2 tomatoes, pureed in a blender

6 hard-boiled eggs, shelled

½ cup coconut cream

¼ cup low-fat buttermilk

2 tablespoons minced fresh mint

For tempering

1 tablespoon coconut oil

¾ teaspoon mustard seeds

1 or 2 dried red chilies, broken

2 or 3 star anise

10 curry leaves

Preparation

1. In a small skillet, lightly dry roast the coriander seeds, black peppercorns, and dried chilies until fragrant. Grind to a smooth paste.

2. Heat a wok or skillet and add the ground spices, magic trinity masala, turmeric, and salt and mix well.

3. Add the pureed tomatoes and cook until the mixture begins to simmer and thicken.

4. Add the hard-boiled eggs and cook until the sauce coats the egg and thickens slightly, about 3 minutes.

5. Add the coconut cream, buttermilk, and mint and simmer lightly for a few minutes.

6. In a small skillet, heat the oil and add the mustard seeds and cook until they begin to pop. Add the dried chilies and star anise and cook for about 10 seconds. Add the curry leaves and remove from the heat. Remove the star anise and pour the oil over the egg mixture and simmer for about 3 minutes.

7. Serve hot with rice or flatbreads.

Tips and Tricks
It is important to remove any broken pieces of the star anise from the tempered oil before using as they can take someone by surprise if they eat it by mistake.

Eggs Tossed in a Sweet and Tangy Sauce
(GF)

Every now and then, I have extra hard-boiled eggs around. This tends to happen in my household when the soft-boiled eggs my children prefer for breakfast get overcooked. I invented this dish to use the "mistakes" up. It brings a colorful meal to my table without much fuss. The curry has both sweet and savory notes, a quality that is characteristic of the western state of Goa.

Prep Time: 10 minutes | Cook Time: 20 minutes | Serves: 6

Ingredients

3 cloves garlic
1-inch piece fresh ginger, peeled
3 dried red chilies
1 teaspoon cumin seeds
1 teaspoon coriander seeds
3 tablespoons oil
1 large red onion, thinly sliced
2 tomatoes, chopped
1 teaspoon raw cane sugar
¼ cup vinegar
½ teaspoon salt or to taste
6 hard-boiled eggs, peeled and cut in half
1 tablespoon freshly ground black pepper
2 to 3 tablespoons chopped cilantro

Preparation

1. Place the garlic, ginger, red chilies, cumin seeds, and coriander seeds in a small blender and process to a smooth paste.

2. Heat the oil on medium heat for about 1 minute. Add the onion slices and cook, stirring occasionally, until soft and turning slightly brown on the edges, about 6 to 7 minutes.

3. Add the spice paste, mix well and cook for about 1 minute.

4. Add the tomatoes and cook for 3 to 4 minutes, until softened.

5. Dissolve the sugar in the vinegar and add to the tomato mixture along with the salt. Bring to a simmer and cook for about 1 to 2 minutes, until the sauce is well mixed.

6. Gently fold the egg halves into the sauce and cook for 3 minutes.

7. Add the black pepper and garnish with cilantro. Serve with some bread for a quick and satisfying meal.

Masala Omelet Frittata
(GF)

This is a basic riff on the Indian-style masala omelet that makes it hearty enough for a light dinner with a salad or a brunch on a leisurely weekend afternoon.

Prep Time: 10 minutes | Cook Time: 20 minutes | Serves: 4

Ingredients

6 tablespoons oil

1 teaspoon cumin seeds

½ teaspoon mustard seeds

1 medium white or yellow onion, chopped

1 teaspoon freshly grated ginger (optional)

1 potato, grated

½ teaspoon turmeric

1½ teaspoons salt

3 tomatoes, chopped

2 green chilies, minced

4 eggs, beaten

4 tablespoons grated cheese (optional)

2 tablespoons chopped cilantro

Preparation

1. Heat 3 tablespoons of the oil in a heavy-bottomed hard-anodized skillet.

2. Add the cumin seeds and mustard seeds and wait until the mustard seeds begin to crackle. Add the onion and ginger, if using, and cook for 3 to 4 minutes until the onion softens and begins to turn pale golden at the edges.

3. Add the potato and cook until partially soft. Cool and place mixture in a mixing bowl.

4. Add the turmeric, salt, tomatoes, and green chilies. Add the eggs and cheese, if using, and mix well.

5. Heat the remaining 3 tablespoons oil in the skillet. Pour in the egg mixture and cook on medium-low heat for about 10 minutes, until the mixture is beginning to set but still moist. Stir in the cilantro.

6. Place the pan in the broiler and broil on low heat for 2 to 3 minutes, until the eggs are slightly puffy and lightly browned in spots. Sprinkle with black pepper and cool slightly.

7. Turn the mixture out onto a serving plate, cut into wedges and serve.

Seasonal Greens with Paneer
(V, GF)

In the past several years of teaching cooking, there are very few classes where I have not taught this recipe. I make it most of the time with tofu rather than the traditional paneer, however paneer affords for a richer dish. The sauce is comprised of simple, pure flavors that envelop the ingredients in simple harmony and is a little different from the classic restaurant-style recipe as I use a lot less cream. The greens can be a combination of your favorite seasonal greens or just spinach. This recipe is dedicated to my first student, Bob, who has perfected it so beautifully that my family looks forward to sampling it whenever we visit him.

Time: 10 minutes | Cook Time: 20 minutes | Serves: 4

Ingredients

1 tablespoon oil

1 teaspoon cumin-coriander powder (page 353)

1 small onion, finely chopped

1 tablespoon freshly grated ginger

6 cups chopped fresh spinach or other seasonal greens (about 12 ounces)

3 tomatoes, chopped

1 teaspoon salt or to taste

½ teaspoon red cayenne pepper powder

4 tablespoons fresh heavy cream

½ cup cashew nuts

¾ cup cubed Indian paneer cheese

1 lime, halved

Cilantro to garnish

Preparation

1. Heat the oil in a large pot on medium heat for about 1 minute.

2. Add the cumin-coriander powder and cook for a few seconds. Add the onion and ginger and sauté for 2 to 3 minutes until the onion is translucent.

3. Add the spinach or seasonal greens and tomatoes and mix well. Turn the heat to low, cover the pot and let the spinach wilt and the tomatoes soften. This process takes about 3 minutes.

4. Turn off the heat (at this point the spinach should be wilted and there should be some water released from both the spinach and the tomatoes). Stir in the salt and red cayenne pepper powder and let the mixture cool just a little.

5. Place the spinach mixture, cream, and cashews in a blender and blend for 2 to 3 minutes, until very smooth and thick (it will take some stirring and pushing to get the spinach down to a smooth paste).

6. Pour the spinach mixture back into the pot and bring to a gentle simmer. Stir in the paneer and cook for 3 to 4 minutes.

7. Turn off the heat. Squeeze in the juice of half a lime, stir and garnish with cilantro.

Green Tip:
A lot of vegetables, such as radishes and beets, come with flavorful greens when procured fresh. Do not throw these greens away, use them in your favorite recipe in lieu of or in addition to spinach. Beet greens in particular tinge other ingredients with shades of red making them a very pretty addition to salads and stir-fries.

Grilled Tandoori Tofu with Onions
(VE, GF)

Tandoori Tofu is another crowd pleaser—simple, healthy, and beautiful. The kids can get involved in its preparation. I like to make this dish with my daughter, who when she was little called it "the big stick, small stick tofu." To assemble, I first thread the tofu onto 8-inch or 12-inch skewers for cooking, and then thread them onto toothpicks for serving, thus her name. It makes a lovely, kid-friendly snack, or you can leave everything on the large skewers and serve it as a main dish. Adding multi-colored peppers to the mix in autumn adds additional flavor and color to the dish, but they can be left out if not available.

Prep Time: 20 minutes, plus 3 to 4 hours for marinating | Cook Time: 15 minutes | Serves: 6 to 8

Ingredients

1 cup loosely packed mint leaves

½ cup chopped cilantro leaves

1 or 2 green chilies

1-inch piece fresh ginger, peeled

1 tablespoon tandoori masala (page 349)

1 teaspoon salt or to taste

½ cup fresh lime juice

1½ pounds extra-firm tofu, cubed

2 medium red onions

½ green bell pepper (optional)

½ red bell pepper (optional)

8-inch bamboo skewers, soaked in water for 30 minutes

Non-stick cooking spray

Cocktail toothpicks (if serving as an appetizer)

1 tablespoon chaat masala (see page 348)

Extra cilantro and chopped scallions to garnish

Preparation

1. Place the mint, cilantro, green chilies, ginger, tandoori masala, salt, and lime juice in a blender and blend until smooth. Toss with the tofu cubes. Marinate for 3 to 4 hours at room temperature or up to overnight in the refrigerator.

2. Cut the onions into eighths and separate the layers. Cut the peppers, if using, to match the size of the onion pieces. Thread the tofu, onions, and peppers onto the soaked skewers and spray with the cooking spray.

3. Fire up the grill and place the skewered tofu onto the grill and cook for about 5 to 7 minutes on each side. Alternatively, cook in the oven on the low broil setting for the same time.

4. If using as a snack, remove from the skewers and arrange on cocktail toothpicks with an onion piece and tofu cube on each. Arrange them on a platter, sprinkle with the chaat masala. Scatter with cilantro and chopped scallions prior to serving.

Tips and Tricks

You could substitute chicken or fish for the tofu in this recipe.

Sliced almonds can be scattered on with the cilantro to add some elegance.

Scrambled Tofu with Colorful Vegetable Medley
(VE, GF)

Masala scrambled eggs, a cousin to the more popular masala omelet, are street fare in the city of Mumbai, served with small buttered rolls. A version of this with whole wheat toast is my breakfast almost every day. Built along the lines of a scrambled egg, this recipe adds in more summer vegetables for good measure. It is great for either breakfast or a main meal. If you do not have any of my tomato starter made, just sauté in some chopped onion and a chopped tomato.

Prep Time: 10 minutes | Cook Time: 15 minutes | Serves: 6

Ingredients

2 tablespoons oil

¾ teaspoon cumin seeds

¾ cup basic tomato starter (page 357)

½ teaspoon turmeric

1 cup diced bell peppers (*I use two different colors, green and red or orange*)

1 to 2 green chilies, minced

⅓ cup fresh corn kernels (about 1 medium ear of corn)

1 cup crumbled or cubed extra-firm tofu

1 teaspoon salt or to taste

2 scallions, finely chopped

2 tablespoons chopped cilantro

Lime or lemon slices to garnish

Preparation

1. Heat the oil in a skillet on medium heat for 1 minute. Add the cumin seeds and cook until the seeds begin to sizzle.

2. Add the tomato starter and turmeric and heat through until the mixture begins to simmer. Add the bell peppers and sauté for 3 to 4 minutes, until soft and fragrant.

3. Stir in the green chilies and corn and mix well. Add the tofu and salt and cook for 5 minutes (the tofu should be well mixed and nicely coated with the vegetables).

4. Stir in the scallions and mix well. Sprinkle with cilantro and serve with lime or lemon slices if desired.

Tips and Tricks

I either crumble a block of extra-firm tofu or buy the pre-cubed variety usually made by Nasoya.

Quick-Fix Lovely Red Spinach Tofu
(VE, GF)

A lot of people ask me for a vegan alternative to the creamy palak paneer. I am not a fan of modifying an original with substitute ingredients. I feel that it somehow suggests the new dish is an inferior makeover of the original. So I created a version that is a little different in taste, but will win your heart with its beauty and light flavors. This dish can also be served on small plates as an appetizer.

Prep Time: 5 minutes | Cook Time: 10 minutes | Serves: 4 to 6

Ingredients
1 tablespoon oil

1 teaspoon cumin seeds

1 teaspoon fresh ginger paste

½ cup roasted bell pepper chutney (page 71)

1½ cups cubed tofu

Salt to taste

3 cups baby spinach leaves (about 8 ounces)

Preparation
1. Heat the oil in a medium skillet and add the cumin seeds and stir lightly until they sizzle.

2. Add the ginger paste and stir lightly. Gently stir in the chutney, tofu, and salt and simmer for 2 minutes.

3. Gently stir in the spinach leaves and cook for about 4 minutes, until the spinach is wilted but still bright green (the spinach leaves reduce to about one-third of their volume).

Cubed Paneer Stir-Fry with Kale and Bell Peppers
(V, GF)

When the garden is at its brightest and most colorful peak in late summer, vivid greens, colorful peppers, and ripe tomatoes are among the many gifts our little backyard brings us. This recipe needs very little besides tossing the fresh vegetables together with a kiss of heat and a light caress of spices. It is an easier, healthier take on the classic *jhalferazi*.

Prep Time: 15 minutes | Cook Time: 20 minutes | Serves: 4 to 6

Ingredients

2 tablespoons oil

¾ teaspoon cumin seeds

1 tablespoon ginger-garlic paste (page 14)

1 medium red onion, chopped

¾ pound paneer, cut into 2-inch pieces

2 tomatoes, cut into eighths

1 red or yellow bell pepper, cut into eighths

Salt to taste

½ teaspoon red cayenne pepper powder

½ teaspoon turmeric

1½ cups tender kale leaves, cut into small pieces

1 tablespoon chopped cilantro

Preparation

1. Heat the oil in a large non-stick pan (a wok-like pan works well, since it allows adequate surface area to stir the ingredients quickly).

2. Add the cumin seeds and wait for them to sizzle and darken slightly. Add the ginger-garlic paste and stir lightly for about 30 seconds, to allow some of the moisture to dry out.

3. Add the red onion and stir well, cook for about 4 minutes, until the onion has softened and turned translucent (the mixture should be fragrant and begin to turn pale golden at spots).

4. Add the paneer and stir well. Cook for a few minutes, to let the paneer soften and turn pale golden in spots.

5. Stir in the tomatoes, bell pepper, some salt, the cayenne pepper powder, and turmeric and cook for 3 to 4 minutes, until the tomatoes soften and the juices begin to flow.

6. Stir in the kale and cook until just wilted.

7. Stir in the cilantro and enjoy. This dish is great over rice, or with warm bread, but it works well just by itself as a warm starter salad.

Summer — Season of Vibrant Bounty

Then followed that beautiful season ... Summer ...
Filled was the air with a dreamy and magical light; and the landscape
Lay as if new created in all the freshness of childhood.

—Henry Wadsworth Longfellow

To return to the musical analogy I used when I talked about spring (see page 48), once the *raag* (song) has been introduced to you, the musician begins exploring and developing the mood of the song, showing you the depths and dimensions of the *raag*. Nature does this with the Summer.

Summer is the season of lush bounty and the fulfillment of the promise of spring. The bees and butterflies have finished their dance, leaving the markets and gardens filled with vegetables: tomatoes, zucchini, kale, okra—the list could stretch to fill pages. I do not like very hot weather and so the insulated lush green Summers of New York are just fine for me, veering to those slightly hotter days in August that make me anxious for autumn. Summer is the season that brings me the joy of freshly opened zucchini blossoms, ripe tomatoes, bright and colorful peppers, and an assortment of other vegetables that could keep me busy cooking for a lifetime.

I can never keep up with the pace of the garden in the peak of Summer, so I like to chop and freeze excess produce to tide us through the cooler weather. Tomatoes, green beans, chilies, kale, and spinach all freeze well, and ensure that we are equipped for the wintry days when there is not much to fill the seasonal coffers. I have discovered that quite a lot of vegetables freeze well in their uncooked state and can be used in stir-fries, thrown into lentils, or added to many other creations.

I welcome the opening of the farmers markets (we do not have them year round). I love being able to pick up fresh bread, artisanal cheeses, eggs, chickens, and other provisions from local farmers. I usually make the market my first stop of the morning and enjoy picking up a quick breakfast of local wares. The profusion of food makes for a full kitchen and the best time to cook and share with friends. We love to share our table and catch up with friends in summertime.

I love the rain, particularly when it is not too cold. I conjure up romantic images of peacocks dancing and cozy afternoons spent with a good book and something warm to snack on. In Summer my children stay busy at camp and helping their father in the garden. They love to run in with the fresh vegetable "catch of the day." We take short trips to go berry picking or visit local wineries to enjoy fruit wines, which are usually seasonal and best this time of the year. I love the assortment of berries that we find on the farms and around the yard: juicy blackberries, raspberries, and strawberries offer me some consolation for the fact that the Northeast U.S. does not have the proliferation of mangoes that I would find in India this time of year. I enjoy the colorful berries mostly in their natural state, using them for accents as needed rather than dousing them with sugar for jams and other sweet desserts, which often mask their natural depth of flavor.

The proverbial Summer in India brings memories of mangoes, litchis, and slow-paced days with ample time for repose. Decent mangoes are available in the U.S. thanks to imports from Mexico and Haiti, but nothing really matches the prolific number of varieties that you can find in India. There are a few religious festivals scattered across the country in summertime. Ganesh Chatturthi celebrating the elephant god Ganesh in Western India and Buddha Purnima celebrating the birth of Buddha for Buddhists across the country. Most other festivals tend to be of an austere nature involving fasts and simple diets to purify the body, such as the Navaratri (nine days) in northern India. This makes perfect sense since the hot weather often leads to a craving for lighter foods. In certain parts of India, the Summer months also bring the famous monsoon season of rain. The Indian year celebrates six seasons, with the rainy season having its own distinct identity. Monsoon season, with its cooling rain, offers a perfect time to enjoy crisp, hot munchies such as *pakoras* (page 21), or crisp fried fish (page 207), or tempting North Indian savory salads, such as the *chaat* on page 61.

Green Tip:

This summer allow yourself to explore the markets, find your farmers, and experiment with new vegetables and learn to use them to their fullest. Try to subscribe to a CSA or Community Supported Agriculture initiative. Most of my friends who do often find themselves enhancing their creativity to use some of the interesting and unknown produce that comes their way. This is a guaranteed way to introduce spontaneity and healthy eating into your lives. Personally speaking, I enjoy the rhythm of our growing season just for this reason. Nature is spontaneous and giving and in turn brings its vibe into my kitchen and household.

Tips for freezing summer produce for winter and leaner times:

• Seasonal greens, such as spinach, beet or turnip greens, or even kale, can be chopped and frozen in freezer-safe bags. Freezing does give them a more watery consistency, but they still work well added to stir fries or lentils.

• Fresh corn kernels and chopped beetroots and turnips also keep well in the freezer.

• To freeze tomatoes, I recommend quartering them before putting them into freezer-safe bags. Alternately you can make the basic tomato starter on 357 and freeze it. Frozen tomatoes cannot be used in lieu of fresh tomatoes for salads, etc., but they can be used effectively for any of the sauce recipes, since in Indian cooking the tomatoes are cooked down to a soft texture.

• Green beans need to be chopped and blanched (one minute in boiling water followed by a few minutes in ice water) before they are put into freezer-safe bags.

• Excess herbs can also be chopped and frozen. I find ice cube trays very handy for this purpose.

• Hot cayenne or other chili peppers can be frozen whole. (I usually take the tops off, before doing this.)

Chapter Five

The Wealth of the Soil: Vegetables

The essential beauty of Indian cooking is found in its vegetarian offerings. I am not vegetarian, but the wealth of vegetarian dishes that Indian cuisine offers rounds out my table, keeping the food balanced and healthy. I also find that cooking vegetables allows me to feed my visual senses and creative instincts the most in the kitchen.

The Indian cook joyously slices and dices carrots, beets, and cauliflowers in winter, simmers squashes and greens in summer, and enjoys peas in spring and pumpkins in autumn. In fact, the concept of eating the same vegetables all year round is still rather alien to the Indian table, since food is cooked in accordance with seasons and festivals. Except for special occasions, most home cooks tend to cook vegetables simply to showcase natural flavors. I have taken this simplicity even further as I realized that spices should gently complement rather than compete with the flavors of the vegetables. I also tend to keep my vegetables tender-crisp, although most truly traditional Indian cooks will cook their vegetables until they are very soft. They tend to taste fine either way, but they retain more nutrition when not overcooked.

For me there is a certain joy in watching the bustle of the farmers market, experiencing the beauty of picking pumpkins, and tending to your own gardening experiments. Over the years, leading a self-sufficient life, where we eat the bounty of local farms and our backyard for more than eight months of the year, I've worked with a lot of local vegetables to adapt them to my Indian table. I have enjoyed creating recipes for kale, chard, and Brussels sprouts to name a few, enhancing their natural nutrition with the spices of my kitchen. "Eating the rainbow"—choosing a variety of colored vegetable and fruits—gives you not only an eye-catching table, but a wonderful balance of nutrients.

People are often impressed at how much my children enjoy vegetables. I am proud of this fact, and believe the reason for this is simple—they have been taught to enjoy and love the beauty of natural produce from the time they were young. We do not make a big deal about them eating their veggies. Instead I focus on making the options interesting and innovative for them, and consider vegetables a natural part of their diet. I think that if we foster the mindset that vegetables are an optional or unusual part of one's diet, we set the vegetables up for failure right from the beginning.

Green Tip:

Teaching children how to eat healthy begins at home. In order to do this, it is important to not assume that children need persuasion to eat vegetables. If this is a natural part of their diet, they usually do not protest. Take for example, as a child the bitter melon was present on most days on our table and my father often espoused it's many benefits. I grew up learning to love and accept the vegetable as a normal part of my diet rather than questioning its bitter overtones. In today's environment of processed foods and other bad food choices, it is more important than ever to teach children how to eat well. This can be done by encouraging them to get involved in the food preparation and procurement process.

- If you have a garden, carve out a spot for the children. They will be very enthusiastic about eating what they grow.

- Encourage the children to help you with food preparation; this is especially fun with salads and other meals that require "tossing."

- Teach your children how to read food labels. The rule in our house is that if the children do not recognize many words on the food label, they should avoid it.

- Make dinnertime fun with games about the food groups and discussion of what a balanced meal is so that they can learn to eat balanced when you are not around.

Stir-frying with Indian spices

The key to getting an assortment of vegetables on the table on short notice is to learn a few spice combinations for basic stir-frying. Several Indian vegetable dishes are stir-fries or begin with a tempering mixture. The difference between the Indian method of stir-frying and other Asian stir-fries, other than the spices, is the length of cooking time—Indians tend to prefer their vegetables soft. In the relationship between fresh vegetables and spices, less is more. In Indian cooking, whole spices are usually mixed with aromatics like ginger and garlic. Below are a few fun combinations of tempering mixture flavors that work for most vegetables, and offer them a distinctly Indian touch:

• Whole mustard seeds popped in hot oil with a teaspoon of ginger

• A few whole dried red chilies and curry leaves sautéed with chopped garlic

• A teaspoon of the five spice blend (page 75) with sautéed onions

• Turmeric can be added with any of the above combinations or with a touch of lemon and salt.

Tips and Tricks

This recipe also works well with green beans.

One tablespoon of dried unsweetened coconut can be added instead of the sesame seeds if desired to offer a variation of flavor that would work with either the green beans or asparagus.

Stir-Fried Asparagus with Garlic and Sesame Seeds
(VE, GF)

This quick stir-fry is perfect in spring when asparagus is plentiful. I like to use a combination of white and green asparagus for the variation in colors, but either one would be fine on its own. A hint of spices drizzled with a little maple syrup adds unique character to the recipe. This recipe works well as a side dish or as a warm salad to begin a meal.

Prep Time: 5 minutes | Cook Time: 10 minutes | Serves: 4 to 6

Ingredients

1 tablespoon oil
2 cloves garlic, minced
1 teaspoon red pepper flakes
1 tablespoon grated fresh ginger
2 pounds asparagus, trimmed
1 tablespoon soy sauce
1 tablespoon maple syrup
1 teaspoon sesame seeds

Preparation

1. Heat the oil in a wok or skillet on medium heat for 1 minute. Add the garlic, red pepper flakes, and ginger and cook for 1 to 2 minutes.

2. Add the asparagus and sauté well for 1 minute. Mix in the soy sauce and cover and cook for 5 minutes, until the asparagus is tender but crisp.

3. Stir in the maple syrup and cook for 2 minutes, stirring frequently.

4. Place the asparagus on a serving dish and sprinkle with sesame seeds before serving.

Potatoes or Turnips with Garlic, Parsley and Nigella Seeds
(VE, GF)

A classic brunch or even post-fast meal on a religious day, this comforting dish from Eastern India is often served with crisp, hot puffed bread. I make a healthier spring version of this recipe with turnips and my family tends to like the turnips almost as much as the potato version. I find myself making this dish on cold winter days, usually right after the holidays. On a cold, lazy morning a simple stir-fry such as this one is very indulgent.

Prep Time: 5 minutes | Cook Time: 20 minutes | Serves: 4 to 6

Ingredients

2 tablespoons oil

1 teaspoon nigella seeds

1 shallot, finely chopped

2 cloves garlic, minced

2 dried red chilies

1 teaspoon salt

½ teaspoon sugar

8 medium potatoes (red-skinned or russet; about 1½ pounds; your choice whether to peel or not), diced; or 12 medium turnips (about 1½ pounds), peeled and diced

1 tablespoon chopped parsley (optional)

Preparation

1. Heat the oil in a skillet or wok on medium heat for 1 minute. Add the nigella seeds and when they begin to sizzle stir in the shallot and garlic. Cook for 1 to 2 minutes until the shallots are soft and translucent.

2. Add the red chilies, salt, sugar, and potatoes or turnips with ½ cup water. Cover and cook on low for about 15 minutes for the potatoes or 10 minutes if using the turnips.

3. Remove the cover, the potatoes should be nice and soft, and the liquid fairly dry. Turn off the heat and stir in the parsley before serving.

Tips and Tricks

These potatoes are also nice as an alternative to hash browns and can be eaten with eggs.

If you do not have nigella seeds, you can use cumin seeds instead.

Mushrooms in a Spicy Tomato Masala Sauce
(VE, GF)

This dish cooks quickly with constant stirring (I know, constant does not sound easy, but it's only for about 15 minutes). It tastes like it has been cooked for hours to slow perfection. The general technique here is called *bhuna* in Indian parlance or "cooking without water," and it essentially yields a rich-tasting gravy. The catch here is that, since you are doing this with mushrooms, you do not actually have to wait till the dish cooks down or until the meat is a super tender consistency, but it still offers a nice and satisfying taste. A Sunday kind of dish, but with a Friday kind of time commitment!

Prep Time: 10 minutes | Cook Time: 20 minutes | Serves: 4

Ingredients

1 large red onion, peeled

3 cloves garlic

1-inch piece fresh ginger, peeled

2 fresh green chilies

4 tablespoons oil

½ teaspoon cumin seeds

2 tomatoes, chopped

1 teaspoon cumin-coriander powder (page 353)

3 cups halved cremini (baby bella) mushrooms

¾ teaspoon salt or to taste

½ teaspoon sugar

1½ tablespoons chopped cilantro

Preparation

1. Quarter the onion and place in a food processor with the garlic, ginger, and green chilies. Process until finely chopped.

2. Heat the oil in a skillet on medium heat for 1 minute. Add the cumin seeds and wait until they begin to sizzle, this will take a few seconds.

3. Add the onion mixture and cook on high heat, stirring frequently, for about 5 minutes. At this point, the onion should turn dry and begin to turn translucent.

4. Stir in the tomatoes and cook on high heat for 5 to 6 minutes, until the mixture begins to thicken.

5. Stir in the cumin-coriander powder and cook for another 1 to 2 minutes.

6. Add the mushrooms and mix well. Stir in the salt and sugar and cook for 3 to 4 minutes, until the mushrooms darken and the sauce clings to them.

7. Garnish with the cilantro and serve.

Comforting Cauliflower and Potato Medley
(VE, GF)

Potatoes and cauliflower (*Alu Gobi*) are a comforting and well-tested Indian combination. It is a classic that complements most other dishes, but is robust enough on its own as a light vegetarian entrée. This is one of those simple, foolproof recipes with great results and is one of the first recipes that I teach my students. More often than not, it becomes a part of their everyday cooking. My friend Helen even likes to serve this dish at room temperature as a salad.

Prep Time: 5 minutes | Cook Time: 25 minutes | Serves: 6

Ingredients

2 tablespoons oil

2 cloves garlic, grated

1-inch piece fresh ginger, grated

1 teaspoon cumin seeds

1 medium head cauliflower, chopped

2 medium Yukon gold potatoes, cut into eighths

1 teaspoon turmeric

1 teaspoon cumin-coriander powder (page 353)

½ teaspoon red cayenne pepper powder

1 teaspoon salt or to taste

1 large tomato, coarsely chopped

½ cup frozen green peas

½ cup chopped cilantro

½ teaspoon garam masala powder (page 350)

Preparation

1. Heat the oil in a large pot on medium heat for about 30 seconds. Add the garlic and ginger and sauté very lightly until they darken slightly and turn aromatic.

2. Add the cumin seeds and gently heat till they begin to sizzle.

3. Add the cauliflower, potatoes, turmeric, cumin-coriander powder, cayenne pepper powder, and salt and mix well. Stirring frequently, cook for 2 to 3 minutes.

4. Stir in the tomato, cover the mixture, and reduce the heat to low. Cook for 12 to 13 minutes. Removing the lid, you should find the vegetables soft but not mushy, a nice yellow color with flecks of orange-red from the tomatoes.

5. Mix in the peas, cover, and cook for another 1 to 2 minutes.

6. Turn off the heat, stir in the cilantro and sprinkle with the garam masala.

Tips and Tricks

For a healthier and more colorful variation of this dish, you can substitute sweet potatoes for the cauliflower as I sometimes do. You will enjoy the color and the touch of sweetness that they add.

Stir-Fried Radishes with Radish Greens
(VE, GF)

My husband was very fond of his mother's version of radishes mixed with radish greens. I did not know her recipe, but took a stab at combining the two ingredients and judging from the family's reaction, I had a winner! This is a very simple recipe that I make to use the radishes that we grow in our garden. I make this with regular red radishes and their tops or tiny white early radishes, but any radish will do.

Prep Time: 5 minutes | Cook Time: 15 minutes | Serves: 4

Ingredients

3 to 4 tablespoons oil

1 teaspoon mustard seeds

3 or 4 cloves garlic, minced

1 teaspoon freshly grated ginger

1 teaspoon salt or to taste

1 teaspoon red cayenne pepper powder

½ teaspoon turmeric

1½ cups chopped radish greens

2 cups red radishes, cut into wedges

Preparation

1. Heat the oil in a skillet or wok on medium heat for 30 seconds.

2. Add the mustard seeds and when they start to crackle stir in the garlic and ginger and cook for 1 to 2 minutes.

3. Add the salt, cayenne pepper powder, turmeric, and radish greens. Stir well and cook for 3 to 4 minutes until the greens are nice and wilted.

4. Add the radish wedges and cover and cook for another 2 to 3 minutes. Serve immediately.

Green Tip:

I have generally mentioned my preference for organic produce, but this is especially important with anything that is eaten with the skin on. Commercial production adds in a significant amount of pesticides and these can be ingested when you are consuming fruits and vegetables. Highly susceptible fruits and veggies fall into the categories of berries, bell peppers, greens, such as spinach, collards and kale, and tomatoes. There are other products such as garlic and onions where we do remove several outer layers, but I for one have noticed a marked difference in the taste between conventional and organic varieties of these items.

Crisp Turnips with Greens and Caramelized Onions
(VE, GF)

Tender Japanese turnips make their way to the farmers markets in late spring. I was so fascinated by their snow white appearance the first time I saw them that I brought home a bunch and came up with this recipe. This year we even grew our own Japanese turnips. I like to use the turnip greens along with the turnips for this recipe.

Prep Time: 10 minutes | Cook Time: 15 minutes | Serves: 4

Ingredients

3 tablespoons oil

½ teaspoon mustard seeds

10 small onions, or 1 red onion, thinly sliced

2 cloves garlic, pressed

1 cup chopped small white turnips

¾ teaspoon turmeric

¾ teaspoon red cayenne pepper powder

1 cup very finely chopped turnip greens or kale

¾ teaspoon salt or to taste

Preparation

1. Heat the oil in a pot on medium heat for 1 minute. Add in the mustard seeds and wait till they crackle and then add the onions and garlic and sauté till they soften, about 3 minutes.

2. Add the turnips and sauté them for 3 to 4 minutes (they should soften and begin to turn slightly crisp at the edges).

3. Stir in the turmeric and cayenne pepper powder and cook for 1 more minute.

4. Stir in the greens and salt and cook for 3 to 4 minutes, until the greens have wilted and are well sautéed. Serve immediately.

Tips and Tricks

While you can use regular turnips in this recipe, I have found their greens to be harsher than the smaller Japanese variety, so while they are edible I do not like using them. You can use something like baby spinach or kale paired with regular turnips, if you are looking for a substitution.

South Indian Potato and Mixed Vegetable Curry
(V, GF)

The simple, comforting potato serves as a backdrop to a variety of seasonal vegetables in this recipe. The vegetables can vary according to seasonal availability. The spices, potatoes, and greens remain consistent. This colorful, satisfying medley works well as a filling for *dosas* (page 311) or served with *puris* (page 309).

Prep Time: 10 minutes | Cook Time: 25 minutes | Serves: 4 to 6

Ingredients

2 tablespoons oil

1 teaspoon mustard seeds

⅛ teaspoon asafetida

8 to 10 curry leaves

2 or 3 dried red chilies

2 medium russet potatoes, peeled, boiled with ½ teaspoon turmeric and salt, coarsely mashed

1 teaspoon turmeric

2 tomatoes, chopped

2 medium carrots, peeled and grated

¾ cup fresh or frozen corn kernels

½ cup finely chopped spinach, fenugreek, or chard

1 teaspoon salt or to taste

¾ cup buttermilk

1 to 2 tablespoons chopped cilantro

Preparation

1. Heat the oil in a pot on medium heat for about 1 minute and then add the mustard seeds and when they begin to pop, usually right away, add the asafetida and stir lightly.

2. Add the curry leaves and red chilies and stir well.

3. Mix in the potatoes and turmeric and stir well and cook for about 2 minutes.

4. Add the tomatoes, carrots, corn kernels, and spinach and cook for a couple of minutes.

5. Stir in the salt and buttermilk and simmer, stirring frequently, for 5 to 7 minutes, until the mixture is a coarse textured and soft medley.

6. Stir in the cilantro and serve.

Variation: Turnips and Mixed Vegetable Curry
Turnips would be a delicious substitute for the potatoes in this dish.

Tempered Zucchini with Creamy Yogurt and Pine Nuts
(V, GF)

This recipe originated in the eastern Indian state of Orissa, where it is made with eggplants. I kept the seasonings intact but substituted tender, prolific summer zucchini for the eggplant. Pine nuts add a touch of richness that compensates for the lighter texture of the zucchini.

Prep Time: 10 minutes | Cook Time: 5 minutes | Serves: 4 to 6

Ingredients

1 cup whole plain yogurt

¾ teaspoon salt or to taste

½ teaspoon sugar

3 tender young zucchini

¼ teaspoon turmeric

½ teaspoon red cayenne pepper powder

2 tablespoons oil

¾ teaspoon black mustard seeds

⅛ teaspoon asafetida

8 to 10 curry leaves

¼ cup pine nuts

Preparation

1. Beat the yogurt with the salt and sugar in a medium mixing bowl and set aside.

2. Remove the zucchini tops and cut crosswise into slices (about ¼ inch in thickness). Rub the zucchini with the turmeric and cayenne pepper powder.

3. Heat the oil in a skillet and add the mustard seeds and cook until the seeds begin to pop and crackle.

4. Add the asafetida and curry leaves and immediately add the zucchini. Stir-fry the mixture for about 2 to 3 minutes.

5. Pour the mixture over the yogurt and mix lightly. Place in a serving bowl and garnish with the pine nuts before serving.

Smoky Roasted Eggplant in Tomato Puree
(VE, GF)

Most people I know love *Baigan Bharta*, a comforting classic Indian dish where the eggplant is cooked until its outer skin is charred, imbuing it with a deep, smoky taste. I've added roasted tomatoes to my version to pay homage to both summer vegetables: the eggplant and the tomato.

Prep Time: 10 minutes | Cook Time: 25 minutes | Serves: 4

Ingredients

1 large or 2 medium eggplants (about 1½ pounds)

3 tablespoons oil

4 medium ripe tomatoes (about ¾ pound)

1 teaspoon cumin seeds

1 medium red onion, finely chopped

2 teaspoons crushed coriander seeds

2 teaspoons ginger paste

6 cloves garlic, minced

1 teaspoon salt or to taste

¾ teaspoon red cayenne pepper powder

2 tablespoons finely chopped cilantro

Preparation

1. Place the eggplant(s) on an open flame and cook for about 6 to 7 minutes (the flame on a gas stove works well for this). When the exposed side is completey charred, turn the eggplant(s) and roast on the other side for 6 to 7 minutes until well charred. Place the eggplant(s) on a plate to cool. Carefully remove the skin from the eggplant(s) and mash coarsely.

2. In the meantime, drizzle about 1 tablespoon of the oil on a baking dish. Place the tomatoes in the dish and begin broiling them on low heat. Turn the tomatoes a couple of times to ensure that they are cooked evenly and the skin is uniformly darkened. When the tomatoes are charred, remove from broiler and cool slightly. Carefully remove their skin and place the tomatoes in a blender or food processor and coarsely puree.

3. Heat the remaining 2 tablespoons oil in a pot. Add the cumin seeds and cook for about 45 seconds. Add the red onions and lightly sauté for about 5 to 6 minutes, until they wilt and begin to turn soft and crisp at the edges. Add the coriander seeds, ginger paste, and garlic and cook until the garlic is fragrant and toasty.

4. Add the mashed eggplant and mix well. Add the tomato puree, salt, and cayenne pepper powder and cook and stir until they are well mixed.

5. Stir in the cilantro leaves and serve immediately.

Fragrant Pan-Roasted Green Beans with Coconut and Pine Nuts
(VE, GF)

I confess I am not very fond of green beans, so I suppose it is divine justice that my friends and family constantly request this recipe. But since it can be tossed together in about 15 minutes, I am happy to oblige. I like to use a combination of green and yellow beans, but it tastes just fine with just one variety. The magic of this recipe rests in the lightly toasted medley of whole spices, garlic, and coconut enveloping the green beans in a happy comforting package.

Prep Time: 10 minutes | Cook Time: 15 minutes | Serves: 4

Ingredients

2 tablespoons oil

1½ teaspoons Bengali Five Spice Blend (panch phoron)

6 cloves garlic, minced

2 cups (about 1 pound) green beans (or a combination of green and yellow beans), trimmed and cut into 1-inch pieces

1 teaspoon salt or to taste

2 tablespoons grated unsweetened coconut (can be frozen)

2 tablespoons pine nuts

½ cup finely chopped chives, green garlic, or cilantro

Preparation

1. Heat the oil on medium heat for about 1 minute and then add the five spice blend. When the spices crackle, add the garlic and stir lightly for a few seconds to allow the garlic to get fragrant and toasty.

2. Add the green beans and salt and mix well. Cover and cook for about 6 minutes on low heat.

3. Remove the cover and stir in the grated coconut, pine nuts, and chives and mix well. Serve hot or warm.

Crisped Okra with a Dry Spice Rub
(VE, GF)

I had to make a few compromises before this recipe for *Bhindi Masala* became a staple on my table. Although I usually like vegetables to retain their bright green color through cooking, the spices in this recipe add just the right dimension of flavor so I made peace with the darker hues of the dish. Secondly, this recipe uses a little more oil than I would like for everyday cooking. But the oil policeman in our house (my husband) accepts this since he loves his okra. To keep the okra nice and silky, it is very important to add the tomato (if using) right before removing from the heat.

Prep Time: 10 minutes | Cook Time: 15 minutes | Serves: 4

Ingredients

⅓ cup oil

1 teaspoon cumin seeds

2 red onions, finely chopped

1 tablespoon cumin-coriander powder (page 353)

1½ tablespoons minced ginger

1½ pounds okra, cut into ½-inch pieces, tips and tops removed (wash and thoroughly dry the okra before cutting)

1 teaspoon salt or to taste

½ teaspoon turmeric

½ teaspoon amchur (dried mango powder) or 1½ tablespoons fresh lime juice

½ teaspoon red cayenne pepper powder

1 tomato, finely chopped (optional)

2 tablespoons finely chopped cilantro

Preparation

1. Heat the oil in a heavy-bottomed pan and sauté the cumin seeds until they sizzle.

2. Add the onions and cook for about 5 minutes, until soft and crisp.

3. Add the cumin-coriander powder and ginger and cook lightly for 1 minute.

4. Add the okra and cook on medium-high heat for about 5 minutes, stirring until the okra is fairly soft and nicely coated with the golden spice mixture.

5. Stir in the salt, turmeric, amchur or lime juice, and cayenne pepper powder.

6. Add the tomato, if using, and cook for 2 minutes, until the tomato softens and mixes in with the okra (you should see the spices and the oil clinging to the okra).

7. Garnish with cilantro before serving.

Zucchini Dumplings in Tomato Gravy
(VE, GF)

The connections between childhood, food, and comfort are elusive. Somewhere in the midst of all the cooking, a heavy dose of love gets mixed in with the food that we cook for our children. This process can form memories that shape our lives, thoughts, and sensibilities years later. For my husband, bottle gourd dumplings were a regular at his family meals. This recipe is adapted from my mother-in-law's kitchen, and a serving of these dumplings still can cheer my husband up. They are simmered in a light tomato-based broth with a gentle hint of spices. I use zucchini most of the time as it is readily available and works as an acceptable substitute for bottle gourds.

Prep Time: 10 minutes | Cook Time: 30 minutes with pressure cooker • 45 minutes on the stovetop | Serves: 6 to 8

Ingredients

For the dumplings

4 young green zucchinis, cut in large pieces

5 scallions (optional)

1 cup chickpea flour (besan)

1 teaspoon salt

¼ teaspoon red cayenne pepper powder

Oil for frying

For the tomato gravy

2 tablespoons oil

1 teaspoon cumin seeds

1 teaspoon cumin-coriander powder (page 353)

½ teaspoon turmeric

¼ teaspoon asafetida

1 teaspoon salt

¼ teaspoon red cayenne pepper powder

2 teaspoons ginger paste

3 tomatoes, finely chopped

3 tablespoons finely chopped cilantro

½ teaspoon garam masala (page 350)

Preparation

1. For the dumplings, place the zucchini and scallions (if using) in a food processor and process until well chopped but not pureed.

2. Mix the zucchini (do not squeeze out the natural liquid) with the chickpea flour, salt, and red cayenne pepper powder. You will get a mixture that can be shaped into free-style dumplings.

3. Heat some oil on medium heat for a couple of minutes to ensure that the oil is hot. Add the dumplings by tablespoonful or loosely shaped by hand, a few pieces at a time and fry until golden brown. Set aside to drain on paper towels while you fry the rest and make the tomato gravy.

4. For the tomato gravy, heat the oil in the base of a pressure cooker or a heavy-bottomed pan on medium heat for about 30 seconds. Add the cumin seeds and when they sizzle add the cumin-coriander powder, turmeric, asafetida, salt, red cayenne pepper powder, and ginger paste, all within seconds of each other. Cook this mixture for about 20 seconds, the ginger should darken very slightly and be well mixed with the dry spices.

5. Stir in the tomatoes and cook for 5 minutes and then add 1 cup of water. Cover and cook under pressure for 4 minutes (once the cooker reaches pressure) or for 15 to 20 minutes on the stovetop.

6. Remove the lid and add the dumplings and simmer for 5 minutes. Stir in the cilantro and garam masala and serve.

Tips and Tricks
The dumplings can be made in large batches, frozen, and then thawed and simmered in the gravy just before serving

Curried Summer Eggplants and Potatoes
(VE, GF)

This vivid, gently-spiced concoction melts in your mouth and is a summer staple in my house. I adapted my mother-in-law's recipe for *Alu Baigan* (eggplant and potatoes) using garden fresh eggplants and was thrilled with the results. She uses very finely diced eggplant and loads of tomatoes and just the right amount of potatoes, to create a dish that is much like an Indian version of a caponata.

Prep Time: 10 minutes | Cook Time: 40 minutes | Serves: 4 to 6

Ingredients

2 medium eggplants, cut into
  1- to 2-inch wedges

2 medium potatoes, cut into
  1- to 2-inch wedges

1 teaspoon salt or to taste

½ teaspoon turmeric

¼ cup oil

1 teaspoon cumin seeds

1 tablespoon ginger-garlic paste
  (page 14)

1 teaspoon cumin-coriander powder
  (page 353)

4 tomatoes, chopped

2 green chilies, finely chopped

½ teaspoon sugar (optional)

2 tablespoons finely chopped cilantro

Preparation

1. Rub the eggplant and potato wedges with half the salt and the turmeric and set aside in separate bowls.

2. Heat the oil in a large skillet. Add the cumin seeds and when they begin to sizzle add the ginger-garlic paste and cumin-coriander powder and stir well. Mix in the seasoned potatoes and stir well for 1 to 2 minutes. Cover and cook for 5 minutes, until the potatoes are almost cooked and a pale golden yellow.

3. Add the seasoned eggplant and mix well. Cook on medium-high heat for about 5 minutes, until the eggplants and potatoes are mixed well with the spices.

4. Reserving about 1 tomato, add the rest of the chopped tomatoes, the green chilies, the sugar, if using, and the remaining ½ teaspoon salt and stir well. Cover and cook the mixture for 15 to 20 minutes on low heat, stirring occasionally.

5. Remove the cover and mix well. The eggplants should be soft and cooked through. Continue to cook uncovered until fairly dry and mixture is sizzling at the edges of the pan.

6. Stir in the reserved chopped tomato and cook for 3 to 5 minutes, until the tomato is soft and melting.

7. Mix well and stir in the cilantro and taste to see if it needs more salt. Serve with a flatbread of your choice.

Tips and Tricks
This recipe freezes well and the flavors deepen when re-heated, although some of the heady color gets lost in the re-heating.

Cabbage Tossed with Pan-Toasted Spices
(VE, GF)

In many parts of the world, cabbage sustains people through winter and here is a really easy way to add some character to the vegetable. If you are nervous about attempting Indian cooking, this should be one of your first tries as it is one of the simplest recipes in this book—fresh, crisp cabbage sautéed until just tender. Chopped cabbage keeps very well in the refrigerator, so I often keep pre-chopped cabbage handy to use on a busy weeknight.

Prep Time: 5 minutes | Cook Time: 15 minutes | Serves: 4

Ingredients

2 tablespoons oil

1 teaspoon mustard seeds

⅛ teaspoon asafetida

1 tablespoon grated fresh ginger

1 teaspoon dried red pepper flakes

2 cups finely shredded cabbage

2 to 3 medium carrots, peeled and cut into 3-inch julienne slices

½ teaspoon turmeric

1 teaspoon salt or to taste

½ cup fresh or frozen green peas

2 tablespoons chopped cilantro

Preparation

1. Heat the oil in a skillet on medium heat for 1 minute. Add the mustard seeds and when they start to crackle add the asafetida and ginger and sauté lightly.

2. Add the red pepper flakes, shredded cabbage, and julienned carrots and mix well. Stir in the turmeric and salt. Cover and cook the cabbage on low heat for 5 to 7 minutes.

3. Remove the cover, the cabbage should have shrunk and wilted slightly but still retain a little crunch. Stir in the green peas; if using frozen just heat through, if using fresh cook for about 4 more minutes. Stir in the cilantro and taste to see if it needs more salt before serving.

Tips and Tricks

This cabbage dish can be served at room temperature as well as warm.

The technique and flavors of this recipe can be adapted to cook almost any vegetable or even fish.

Pan-Roasted Rutabaga and Brussels Sprouts
(VE, GF)

It has taken me some trial and error to convert Brussels sprouts into a good Indian vegetable. In this recipe, I pair two relatively humble winter vegetables in a wonderfully nourishing dish that is very attractive to behold. The rutabaga should be pan roasted until crisp so it can blossom to its full potential. Once roasted, it complements the slight bitterness of the Brussels sprouts very well.

Prep Time: 15 minutes | Cook Time: 20 minutes | Serves: 4 to 6

Ingredients

½ medium rutabaga, peeled (about ½ pound)

25 small tender Brussels sprouts (about ¾ pound)

2 tablespoons oil

¾ teaspoon mustard seeds

½ teaspoon cumin seeds

⅛ teaspoon asafetida (optional)

1 medium red onion, chopped

½ teaspoon turmeric

¾ teaspoon salt or to taste

1½ teaspoons freshly grated ginger

2 dried red chilies

10 to 15 curry leaves

2 tablespoons chopped cilantro to garnish

Preparation

1. Finely chop the rutabaga or cut it into quarters lengthwise and then thinly slice the quarters into wedges. Set aside in a colander.

2. Cut off the tops of the Brussels sprouts and thinly slice them and set aside.

3. Heat the oil in a skillet on medium heat. Add the mustard seeds and when they crackle, working in quick succession, add the cumin seeds, asafetida and red onion and stir well. Cook for about 3 to 4 minutes until the onion softens and begins to turn pale golden.

4. Add the chopped rutabaga along with the turmeric, salt, and ginger and cook, stirring frequently, until rutabaga is soft and fairly crisp on the sides, about 6 to 7 minutes.

5. Stir in the dried red chilies and curry leaves, followed by the Brussels sprouts and cook until the sprouts have softened and wilted, about 3 minutes.

6. Taste for salt and garnish with the cilantro and serve immediately.

Whole-Spice Roasted Butternut Squash with Sage
(V, GF)

There is something right about turning on the oven in autumn. It fits in with the chilly evenings, the time for bright, simple, home-style meals that remind you that the holidays are around the corner. One of the last vestiges of green in my garden are hardy sage and its companion thyme. Fragrant and soft, sage adds the perfect balance to butternut squash. Sometimes even simplicity takes time and testing to accomplish. It took me quite a few iterations to create a recipe that balanced spices and allowed the flavor of the sage to shine without loads of unnecessary butter. I hope you will agree that the effort was worthwhile!

Prep Time: 5 minutes | Cook Time: 45 minutes (mostly unattended) | Serves: 6

Ingredients

1 large butternut squash (about 2 pounds)

2 tablespoons oil

1 teaspoon Bengali Five Spice Blend (panch phoron)

1 teaspoon freshly ground black pepper

1 tablespoon ginger paste

Salt to taste (optional, *I really do not think that this dish needs it*)

1 tablespoon salted butter

15 fresh sage leaves

Preparation

1. Heat the oven to 375°F. Peel the squash, remove the seeds, cut the squash into 2-inch chunks.

2. Heat the oil in a skillet. Add the five spice blend and when it crackles mix in the black pepper and ginger paste and mix well. Add the squash and stir well to coat. Place the seasoned squash on a greased baking sheet.

3. Roast the squash in the oven for about 35 minutes. It should be soft and beginning to get flecks of golden brown at spots. Taste to check if needs any salt.

4. Heat the butter in a small skillet on low heat for about 2 to 3 minutes, until it melts and gradually acquires a shade of pale gold. Add the sage leaves and cook until they turn dark and almost crisp. Pour over the squash and mix lightly. Serve on a flat plate to showcase the spices and sage.

Broccoli with Toasted Cashew Nuts
(VE, GF)

This recipe is a favorite in our household throughout the year since broccoli grows in spring and lasts through autumn until the winter frost hits. It is a quick stir-fry with a simple adornment—toasted cashews. The ginger is finely chopped rather than ground to a paste and this makes a difference in the flavors of the dish. Sometimes less is more!

Prep Time: 5 minutes | Cook Time: 15 minutes | Serves: 4

Ingredients
2 tablespoons oil (preferably olive oil)

1 red onion, finely chopped

½ teaspoon sugar

1 tablespoon finely chopped fresh ginger

2 cloves garlic, minced

1½ pounds tender broccoli, cut into medium-size pieces

1 teaspoon salt or to taste

½ teaspoon dried red pepper flakes

2 tablespoons fresh lime juice

½ cup cashews, lightly toasted and coarsely broken

Preparation
1. Heat the oil in a large skillet on medium heat for about 30 seconds. Add the onion and stir-fry for 1 to 2 minutes. Stir in the sugar and cook for another 2 minutes, until the onion wilts and begins to turn golden.

2. Stir in the ginger and garlic and cook for another minute or so, until they turn golden and toasty.

3. Stir in the broccoli and salt and cook on medium to low heat for about 7 minutes, stirring frequently to make sure that the onion mixture does not burn. The broccoli softens and gets fragrant and lightly browned in spots.

4. Stir in the red pepper flakes and lime juice. Sprinkle the cashews over the broccoli and serve.

Tips and Tricks
The raw cashew nuts can be roasted in a pan until they are gently browned while the broccoli is cooking.

Roasted Brussels Sprouts and Winter Squash Pizza
(V)

I must confess how I hesitantly ventured to make the crust for this pizza. The recipe from Suvir Saran's book *Masala Farm* looked so simple that I really did not think it would work. After some persuasion from the online foodie congregation, however, I tried it and sure enough I was not disappointed. Over time, I modified it with some whole wheat flour and herbs. This dough improves in flavor as it rests. I encourage you to make the dough ahead, pull it out when needed, and have a pizza on the table in less than thirty minutes. Luckily, by the time I am writing this book I had met Suvir and actually got a demo on the rolling. It is a simple process, but the dough does get rolled out very thin. The best part is that most kids I know love this and eat it without realizing they are eating a load of healthy winter vegetables. After playing around with a bunch of toppings, this combination became my family's favorite.

Prep Time: 4½ hours (includes 4 hours for dough to rise) | Cook Time: 20 minutes | Serves: 4

Ingredients

For the pizza dough (makes one 10-inch thin crust pizza)

¾ cup whole wheat flour (atta)

¾ cup all-purpose flour

1 teaspoon salt

1 tablespoon dried fenugreek leaves (kasuri methi)

Several grinds of black pepper

1½ teaspoons rapid rise (bread machine) yeast

2½ tablespoons olive oil

¾ cup lukewarm water

Cornmeal and extra flour for rolling

For the toppings

2 tablespoons olive oil

15 to 20 medium Brussels sprouts, sliced

1 small winter squash (delicata or acorn) , peeled, seeded, and cut into thin slices (*best done with a peeler or mandolin*)

8 ounces goat cheese, crumbled

Preparation

1. Make the dough: Place the flours in a food processor with the salt, fenugreek leaves, and black pepper and pulse a few times to mix. Add the yeast and pulse a few times. Pour in the oil and lukewarm water in a single stream and process until a smooth ball is formed. Remove dough into a bowl and knead lightly for a minute or so to smooth it out. Cover and let the dough rest and rise in a warm place for about 2 hours.

2. Knead dough again and then cover and let it rise for another 2 hours.

3. Place a pizza stone in the oven at 450°F and heat for at least 30 minutes.

4. Flour a flat surface with some cornmeal and flour. Roll out the dough to a thin 10-inch round circle. Place the dough on the heated stone, spread a little olive oil on top, line with the squash and Brussels sprouts. Sprinkle with the goat cheese and drizzle with the remaining olive oil.

5. Bake for about 15 minutes. The crust should be crisp and golden and the the sprouts should be golden and roasted. Cut into six slices using a pizza cutter and serve immediately.

Tips and Tricks

If making dough ahead and storing overnight you can put the dough covered in the refrigerator after the first 2-hour rise. Then proceed with steps 3 and 4 after bringing the dough out of the refrigerator and letting it rest for about 30 minutes.

Tandoori Spice Roasted Baby Potatoes with Mint
(V, GF)

This recipe merges two favorites: deep-fried North Indian crispy potatoes and tandoori seasoned potatoes. I reduced the effort and the fat for this dish significantly by roasting the potatoes in the oven. For best results roast the potatoes undisturbed for the prescribed time.

Prep Time: 7 minutes | Cook Time: 1½ hours (mostly unattended) | Serves: 4 to 6

Ingredients

1½ pounds baby white potatoes

1 tablespoon tandoori masala (page 349)

4 cloves garlic, minced

½ teaspoon red cayenne pepper powder

4 tablespoons plain yogurt

½ teaspoon salt or to taste

½ teaspoon powdered mint

4 tablespoons oil

1 tablespoon chopped cilantro

Preparation

1. Heat the oven to 350°F. Boil the potatoes for 10 minutes. Drain, cool, and peel.

2. Toss the potatoes with the tandoori masala, garlic, cayenne pepper powder, yogurt, salt, and mint. (The potatoes will be in a fairly moist marinade.)

3. Place the potatoes in a baking dish and drizzle with the oil. Bake for 45 to 50 minutes, stirring and basting them occasionally.

4. Garnish with the cilantro and serve.

Tips and Tricks

I suggest cooking these potatoes with one of the roasts in this book to make the best use of the oven. Or they can be pan-fried for convenience. In this case, pan-fry the potatoes for 10 minutes without adding the mint. Once they are golden brown, toss with mint and cilantro.

Autumn — Season of Harvest & Fragrant Spices

"Autumn is the mellower season, and what we lose in flowers, we more than gain in fruits."
—Samuel Butler

The lightness of summer eases into Autumn, a season with more color and in some ways a season with more energy and brightness. Autumn's melody is heady and potent, with layers of slow softness. Going back to my analogy of the song when talking about spring and summer, by the time Autumn emerges, we know the notes of the song, we are ready to listen to it just a little more, before we let the music slow down.

I love the warmth of the August months easing into cooler, crisper September mornings. The sight of yellow school buses carrying a new flock of children into their back-to-school routines always signals the advent of Autumn. My children are still young enough to welcome the school year and eagerly anticipate meeting a new teacher, checking out their classmates, and catching up on their summer tales.

As a child in India, I had calendars from the U.S. filled with photos of red- and yellow-leaved trees and I used to marvel at their stunning colors. During my first Autumn in the U.S., my biggest consolation for being away from family was indeed seeing the greens melt into a palette of yellow, red, and golden orange.

In Autumn markets are still prolific here in New York and beautiful apples and pears join the rows of peppers and eggplants. These fruits are perfect for making pies, and in simpler form they work well for chutneys. I also often throw sweet, tart early apples into a lighter curry. There is a certain special happiness in walking through rustling leaves and savoring the crisp, fresh air. Autumn brings its own holidays and the beginning of the Jewish New Year, Rosh Hashanah, observed by several of my friends. If you live in a house with children, one of the most important Autumn holidays is Halloween, which is a fun day to dress up and indulge in the comfort of sugar. And Autumn ends with the all important holiday feast of Thanksgiving.

In India, gorgeous orange flowers called *gul mohors* filled the Autumn air with heady colors and their unique fragrance. Autumn is the time of festive family celebrations in India. The traditional holidays Navaratri and Durga Puja both celebrate nine days of the mother goddess. These festivals culminate with the tenth day called *Dushera* or *Dashami*, a day which commemorates the victory of good over evil and is celebrated with sweets and visiting family. The grand finale of the festivals is Diwali or Deepavali—the festival of lights. There are so many ways to celebrate Diwali, but at heart it is yet another symbolization of the victory of light over the darkness of evil. In northern India, some communities pray to the Goddess of Wealth Lakshmi during Diwali, and mark it as the start of a new year. In eastern India, a traditional way to celebrate the festival is to light twelve lamps to commemorate ancestors, six from each side of the family, and for some unbeknown reason eat a medley made with sixteen varieties of local greens. However we celebrate it, Diwali has become a signature Indian holiday around the globe, with even the White House lighting a symbolic lamp on this occasion. These festivals are a time for new clothes and food, food, and more food. Recipes such as Puffed Balloon Bread (page 309), Beet Halwa (page 323), and Saffron Pistachio Rice Pudding (page 333), and a host of savory dishes are all well-suited to grace your festive Indian table. After all, no festival can be complete without the celebration of food.

Whether in the U.S. or India, Autumn nudges me to the kitchen to turn on the oven and replenish my supplies of fragrant spices. Cinnamon, star anise, and cardamom are all evocative of this season and feature in my favorite Autumn recipes. I savor the fragrance of these spices in my foods or well-loved cup of tea rather than in a scented candle. Although candles certainly have their place on a celebratory dining table, as with all forms of combustible indulgence, less is more.

Chapter Six

Fruits of the Sea: Fish & Shellfish

With increasing attention to healthier proteins, people are eating more fish with their lean protein and omega-rich oils. Since it is difficult to understand what the conditions of "farming" really are, wild-caught fish varieties are always preferred. Most importantly, for fish to produce their natural, healthy nutrients, they need to be able to grow, breed, and eat as they would in nature.

Most Indian restaurants in the U.S. do not do justice to the wealth of fish and seafood that abound along the coastlines of India. Indian fish cuisine is subtle and nuanced and therefore often does not lend itself to mass production. Coastal areas of India thrive on a diet rich in fish and seafood. In eastern India, purchasing fresh fish is a task of such utmost importance that it is usually performed by the gentleman of the family before he leaves for work. Good fish is believed to be available only in the very early mornings, right when the fishmonger reaches the market. On the plus side, the fish market trip is usually combined with morning tea at the local sweet shop and bringing back breakfast samosas for the rest of the family.

Fish delicacies are as diverse as the regions of India; they are cooked in coconut milk in the Deccan and Konkan regions of Maharastra and Kerala, drenched with chilies and vinegar in Goa, and simmered in mustard or yogurt in eastern India. The options are endless. In the coastal state of Kerala, to be considered worth his or her salt, a chef must be skilled in selecting and preparing the fresh daily catch.

In the recipes I give here, I suggest readily available types of fish to substitute for some of the harder-to-find Indian varieties. As a rule of thumb, milder, firm-fleshed varieties of white fish such as tilapia, cod, and halibut, as well as salmon (wild-caught) and shrimp work well for my recipes. I also like to experiment with red snapper, mussels, and scallops. But these recipes are quite flexible, so feel free to mix and match with any fish of your choice.

In my opinion the freshness of the fish is more important that the type of fish. In India, where home refrigerators are less common, we often deep-fry fish before further cooking it to preserve the final dish longer. I use a more delicate approach in my cooking, since it is simpler, healthier, and certainly works better with the fish fillets we tend to use in the U.S. more frequently than the steaks and whole fish found in India.

Weeknight Baked Black Pepper and Fenugreek Shrimp
(F&S, GF)

With my essential black pepper and fenugreek rub handy, this dish requires less than 15 minutes of active cooking time and comes to the rescue for weeknight family meals or simple parties with no fuss at all.

Prep Time: 35 minutes (including 30 minutes marinating time) | Cook Time: 10 minutes | Serves: 4 to 6

Ingredients

1½ pounds medium or large shrimp, shelled and deveined

4 tablespoons sour cream

1½ tablespoons fenugreek and black pepper rub (page 351)

Extra salt to taste

2 tablespoons oil

2 tomatoes, diced (*I like to mix red and yellow*)

Preparation

1. Place the shrimp, sour cream, and fenugreek and black pepper rub, and extra salt if using in a ziplock bag and mix well to coat the shrimp. Set aside for 30 minutes.

2. Pre-heat the broiler. Grease a baking sheet with 1 tablespoon of the oil.

3. Arrange the seasoned shrimp in a single layer on the baking sheet and scatter with the tomatoes. Drizzle with the remaining tablespoon of oil.

4. Broil the shrimp on low for about 4 minutes, turn and cook for another 2 to 3 minutes. By now, the shrimp should be crisped and the tomatoes should have released their juices and be slightly roasted.

5. To serve, arrange the tomatoes and shrimp on a platter, garnish with herbs if desired and serve immediately.

Fragrant Shrimp with Whole Spices and Coconut Milk
(F&S, GF)

This shrimp curry, known as *malaikari*, is a classic from Eastern India. This version is an adaptation of my great aunt's signature dish, something that she reserved exclusively for festive occasions. Don't be daunted by the list of ingredients—I have broken the recipe down for you in fairly simple steps. The seasoning base is close to my aunt's recipe, but she used whole prawns that were almost as big as small lobsters. So if you are feeling indulgent, feel free to use lobsters or lobster tails for this recipe.

Prep Time: 15 to 20 minutes | Cook Time: 35 to 40 minutes | Serves: 6

Ingredients

2 pounds large or colossal shrimp, shelled and deveined

1½ teaspoons turmeric

1½ teaspoons salt

⅓ cup oil

2 medium onions, finely chopped, plus 1 medium onion, grated with the coarse side of the grater

2 teaspoons fresh ginger paste

2 or 3 mild dried red or kashmiri chilies

2 teaspoons coriander seeds

1½ teaspoons cumin seeds

½ teaspoon whole black peppercorns

1½ teaspoons sugar

2 or 3 bay leaves

1 cup coconut milk (for a richer effect you can make ⅓ cup of this coconut cream)

2 teaspoons ghee

1 (2-inch) cinnamon stick, coarsely broken

3 or 4 green cardamom pods, bruised

4 cloves

Preparation

1. Rub the shrimp with half the turmeric and half the salt and set aside for about 10 minutes.

2. In a large skillet, heat about 2 tablespoons of the oil. Add the shrimp in a single layer without crowding the skillet and cook for about 2 minutes on each side. The shrimp should be just partially cooked. Remove the shrimp and set aside.

3. Add the remaining oil to the skillet and heat. Add the chopped onions, and gently cook them on low heat, softly stirring the mixture until it reaches a uniform toffee color. This process will take a good 7 to 8 minutes and needs to be done with care and love.

4. Add the grated onion and ginger paste and continue cooking the mixture for another 6 minutes, until the onions are pale golden and fragrant.

5. Grind the dried red chilies, coriander seeds, cumin seeds, and peppercorns into a fine powder in a spice mill or coffee grinder. Mix into the onion mixture and cook for 1 to 2 minutes, until the spices are fragrant and the mixture gets a somewhat reddish tint.

6. Add the remaining ¾ teaspoon salt, remaining ¾ teaspoon turmeric, the sugar, bay leaves, and coconut milk and bring to a simmer. After 5 minutes, add the shrimp. Let the shrimp simmer for 10 minutes.

7. Heat the ghee separately in a small pan and add the cinnamon stick, cardamom pods, and cloves and pour over the simmering sauce and mix well. Cook for another 2 minutes. Serve with rice.

Salmon in a Tomato, Thyme and Ginger Sauce
(F&S, GF)

Pondicherry (or Podduchery) is a small area in southern India. A former French colony, the town retains a very prominent French influence on the culture, traditions, and food of this region which results in a unique cuisine that combines French flavors with traditional South Indian spices. This simple, tangy fish creation, with light overtones of thyme, is based on something I chanced on several years back in a New York restaurant named Pondicherry. If you do not have thyme, you can use ajowain or carom seeds.

Prep Time: 10 minutes | Cook Time: 20 minutes | Serves: 4 to 6

Ingredients

2 pounds wild-caught salmon fillets, skin on

½ teaspoon turmeric

2 teaspoons salt

2 to 3 tablespoons olive oil

¾ teaspoons mustard seeds

8 to 10 curry leaves (optional)

1 medium white onion, chopped

1 tablespoon grated fresh ginger

2 or 3 green Serrano chilies, minced

3 tomatoes, chopped

1 tablespoon chopped fresh thyme leaves

2 tablespoons chopped fresh basil

2 tablespoons red wine vinegar

1 tablespoon chopped cilantro

Preparation

1. Cut the salmon into 2-inch pieces. Rub with the turmeric and half the salt. Set aside.

2. Heat the oil in a skillet. Add the mustard seeds and when they crackle add the curry leaves if using.

3. Add the onion, ginger, and green Serrano chilies and cook for 3 to 4 minutes, stirring frequently, until the onions are soft and translucent.

4. Add the tomatoes, the remaining 1 teaspoon salt, and the thyme and cook on low heat until the tomatoes are nice and soft and pulpy.

5. Stir in the basil and vinegar and gently add the salmon. Poach the salmon on low heat for 7 minutes. Do not overcook, it is important for the salmon to be just moist but not dried out.

6. Garnish with the cilantro and serve over rice, if desired.

Green Tip:

Wild-caught fish is usually the best choice for healthy omega-rich oils. Though more expensive, they are usually healthier and more flavorful than their farm-raised counterparts. Look for fish at a market that has good turnover of inventory and that clearly labels its varieties as farm-raised or wild-caught. To make sure you are getting wild-caught fish, look for fish that is local to your area. It is usually fresher and you can avoid the energy wasted in transporting the fish. For example, in the northeast U.S., I would look for cod or scrod or even haddock and scallops as everyday options.

Salmon or Tuna with a Blood Orange and Tamarind Glaze
(F&S, GF)

Redolent with herbs, this simple salmon or tuna preparation results in a very flavorful and versatile dish, partly because the herbs mimic the scent of the spices. This recipe is one of the staples for entertaining in my kitchen. It makes for a lovely presentation with relatively little effort.

Prep Time: 10 minutes | Cook Time: 15 minutes | Serves: 4

Ingredients

1½ pounds salmon or tuna steaks

1 teaspoon salt

1 teaspoon turmeric

1 teaspoon red cayenne pepper powder

Oil for searing

1 tablespoon fresh oregano leaves

½ tablespoon fresh thyme leaves

1 blood orange, cut in half

4 tablespoons tamarind chutney (page 85 or store bought)

For garnish

2 long green chilies, finely chopped

1 blood orange, peeled and sliced

Preparation

1. Cut the fish steaks into individual serving portions and rub with the salt, turmeric, and cayenne pepper powder. Set aside for 5 to 10 minutes.

2. Heat some oil in a skillet and place the fish in the pan in a single layer. Cook for about 7 minutes (less if using tuna) and then turn and cook for another 5 minutes.

3. Remove skillet from heat and immediately add the oregano leaves and thyme leaves to the skillet. Quickly squeeze some fresh blood orange juice over the fish.

4. Add 2 teaspoons of the tamarind chutney on top of each portion of fish to let the chutney seep in and gently glaze the fish.

5. Put the fish on a serving platter. Garnish with chopped green chilies and blood orange slices and serve.

Tips and Tricks

You can use ½ teaspoon carom seeds in place of the thyme leaves. Add them to the hot oil in the pan right before adding the salmon.

Seared Herb-and-Walnut-Crusted Fish
(F&S, GF)

When I began cooking in earnest, I had a small two-burner stove with a tiny oven. To comfortably work with the available space, I made a lot of simple dishes that could get done in a single pan. Though I have much more cooking space these days, some of these dishes still happily tide me through on busy days. Healthy, quick, and flavorful, this dish is also rather pretty! Dried fenugreek leaves are readily available at Indian grocers and they retain flavor when stored for an extended period of time. I use tuna or swordfish for this recipe.

Prep Time: 30 minutes (including 20 minutes for marinating) | Cook Time: 20 minutes | Serves: 4

Ingredients

1 tablespoon tandoori masala (page 349)

1 tablespoon ginger-garlic paste (page 14)

1 teaspoon red cayenne pepper powder

1½ teaspoons amchur powder or juice of 1 lime

2 tablespoons plain yogurt (*this can be reduced or eliminated if using lime juice*)

2 or 3 medium tuna or swordfish steaks (1½ to 2 pounds)

4 to 5 tablespoons oil

For the crust

1 tablespoon dried fenugreek leaves (sold as *kasuri methi*)

1½ tablespoons finely chopped mixed herbs (mint, chives, and/or cilantro)

½ teaspoon salt

½ cup finely chopped walnuts

Preparation

1. Place the tandoori masala, ginger-garlic paste, cayenne pepper powder, amchur powder or lime juice, and yogurt in a mixing bowl. Add the fish steaks and mix well to coat evenly. Set aside for 20 minutes.

2. In the meantime, toss together the fenugreek leaves, mixed herbs, salt, and walnuts for the crust.

3. Place each steak in the herb mixture and coat uniformly.

4. Heat the oil in a large heavy-bottomed skillet until fairly hot but not smoking. Add a fish steak and cook for about 1½ minutes, turn and cover and cook for another 2 minutes. This amount of time should cook the fish and not dry it out. Repeat with the other fish steaks.

5. To serve, cut fish into wedges and garnish with additional cilantro before serving.

Tips and Tricks

I finding it easier to cook these steaks individually since they need constant attention while cooking.

Coastal Coconut and Tamarind Fish Curry
(F&S, GF)

The Konkan region of India is a strip lining the western coastline from Raigad to Mangalore. As a child I visited this region several times. The food in the area is diverse with a myriad of influences. The fragrant fish curry that my parents loved stands out most in my memory. This Konkani-inspired recipe is from Susan Shanbag, a friend whose husband is from the Konkan region. I tweaked it by substituting tamarind for the star-shaped kokum (because I usually have freshly strained tamarind handy) and coconut cream for the grated coconut, and finally I add some Kashmiri red chili powder to balance the color and heat.

Prep Time: 10 minutes | Cook Time: 35 minutes | Serves: 6

Ingredients

2 tablespoons oil

1 teaspoon black mustard seeds

1 teaspoon cumin seeds

10 to 15 curry leaves

1 red onion, finely chopped

1 tablespoon minced fresh ginger

1½ tablespoons cumin-coriander powder (page 353)

2 teaspoons Kashmiri red chili powder

1 teaspoon red cayenne pepper powder

2 tablespoons tamarind paste (not concentrate)

⅓ cup coconut cream

1 teaspoon salt or to taste

1½ pounds white fish fillets (such as tilapia, perch, or halibut), cut into 2 or 3 pieces each

2 tablespoons chopped cilantro

Preparation

1. Heat the oil in a skillet on medium heat for about 30 seconds. Add the mustard seeds and cumin seeds and when the mustard seeds begin to pop, add the curry leaves and onion and sauté for 5 to 6 minutes.

2. Add the ginger, cumin-coriander powder, kashmiri red chili powder, and cayenne pepper powder and stir well for about 1 to 2 minutes.

3. Add the tamarind paste and ½ cup of water and bring to a simmer. Let simmer for about 15 minutes, until the flavors have mixed and the mixture is thick and a deep shade of red.

4. Stir in the coconut cream, salt, and another ½ cup water and bring to a simmer.

5. Add the fish and simmer for about 10 minutes until cooked through.

6. Stir in the cilantro and serve with hot steamed rice.

Seared Scallops in a Blueberry Ginger Sauce
(F&S, GF)

I created this height-of-summer recipe for my "Spices and Seasons" column in the *Journal News*. It is impossible to ignore summer blueberries —plump and sweet with a touch of tartness. The flavors of this dish are simple, clean, and vibrant and pair beautifully with a glass of chilled white wine. The dish may sound complex, but gets tossed together in less than 30 minutes, just what you want for summer fun.

Prep Time: 15 minutes | Cook Time: 10 minutes | Serves: 4

Ingredients

For the scallops
1 pound medium or large scallops
   (about 20 medium or 12 large)
½ teaspoon sumac
½ teaspoon raw cane sugar
¼ teaspoon salt
1 tablespoon butter
2 tablespoons olive oil

For the blueberry sauce
½ cup fresh blueberries
2 teaspoons freshly grated ginger
½ teaspoon raw cane sugar
¼ teaspoon salt or to taste
¼ teaspoon coriander powder

For garnish
1 tablespoon finely chopped basil

Preparation

1. Pre-heat oven to 400°F.

2. Prepare the scallops: Rinse the scallops in cold water and blot until very dry with paper towels. Toss the scallops with the sumac, sugar, and salt. Set aside.

3. Prepare the blueberry sauce: In a baking dish put the blueberries, ginger, cane sugar, salt, and coriander powder and toss lightly. Put in the oven and bake about 10 minutes, until the blueberries have popped and formed a bubbling sauce.

4. Meanwhile, in a large flat skillet, heat the butter and olive oil on medium heat for at least 1 minute. Carefully place the scallops in a single layer with some space between each scallop. Cook for 3 minutes and then turn and cook on the other side for about 4 minutes. The scallops should turn just a little golden on each side.

5. To serve, spread some of the sauce on each of 4 plates and place 5 medium scallops (or 3 large) on top of the sauce on each plate. Sprinkle with basil leaves before serving.

Super Simple Fish Curry
(F&S, GF)

You can make this with any fresh firm fish, but my choices are usually mackerel steaks, rainbow trout, or halibut. As long as the fish is the freshest possible, the key element in Indian cooking is getting the seasonings right. This recipe merges the five-spice blend of eastern India with flavors from the northern state of Punjab, resulting in an interesting medley of regional Indian flavors. It is inspired by my friend's mother, who is a Punjabi married into a Bengali family—hence the juxtaposition of flavors. Sometimes the most interesting nuances in Indian food emerge when flavors from two different parts of India are blended.

Prep Time: 10 minutes | Cook Time: 20 to 25 minutes | Serves: 4 to 6

Ingredients

2 tablespoons oil

1 teaspoon Bengali Five Spice Mixture (panch phoron)

1 small to medium red onion, finely chopped

1 tablespoon ginger-garlic paste (page 14)

½ teaspoon turmeric

1 teaspoon salt or to taste

2 tomatoes, chopped

2 pounds fish steaks or fillets, cubed

2 green chilies, minced

1 tablespoon finely chopped fresh thyme or ½ teaspoon carom seeds

1 to 2 tablespoons chopped cilantro to garnish

Preparation

1. Heat the oil in a wok or skillet on medium heat spreading in the pan until the oil shimmers. Add the five-spice blend and cook until the spices begin to crackle and the mixture is fragrant, about 30 seconds if the oil is well heated.

2. Add the onion and ginger-garlic paste and sauté for about 3 to 4 minutes.

3. Stir in the turmeric, salt, and tomatoes and cook for a couple of minutes until the tomatoes begin to release their juices.

4. Add the fish, green chilies, and thyme. Cook for 7 to 10 minutes until the fish is cooked through, stirring gently to allow the sauce to coat the fish.

5. Garnish with cilantro and serve over steamed white rice.

Shrimp in a Mango Basil Sauce
(F&S, GF)

Once upon a time, someone gave me a mango that was too hard to eat but had the potential to ripen. I placed it in a brown paper bag and forgot about it for a week. When I finally checked, the mango had morphed into a soft, fragrant, tempting, orange fruit. I decided to cook it in a different way. This shrimp recipe is the result and brings out the best of the plump gift of the sea and the plumb luscious mango.

Prep Time: 5 minutes | Cook Time: 20 minutes | Serves: 4

Ingredients

2 to 3 tablespoons oil

¾ teaspoon black mustard seeds

1 teaspoon coarsely ground cumin seeds

1 small red onion, finely chopped

1 tablespoon freshly grated ginger

3 or 4 green chilies, minced

1 pound large shrimp, peeled and deveined

1 ripe mango, seeded and chopped

1 teaspoon black salt

1 teaspoon driedred pepper flakes

20 large fresh basil leaves

1 tablespoon chopped cilantro

Preparation

1. Heat the oil in a skillet or wok on medium heat for about 30 seconds. Add the mustard seeds and when they begin to crackle add the coarsely ground cumin seeds and red onion and cook for 5 minutes, stirring frequently until the onion is soft and translucent.

2. Add the ginger and green chilies and cook for another minute.

3. Add the shrimp and cook, stirring, for about 3 minutes, until the shrimp change color.

4. Gently mix in the mango, black salt, and red pepper flakes and cook for 6 to 7 minutes, until the mango is somewhat saucy.

5. Stir in the basil and cook for about 1 minute. Garnish with the cilantro and serve immediately.

Chickpea Flour-Crusted Fish
(F&S, GF)

Fresh fish encased in a crisp, well-seasoned chickpea flour batter is a classic Punjabi recipe called *Amrisari Macchi*. I played around with the flavors and seasonings just a little, to create magical deliciousness. My version features a gentle, clingy coating that does not weigh the fish down with extra heaviness. I like to serve this fish as I'm frying it. So for a truly casual and delicious experience, hand your guests their choice of a chilled drink, and tell them to gather around while you cook. Set aside small plates with some salad and serve the fish as soon as you get it out of the wok—fresh, crisp, and amazingly flavorful. I love to use whiting chunks for this recipe, however, any mild-tasting white fish would work.

Prep Time: 25 minutes (including 20 minutes marinating time) | Cook Time: 20 minutes | Serves: 4 to 6

Ingredients

2 pounds whiting fish fillets, cut into 1½-inch pieces

½ teaspoon turmeric

1½ teaspoons salt

1 large lime, cut in half

1 tablespoon ginger paste

2 teaspoons minced garlic cloves

1 red onion, very finely chopped

3 tablespoons minced cilantro

2 tablespoons finely chopped fresh thyme or ½ teaspoon ajowain or carom seeds

2 green chilies, minced

¾ cup chickpea flour (besan)

¼ cup cornmeal

Oil for frying

Preparation

1. Place the fish in a mixing bowl and sprinkle with the turmeric and half the salt. Squeeze on the lime juice. Add the ginger paste, garlic, and red onion and toss well to coat. Add the cilantro, thyme, and green chilies and let the mixture rest for about 20 minutes.

2. In another mixing bowl mix together the chickpea flour and cornmeal. Add to the fish mixture with just enough water to coat, about ¼ cup. (My version does not opt for a heavy batter but rather just a crumbly light-textured crust around the fish.)

3. Heat some oil in a cast-iron wok or skillet and when the oil is hot (test with a small amount of the batter, it should sizzle and rise to the top) add the fish a few pieces at a time and fry for 3 to 4 minutes, the coating should be golden and the fish should be flaky soft.

4. Remove the fish with a slotted spoon and drain on paper towels. Serve immediately with your choice of a chutney.

Shrimp in a Creamy Bell Pepper Sauce
(F&S, GF)

Here is a seafood-based take on my roasted bell pepper sauce, with soft, delicate avocados adding even more vibrant color and naturally creamy consistency. The colors are just the beginning of what makes this beautiful dish a winner. Something magical happens to the avocados when they absorb the flavors of this delicate sauce. The mild flavors of this dish make it popular with both adults and children.

Prep Time: 10 minutes | Cook Time: 20 minutes | Serves: 6

Ingredients

1½ pounds large or jumbo shrimp, shelled and deveined

1 lime, cut in half

1 teaspoon salt

½ teaspoon turmeric

1½ tablespoons oil

¾ teaspoon mustard seeds

¾ teaspoon cumin seeds

1 medium red onion, chopped

½ teaspoon red cayenne pepper powder

½ cup roasted bell pepper chutney (page 71)

1 medium avocado, peeled and chopped

½ cup coconut milk (optional)

½ cup fresh or frozen sweet corn kernels

1 to 2 tablespoons minced cilantro or basil

Preparation

1. Place the shrimp in a mixing bowl, squeeze in the lime juice and stir in the salt and turmeric. Set aside.

2. In a large pan, heat the oil on medium heat for about 1 minute. Add the mustard seeds and cumin seeds and cook until the mustard seeds crackle and cumin seeds sizzle, about 30 seconds.

3. Add the red onion and cook and stir well for about 4 to 5 minutes, until the onion softens, wilts, and begins to turn pale golden at the edges.

4. Grind the cayenne pepper powder, roasted bell pepper chutney, coconut milk (if using), and ⅓ cup of water into a smooth puree and add to the mixture. (If not using the coconut milk, increase the water to ¾ cup.) Stir in the corn.

5. Gently add the shrimp and simmer for about 12 minutes, until the shrimp are cooked through.

6. Stir in the minced cilantro or basil. Gently mix in the avocado and heat through before turning off the heat. Serve immediately.

Wasabi Ginger Fish with Fresh Blackberries
(F&S, GF)

I love to mingle sweet and sour tastes, and over time I learned to create them with more of a natural accent, such as with the blackberries that are so plentiful through late summer and early autumn. This recipe uses a very common everyday marinade in my kitchen that my kids love. The wasabi is an unusual grown-up kick that I like to add to make things a little lively.

Prep Time: 5 minutes plus 3 hours marinating time | Cook Time: 15 minutes (mostly unattended) |
Serves: 4

Ingredients

1 2-inch piece fresh ginger, peeled

2 tablespoons prepared wasabi

2 tablespoons maple syrup

2 to 3 tablespoons olive oil

½ cup low-sodium soy sauce

2 pounds fish steaks or fillets (salmon or halibut work well), cubed

10 to 12 blackberries

10 grape tomatoes, chopped (optional)

Freshly ground black pepper

Chopped cilantro to garnish

Preparation

1. Place the ginger, wasabi, maple syrup, olive oil, and soy sauce in a blender and blend to a smooth paste.

2. Place the fish in a mixing bowl and pour on the paste and toss to coat. Marinate in the refrigerator for up to 3 hours.

3. Set the oven to 350°F.

4. Arrange the fish in a shallow baking casserole. Bake uncovered for about 10 minutes.

5. Turn the oven to a low broil setting. Baste the fish with any sauce in pan to glaze it, and add the blackberries and grape tomatoes (if using).

6. Broil for about 2 to 3 minutes, until the blackberries just begin to release their juices. Top with lots of freshly ground black pepper and garnish with cilantro and serve.

Mussels in a Rich Shiitake Sauce
(F&S, GF)

There are a few tricks to cooking mussels but once you get the hang of it, you will wonder what the fuss was about. To ensure all my mussels are open and free of any residual sand, I steam them separately in a flavorful broth and then discard the broth. I then drench the mussels in a well-seasoned sauce that can be scooped up with bread or served over rice. As my brother likes to say, "it is the sauce that makes the mussels." These mussels are comforting in any season, but I usually add in some tomatoes if I make them in summer.

Prep Time: 10 minutes | Cook Time: 35 minutes | Serves: 6

Ingredients

For the shiitake sauce
3 tablespoons salted butter
2 tablespoons oil
4 shallots, finely chopped
1 tablespoon basic curry powder
(see recipe on page 354)
½ cup finely chopped shiitake
mushrooms
2 ripe tomatoes, finely chopped
(optional)
¾ teaspoon salt or to taste
1 cup white wine
¾ cup coconut milk
1 tablespoon chopped cilantro

For the mussels
2 cups white wine
4 cups low-sodium chicken or
vegetable broth
4 pounds mussels, cleaned and
debearded

For garnish
Minced chives
Minced cilantro

Preparation

1. In a large skillet, heat the butter and oil for a couple of minutes. Add the shallots and cook on medium-low heat, stirring frequently, for 7 to 8 minutes, until the mixture is a pale golden color.

2. Add the curry powder and shiitake mushrooms and mix well. If using the tomatoes add them at this point and cook for 3 minutes, stirring frequently.

3. Add the salt and white wine and simmer for about 15 minutes on low heat, stirring occasionally. Cool the mixture slightly, and then blend to a smooth puree with the coconut milk. Set aside.

4. While the sauce is cooking, bring the white wine and broth to a simmer in a large pot.

5. Once the sauce is ready, add the mussels to the simmering broth mixture and cook for 5 minutes, just until they are open (do not overcook them). Drain, discarding the cooking liquid and any unopened mussels.

6. Place the sauce back on the heat, bring to a simmer and stir in the cilantro. Add the mussels and cook for another minute. Garnish with the chives and cilantro before serving.

Chapter Seven

The Pride of the Farm: Meat & Poultry

The Indian meat of choice is goat, known as mutton in India. This used to be much harder to find even a few years back in the U.S. so I ended up adapting many goat meat recipes using lamb. So if you are adventurous you can try the lamb recipes in this chapter with goat meat. I encourage you to plan ahead with cooking meat because the flavors of curries improve significantly with longer simmering times, and also taste much better the next day when the meat has absorbed the seasonings.

Beef and pork are limited in Indian cooking due to religious constraints. Beef is not generally eaten or cooked in Hindu households, which are a significant portion of the Indian population, and pork is not eaten by Muslims, who are one of the largest meat-eating groups in India. There are, however, several regional specialty dishes cooked with beef and pork.

Chicken is healthier than red meat and works well in stews and curries and holds its own in stir-fries as well. I personally feel that dark meat from chicken works better for these recipes. It is reasonably easy to find good-quality chicken, including organic free-range varieties, in regular grocery stores in the U.S. Free-range chicken is really more than just a healthy choice; it is also a more flavorful choice, since the free-range chickens are more muscular and their meat holds up better to longer stewing periods which is the key to deep and flavorful curries.

Kashmiri Lamb Stew with Carrots
(M&P, GF)

Inspired by a traditional lamb stew called *Rogan Josh* from the region of Kashmir, this version gets done in the slow cooker. It begins with the help of my tomato starter and is finished off with the addition of carrots. If you do not have a slow cooker, this recipe can be prepared on the stovetop in a heavy pot on low heat. Whatever cooking method you use, I think that you'll enjoy this full-bodied stew.

Prep Time: 10 minutes | Cook Time: 3 hours in a slow cooker | Serves: 4 to 6

Ingredients

1½ cups tomato starter (page 357)

1 tablespoon cumin-coriander powder (page 353)

1½ teaspoons ground fennel seeds

1 teaspoon red cayenne pepper powder

2 teaspoons Kashmiri chili powder or paprika

2 or 3 green cardamom pods

1 (2-inch) cinnamon stick, broken

3 or 4 cloves

2 or 3 bay leaves

2 pounds lamb chops, cut into small 1-inch pieces, or boneless leg of lamb, cut into cubes

Salt to taste

3 medium carrots, peeled and cut into 2-inch pieces

1 tablespoon chopped cilantro

Preparation

1. In a bowl, mix together the tomato starter, cumin-coriander powder, ground fennel seeds, cayenne pepper powder, and Kashmiri red chili powder. Place mixture in a slow cooker or heavy-bottomed pot.

2. Add in the cardamom pods, cinnamon stick, cloves, and bay leaves and mix well.

3. Stir in the lamb and pour in 1 cup of water. Cook in the slow cooker on high for 2½ hours or simmer on the stovetop for 1 hour. At this point the lamb should be fork tender.

4. Adjust the salt as needed. Add the carrots and cook for another 30 minutes.

5. Remove from heat. At this point the stew can be stored in the refrigerator for a few days. When ready to serve, reheat on the stove top and stir in the cilantro.

Lamb Curry with Mint and Apricots
(M&P, GF)

I often create dishes to use up excess or leftover foods. This was the case when I recently bought an entire clamshell of apricots thinking my kids would love them. Well, they refused to touch them. Here I was stuck with a crisper full of lovely, tangy yellow fruit. I ended up making a jam with honey, and then used the remaining apricots in this lamb dish. It is a lovely, spicy dense pairing. I use fiery habanero chilies, but you can use whatever suits your palate.

Prep Time: 10 minutes | Cook Time: 40 minutes with pressure cooker • 80 minutes on stovetop |
Serves: 4

Ingredients

¼ cup oil

1 (2-inch) cinnamon stick

3 or 4 cardamom pods

3 or 4 cloves

1 large onion, finely chopped

3 cloves garlic, minced

2 teaspoons grated fresh ginger

1 teaspoon cumin-coriander powder (page 353)

1 pound boneless lamb, cut into 2-inch cubes

1 teaspoon turmeric

2 teaspoons salt

2 tomatoes, chopped

4 green chilies, finely chopped

4 fresh apricots, chopped (can be replaced with ¾ cup chopped dried apricots)

2 tablespoons chopped fresh mint

1 teaspoon finely chopped cilantro

Preparation

1. Heat the oil in a pressure cooker or heavy-bottomed pot on medium heat for about 30 seconds. Add the cinnamon stick, cardamom pods, and cloves.

2. Add the onions, garlic, and ginger and cook slowly until the onions begin to turn light brown.

3. Add the cumin-coriander powder, lamb, turmeric, and salt and cook stirring slowly for about 10 minutes.

4. Add the tomatoes, chilies, apricots, and mint and cook for another 5 minutes.

5. Add about ½ cup water, cover and cook under pressure for about 15 minutes or on the stovetop for 50 to 60 minutes.

6. Remove the lid, mix well, and cook for another 5 to 7 minutes, until the gravy is thick and fairly dry.

7. Add the cilantro and enjoy with rice or bread.

Red Chili, Garlic and Cardamom Lamb
(M&P, GF)

Last winter my aunt decided to visit us while her husband was in India. This was a really big deal because she rarely ventures outside her comfort zone in New York City. I knew my work was cut out for me. She is fond of lamb, so to honor her visit, I cooked this lamb dish that has its roots in the royal cuisine of the northern state of Rajasthan. This dish is called *Laal Maas* which literally translates to "*red meat*" and its red color is traditionally derived from hot chili peppers. I use a combination of Kashmiri red chili powder and hot dried red chilies to balance the heat. It ends up being just the right amount of spice. The deep, dense flavors are beautiful for the lamb and produce a lovely dish.

Prep Time: 10 minutes | Cook Time: 70 minutes on stovetop • 40 minutes with a pressure cooker (mostly unattended) | Serves: 6

Ingredients

2 teaspoons cumin seeds

1 tablespoon coriander seeds

6 dried red chilies

1 tablespoon Kashmiri red chili powder

1 cup plain yogurt

3 pounds lamb, on the bone

1½ teaspoons garam masala powder (page 350)

2 teaspoons salt

⅓ cup oil

4 onions, chopped

1 clove garlic, sliced

4 black cardamom pods

6 green cardamom pods

⅓ cup chopped cilantro leaves

Preparation

1. Place the cumin seeds, coriander seeds, and dried red chilies in a spice or coffee grinder and grind to a powder. Stir in the Kashmiri chili powder.

2. In a mixing bowl, mix the ground spices with the yogurt, lamb, garam masala, and salt and set aside to marinate while you cook the onions.

3. Heat half the oil in a pot and add the onions and cook until a pale toffee color.

4. Stir in the garlic, cardamom pods, and lamb mixture. Cook the lamb on fairly high heat, stirring frequently, and adding the remaining oil as needed to brown the meat—it takes about 15 minutes of active cooking to obtain the right result.

5. Stir in about ¾ cup of water. Bring to a boil and then reduce to a medium simmer, cover and let simmer for 30 minutes. (Alternately cook this in a pressure cooker for 20 minutes and skip the next step).

6. Remove the cover (at this point the meat should be fairly soft), stir well and cook uncovered for 10 minutes to let the gravy thicken.

7. Stir in the cilantro and serve with rice or bread.

Tips and Tricks

If you have a little extra time on your hands, you can transfer the lamb to a slow cooker during the finishing stages and simmer for an additional 2 to 3 hours.

I have found that the chewier texture of goat meat is also excellent for this dish.

Lamb Stew with Potatoes and Mushrooms
(M&P, GF)

I prefer to make this recipe with goat meat but it is not very easy to find. Instead I use American lamb, which I feel is a little closer in taste to goat meat than the often preferred Australian lamb. After one wintry Sunday of activities—dance class, grocery store, play practice—I felt that I owed myself a treat. So I cooked up this quick, satisfying lamb/mutton stew—spicy, somewhat robust, laced with mushrooms and potatoes.

Prep Time: 15 minutes | Cook Time: 40 minutes using pressure cooker • 70 minutes on stovetop |
Serves: 4 (recipe can easily be doubled)

Ingredients

⅓ cup oil

2 onions, finely chopped

1 tablespoon freshly grated ginger

1 (2-inch) cinnamon stick, broken

2 or 3 cardamom pods

4 to 6 cloves

1½ teaspoons coarsely ground black pepper

1½ pounds lamb, trimmed of fat and cut into cubes

1 teaspoon turmeric

1½ teaspoons salt

2 or 3 tomatoes, cut into small pieces

1 large potato (about ½ pound), peeled and cut into small pieces, or 3 or 4 smaller potatoes, peeled and halved

⅓ cup chopped cilantro

1 cup chopped cremini mushrooms (also called baby bella mushrooms)

2 or 3 dried red chilies

Preparation

1. Heat the oil in a pressure cooker or heavy-bottomed pot and add the onions and ginger and sauté for 4 to 5 minutes.

2. Add in the cinnamon stick, cardamom pods, cloves, black pepper, and lamb. Mix well and add in the turmeric and salt. Cook stirring for a good 10 to 15 minutes, until the lamb is well browned.

3. Stir in the tomatoes, potatoes, and 1½ cups water and bring to a simmer. Cover and cook under pressure for 15 minutes or on the stovetop, uncovered, on low heat for 45 minutes, until the lamb is tender and the gravy is thick.

4. Cool slightly and remove the cover from pressure cooker if used.

5. Add in the cilantro, mushrooms, and red chilies and cook for another 3 to 5 minutes. Serve.

Tips and Tricks

For an interesting variation, you can add some star anise to the stew. The sweet anise undertones add an interesting dimension to this dish.

Red Wine and Chili Pork Curry
(M&P, GF)

Winter evenings leave me craving rich, spicy fare. The cold just begs for extra time spent nursing a comforting pot of curry by the stove. Full-flavored, rich, and robust, this pork curry is inspired by the flavors of Pondicherry, an erstwhile French colony in Southern India. To build a meal around this, you can serve the pork over steamed rice or freshly toasted bread. I came up with the first version of this dish on a stormy night, when we were suddenly left without electricity. I did not want the meat and my curry leaves to spoil, so thanks to my gas stove, I devised this robustly spiced dish that has held its own over time.

Prep Time: 10 minutes | Cook Time: 40 minutes | Serves: 6

Ingredients

⅓ cup olive oil

1½ teaspoons mustard seeds

2 large white onions, finely chopped

4 green chilies, minced

1½ tablespoons ginger-garlic paste (page 14)

1½ pounds pork tenderloin, cut into cubes

20 pearl onions

3 tablespoons soy sauce

2 tablespoons rice vinegar

1 tablespoon sugar or honey

½ teaspoon red cayenne pepper powder

¾ cup red wine (such as a burgundy)

10 to 12 curry leaves

Preparation

1. Place the oil in a large Dutch oven or other similar cooking pot, and heat over medium heat for 1 minute. Add the mustard seeds and wait until they crackle.

2. Add the white onions and sauté for about 5 minutes, until soft and translucent.

3. Add the green chilies and ginger-garlic paste and mix well.

4. Add the pork and pearl onions and continue cooking on medium-high heat for about 5 minutes to allow the pork to sear lightly.

5. Stir in the soy sauce, vinegar, sugar, cayenne pepper powder, and some of the wine. Bring the mixture to a simmer and stir in the curry leaves.

6. Continue cooking, gradually adding in the wine until a smooth, deep and bold sauce is formed and the meat is tender. The sauce will eventually dry out to a thick coating. This will take another 20 to 25 minutes. Serve hot.

Tips and Tricks

This curry can be refrigerated overnight and served the next day, allowing the flavors to deepen and meld with each other.

Pork in a Tangy Spicy Sauce
(M&P, GF)

For some reason, this ended up being one of the last dishes I selected for this book. This recipe for vindaloo, a Goan-style dish, is considered one of my specialties and I just felt that the book would not be complete without it. I received this recipe from my Goan friend Thomas, and other than simplifying it a little here and there this still remains his recipe.

Prep Time: 20 minutes (plus at least 6 hours to marinate the pork) | Cook Time: 35 to 45 minutes | Serves: 6 to 8

Ingredients

½ cup white or red wine vinegar

1 tablespoon coriander seeds

1 teaspoon cumin seeds

6 cloves garlic

1-inch piece ginger, peeled

3 green chilies

2 or 3 dried red chilies

1½ teaspoons salt

2 pounds pork (preferably from the butt or other soft meaty segment), cut into cubes

4 tablespoons oil

4 cloves

1 (2 to 3-inch) cinnamon stick

2 red onions, chopped

⅓ cup coconut milk

Chopped cilantro to garnish

Preparation

1. Place the vinegar in a mixing bowl and stir in the coriander seeds, cumin seeds, garlic, ginger, green chilies, red chilies, and salt and set aside for 10 to 15 minutes.

2. Place the mixture in a wet-dry grinder or blender and blend until smooth. Toss with the pork in a non-reactive bowl. Cover and marinate for 6 hours to overnight.

3. When ready to cook, heat the oil in a pot on medium heat and add the cloves and cinnamon stick. Add the red onions and sauté until beginning to turn a pale toffee color.

4. Add the pork with the marinade and continue cooking the mixture, stirring frequently, for at least 10 minutes, until the spices and onions melt together to form a soft sauce and the oil surfaces through.

5. Stir in the coconut milk and use the milk to effectively deglaze the pan, scraping in any spices that are clinging to the sides. Stir in ½ cup of water and bring to a simmer and cover and cook the pork for 15 to 20 minutes.

6. Remove the cover and reduce the sauce if needed to a thick gravy that loosely coats the meat.

7. Stir in the cilantro and serve.

Slow-Roasted Chicken with Caramelized Onions
(M&P, GF)

This recipe is in the Muslim tradition of cooking using a technique called *bhuna* or *kasha*, a process in which a medley of meat, golden onions, and spices is slow cooked with whole spices without any additional water. The classic preparation of this recipe—traditionally made with goat meat—is called *kasha mangsho*. My version uses chicken, and it is important to note that the chicken should be on the bone (preferably a free-range chicken, skinned and cut up). The trick to the recipe's deep, full flavors is to cook it without any water. The only moisture in this dish comes from a small amount of yogurt. It is best enjoyed with *puris* (page 309) or *naan* (page 305).

Prep Time: 10 minutes | Cook Time: 40 to 45 minutes | Serves: 6

Ingredients

3 pounds chicken on the bone skinned and cut into medium-size pieces

1 lime, cut in half

1 tablespoon ginger-garlic paste (page 14)

3 green chilies, minced

1½ teaspoons salt

⅓ cup oil

4 onions, thinly sliced

1½ teaspoons sugar

1 tablespoon coriander seeds

1 tablespoon cumin seeds

6 whole mild dried red chilies

½ teaspoon fennel seeds

1 teaspoon black peppercorns

2 or 3 bay leaves

1 (2-inch) cinnamon stick, broken

3 or 4 cloves

2 or 3 cardamom pods

½ cup plain Greek yogurt (can be low fat)

Chopped cilantro for garnish

Preparation

1. Place the chicken in a bowl, squeeze in the lime juice, and mix with the ginger-garlic paste, green chilies, and half the salt.

2. Heat the oil in a heavy-bottomed pot. Add the onions and carefully begin frying them. (These onions are at the heart of the recipe, and need to be fried with a lot of tender loving care.) When the onions begin to wilt and soften (after about 3 to 4 minutes) stir in the sugar and continue cooking, stirring fairly frequently, for another 6 to 7 minutes, until the onions reach a shade of deep caramel.

3. At this point add in the seasoned chicken and stir well for 2 minutes.

4. In the meantime, place the coriander seeds, cumin seeds, and 4 of the mild red chilies in a spice or coffee grinder and grind to a powder.

5. Add the spice powder to the chicken along with 2 whole red chilies. Gently bruise the fennel seeds and black peppercorns and mix in along with the remaining ¾ teaspoon salt. Add the bay leaves, cinnamon stick, cloves, and cardamom pods and mix well.

6. Stir in the yogurt and continue cooking the chicken on medium heat, stirring frequently, for a good 20 minutes. The result should be soft well-cooked chicken, coated with shards of golden brown onions and fragrant whole spices.

7. Garnish with the cilantro and serve; or store overnight and serve the next day, since the flavors improve significantly with keeping.

Chili Basil Chicken
(M&P, GF)

Though I am not blessed with my husband's green thumb, I am pretty good with herbs. I grow pots of mint, thyme, oregano, and basil and savor their fresh fragrance through the summer and autumn. This recipe is perfect for the peak of summer, when I like to keep my cooking light. Just a few ingredients yield an unusually festive dish that tastes great heated or at room temperature. I personally like to use Asian purple basil in this recipe, but regular sweet basil is fine too. The flavors are clean, spicy, and refreshing, but the best part is that it gets done in a well-seasoned jiffy.

Prep Time: 10 minutes plus 30 minutes to marinate | Cook Time: 25 minutes | Serves: 4 to 6

Ingredients

2 pounds boneless skinless chicken, cut into 1½-inch pieces

1 teaspoon salt

1 teaspoon turmeric

1 large lime, halved and seeded

3 tablespoons oil

1 teaspoon cumin seeds

1 medium red onion, finely chopped (about ¾ cup)

3 tablespoons very finely chopped fresh ginger

10 green chilies, slit lengthwise

½ cup finely chopped basil leaves, plus 8 to 10 leaves for garnish

3 or 4 dried red chilies

Preparation

1. Rub the chicken with the salt and turmeric. Squeeze the lime juice over it and set aside to marinate for about 30 minutes.

2. Heat the oil in a skillet or wok. Add the cumin seeds and when they sizzle, add the onion and ginger and cook over medium-high heat, stirring frequently, until the onions wilt and soften.

3. Add the seasoned chicken and cook for 12 minutes, stirring frequently, until the chicken is turning fairly brown.

4. Stir in the green chilies and basil leaves and cook until the leaves are wilted. Lightly crush the red chilies and stir in and cook for 2 to 3 minutes.

5. Sprinkle with the whole basil leaves and serve.

Chicken in a Creamy Yogurt Sauce
(M&P, GF)

This classic curry is a traditional North Indian recipe called Chicken Korma. A soft and comforting chicken curry with a soothing assortment of spices, it is practical and simple enough for weeknight dinners, but also great for a party since this recipe is easy to double or triple.

Prep Time: 30 minutes | Cook Time: 30 minutes | Serves: 4 to 6

Ingredients:

For the spice paste
1-inch piece fresh ginger, peeled

4 cloves garlic

2 dried red chilies

2 teaspoons coriander seeds

1½ teaspoons cumin seeds

For the cashew nut paste
½ cup raw unroasted cashew nuts

3 tablespoons low-fat plain yogurt

For the chicken curry
2 pounds boneless skinless chicken thighs

4 tablespoons grapeseed or canola oil

1 large red onion, finely chopped

3 or 4 green cardamom pods

1 or 2 (2-inch) cinnamon sticks

2 or 3 bay leaves

4 cloves

1 teaspoon turmeric

3 tomatoes, pureed (can use canned tomatoes)

1 green chili, minced (optional)

2 tablespoons finely chopped cilantro

Preparation

1. For the spice paste: Place the ginger, garlic, dried red chilies, coriander seeds, and cumin seeds in a blender. Add ⅓ cup water and pulse a few times and then grind to a smooth paste. (To get a good uniform result, you will need to stop the blender a few times and push the ingredients back down with a spoon.)

2. Rub the spice paste onto the chicken and let rest while you prepare the remainder of the dish.

3. For the cashew nut paste: Place the cashews and yogurt in a blender and blend into a smooth paste. Set aside.

4. Heat the oil in a wok or skillet on medium heat. Add the onion and cook for 3 to 4 minutes, until they begin to turn golden.

5. Stir in the cardamom pods, cinnamon stick(s), bay leaves, and cloves and cook for a few seconds.

6. Stir in the chicken with the spice paste and the turmeric and sauté for 6 to 7 minutes.

7. Add the tomatoes and green chili, if using. Bring to a simmer and cook for 10 minutes.

8. Stir in the cashew nut paste and simmer for 3 minutes. You should have a soft chicken curry that is thick and golden yellow in color. Garnish with cilantro and serve with rice.

Chicken Tikka in a Tomato Cream Sauce
(M&P, GF)

I know there are so many versions of this recipe available already, and you may wonder whether you really need another one. After much thought, however, I decided to include it in this cookbook since it is so popular with my family, guests, and students. The finish with the mascarpone cheese is my addition and is worth a try if you have the cheese around. Enjoy!

Prep Time: 5 minutes (not including making the Masala Sauce) | Cook Time: 20 minutes (not including cooking the Chicken Tikka) | Serves: 4 to 6

Ingredients
½ recipe Tikka Masala Sauce (page 359)

1 recipe Chicken Tikka Kebabs (page 39)

⅓ cup heavy cream

3 tablespoons butter or 2 tablespoons mascarpone cheese

Sliced almonds to garnish

Extra cilantro to garnish

Preparation
1. Bring the masala sauce to a simmer. Add the chicken pieces (off the skewers) and the pan drippings, if any (note this is only possible if you make the chicken tikka and this recipe simultaneously), and cook for 3 to 4 minutes.

2. Stir in the cream and simmer for 15 minutes. Turn off the heat.

3. Stir in the butter or mascarpone cheese and let the butter or cheese melt before serving.

4. Add the sliced almonds and extra cilantro for garnishing and serve.

Tips and Tricks
Double the recipe and use half to make "Surprise the Guests" Pink Chicken Biryani on page 279.

Chicken Meatballs in a Light Tomato Gravy
(M&P, GF)

These *koftas* (meatballs) are made with ground chicken or turkey. *Koftas* are balls traditionally made with either meat or vegetables, deep-fried, and then simmered in a flavored gravy. I skip deep-frying the *koftas* because it does not make a huge difference in taste, but does make a dent in the number of calories. The gravy for meat *koftas* is usually much richer than for their vegetarian counterparts. I simplified it to offer you a light, flavorful gravy free from the trappings of excess cream. The star anise in particular leaves the gravy with delicate licorice-like notes that balance out the other flavors.

Prep Time: 15 minutes | Cook Time: 25 to 30 minutes | Serves: 4 to 6

Ingredients

For the meatballs

1 pound ground chicken or turkey

2 teaspoons ground fresh ginger

1 teaspoon ground fresh garlic

2 green chilies, minced

½ teaspoon salt

½ teaspoon sugar

1 lime, cut in half

1 tablespoon chickpea flour (besan)

1 tablespoon oil

For the curry

1½ cups basic tomato starter (page 357)

2 teaspoons cumin-coriander powder (page 353)

2 or 3 pieces star anise

2 cardamom pods

2 or 3 cloves

1 (1½-inch) cinnamon stick, broken

1 teaspoon salt or to taste

4 tablespoons chopped cilantro

Preparation

1. For the meatballs: Mix the ground chicken or turkey with the ginger, garlic, green chilies, salt, and sugar. Squeeze in the lime juice and mix well. Add the chickpea flour and shape the mixture into walnut-size balls.

2. For the curry: Place the tomato starter in a cooking pot and bring to a simmer. Stir in the cumin-coriander powder and cook for 6 to 7 minutes, until the tomatoes are fairly dry and darken considerably.

3. Add the star anise, cardamom pods, cloves, and cinnamon stick and cook on medium-low heat about 7 minutes, stirring occasionally to break the tomatoes down to a smooth consistency.

4. Stir in about 1 cup water and bring the mixture back to a simmer. Stir in the salt. Add the meatballs and cook for 6 to 7 minutes, until the meatballs are no longer pink and are cooked through.

5. Stir in the cilantro and serve.

Classic Chicken Curry
(M&P, GF)

This simple, foolproof dinner party favorite is very satisfying and needs just a little bit of time to plan and cook, with only about 15 minutes of active attention. This recipe can be made with lamb or any other meat and also works well with eggplant for a nice vegetarian variation. It is something my friends and students often ask me to make. I am sure that this will become one of your favorites too!

Prep Time: 10 minutes plus 1 hour marinating time | Cook Time: 50 minutes | Serves: 6

Ingredients

6 medium tomatoes, cut into quarters

1-inch piece ginger, peeled

2 or 3 cloves garlic

3 or 4 dried red chilies

1½ teaspoons salt or to taste

1 teaspoon turmeric

3 pounds skinless chicken, cut into 1½-inch pieces

2 tablespoons butter

3 tablespoons oil

2 onions, finely chopped

1 or 2 bay leaves

6 to 8 green cardamom pods

3 or 4 green chilies, finely chopped

¼ cup chopped cilantro

Preparation

1. Place the tomatoes, ginger, garlic, red chilies, salt, and turmeric in a blender and blend into a paste. Rub the chicken with this mixture and set aside at room temperature for 1 hour.

2. Heat the butter and oil in a wok or skillet on medium-low heat for 1 minute. Add the onions and cook for 5 minutes, stirring frequently, until they soften and begin to turn a pale golden color.

3. Add the bay leaves, cardamom pods, and green chilies and then the seasoned chicken and mix well.

4. Cover and simmer the mixture for 40 minutes, until the sauce is thick and the chicken is falling off the bone. (If you are in a hurry, the chicken can be pressure cooked for 10 minutes, but some of the richness of the sauce will be lost in this quick process.)

5. Stir in the cilantro and serve.

Creamy Mint Chicken Curry
(M&P, GF)

I created this recipe in anticipation of a new friendship, when my co-worker Derek visited with his wife Jane. I was rewarded with a very appreciative lady, and in fact Derek later remarked that his wife was no longer happy with the chicken curry offerings at our local Indian restaurant after she'd had mine.

Prep Time: 10 minutes | Cook Time: 30 minutes | Serves: 4 to 6

Ingredients

2 pounds skinless chicken, cut into 1½-inch pieces

½ teaspoon turmeric

1 teaspoon salt

1 lime, cut in half

3 tablespoons oil

¾ teaspoon mustard seeds

1 teaspoon cumin seeds

1 onion, finely chopped

1 tablespoon freshly grated ginger

1½ teaspoons garam masala (page 350)

½ cup whole Greek yogurt

⅓ cup fresh mint leaves

3 fresh green chilies, minced

Red pepper flakes to garnish

Preparation

1. Rub the chicken pieces with turmeric, salt, and lime juice and set aside.

2. Heat the oil on medium heat for 30 seconds. Add the mustard seeds and cumin seeds and when they begin to crackle, add the onion and sauté until translucent.

3. Add the seasoned chicken pieces and ginger and cook for 15 minutes, until chicken is almost cooked through and turning golden brown at spots and the oil is shimmering through.

4. Stir in the garam masala and cook the chicken for another 5 minutes.

5. Place the yogurt and mint in a blender and blend to a smooth paste. Stir this gently into the chicken and cook for 2 to 3 minutes to heat this through, but do not bring to a boil.

6. Garnish with the green chilies and red pepper flakes.

Chapter Eight

Well-Seasoned Festivities: Indian for the Holidays

There is something about the colder months of the year that gets me into a festive mood. In the U.S. Northeast, mid September is heralded with the beginning of the characteristic color changing. I love when the first few golden leaves peak from a lush green tree, and then over the next few days, more oranges and reds join them until we reach October, when trees are decked with vivid reds, crisp golden yellows, auburn, orange, and only hints of green here and there. At this time of year, the oven lends the whole house a sense of fragrant, comforting warmth, sometimes complemented with the bubbling silence of the slow cooker.

I also love to slow down and catch up with friends before the year is over. The autumn festivals and the winter holidays afford me the perfect opportunity for this. My children love to celebrate everything, so we adopted various cross-cultural holidays along with the Indian festivals of Diwali and Durga Puja to keep the table filled and the house flowing with people. I admit that I make a big deal of celebrations, but I love to build celebrations and fun into my children's lives. Children need the excitement of knowing that some days are different from others. One of my own traditions is my holiday open house that I sneak in between the Indian holidays and Thanksgiving. This is my special opportunity to catch up with friends.

The recipes in this chapter were developed over the years for holidays like Thanksgiving, which is very big in my house, and other winter holidays that give us the excuse to celebrate and eat. Spice-loving people, like my husband, don't always look forward to turkey, which, let's face it, can be a little bland. Thus these holiday recipes have evolved through practice and play with spices, and I've discovered over the years that most ethnic households add their own variety of flavors to the basic recipes for roast turkey or ham. But these recipes are great for any autumn and winter gathering as they can serve a crowd and add a festive note to most occasions. There are other recipes in this book, such as the Golden Harvest Red and Green Quinoa on page 285, that would fit nicely with some of the dishes in this chapter as would some of the vegetable dishes, so please mingle and match for your table as you see fit.

"Fusion" or meshing international flavors with traditional fare has taken off as a culinary trend, and these recipes will appeal to anyone looking to spice up their holidays!

Herb and Spice Roasted Chicken
(M&P, GF)

When someone professes a dislike for a food, I can't help but see it as a challenge. So when my husband threw down the gauntlet—telling me he did not prefer roast chicken—I just had to do something about it. I played around with herbs and spices until I came up with this version. Guess who likes roast chicken now?

Prep Time: 15 minutes | Cook Time: 3 to 4 hours (mostly unattended) | Serves: 6 to 8

Ingredients

¾ cup chopped cilantro

½ cup chopped parsley

3 green chilies

1 (2-inch) piece ginger, peeled

2 or 3 cloves garlic

1 small red onion, peeled and halved

1 teaspoon ground cumin

1½ teaspoons salt

2 limes, cut in half

1 tablespoon grated jaggery or dark brown sugar

1 whole chicken (about 4 pounds)

2 to 3 tablespoons ghee or
    4 tablespoons butter for basting

Preparation

1. Heat the oven to 325°F.

2. Put the cilantro, parsley, chilies, ginger, garlic, onion, ground cumin, and salt in a blender. Squeeze in the lime juice and blend the mixture to a smooth paste. Stir in the jaggery or dark brown sugar.

3. Rub this mixture all over the chicken, taking care to enter all the cracks and crevices and well under the skin. Lightly baste with the ghee.

4. Place the chicken in a deep baking dish and roast for about 3 to 4 hours, basting halfway through the roasting time.

5. Remove from oven and let rest about 15 minutes. Slice into pieces and serve.

Rinku's Pepper, Cranberry and Lemon Chicken
(M&P)

Few things are more symbolic of the holiday season than ruby red cranberries. It does not matter which brand you use, but like most berries, it is good to choose an organic variety. This chicken is perfect for holiday potlucks, winter gatherings, and of course, regular family dinners. The chicken can also be served as an appetizer without the sauce. I am sure that you can find your own special use for it too!

Prep Time: 15 minutes plus at least 2 hours to marinate | Cook Time: 40 minutes | Serves: 6

Ingredients

8 cloves garlic

1½-inch piece ginger, peeled

2 green chilies, minced

1 tablespoon coriander seeds

1½ teaspoons cumin seeds

1½ tablespoons black or multicolored peppercorns

1 teaspoon kosher salt

2 pounds boneless skinless chicken thighs, cut into 2-inch pieces

¾ cup white all-purpose flour

⅓ cup oil

2 red onions, thinly sliced

¾ cup thickly sliced mushrooms

½ cup finely chopped cilantro

1 cup chopped scallions

For the cranberry sauce

6 tablespoons molasses

2 tablespoons sugar

1 cup fresh cranberries

⅓ cup lemon juice

Preparation

1. Place the garlic, ginger, green chilies, coriander seeds, and cumin seeds in the blender and blend to a fairly smooth paste. (To get the mixture to process smoothly, you will need to pulse and scrape it down a few times.)

2. Add the peppercorns and salt and pulse a few times to coarsely crush the peppercorns. (If there is some additional texture from the coriander and cumin seeds that is okay.)

3. Put the chicken pieces in a mixing bowl and toss with the spice marinade. Let marinate for at least 2 hours (if you have the time, marinate for a longer period of time).

4. When ready to cook, dredge the chicken pieces in the flour, and shake off any excess flour.

5. Heat the oil in a heavy-bottomed hard-anodized pan for 1½ minutes on medium heat. Pan fry the chicken pieces in batches for 3 to 4 minutes on each side, until the chicken is golden and well crisped on both sides. Drain on paper towels.

6. Add the onions and mushrooms to the remaining oil and cook for about 5 to 7 minutes, until they are soft, wilted, and turning crisp and golden on the edges.

7. While the onion mixture is cooking, make the cranberry sauce: Combine ⅓ cup water and the molasses and sugar in a saucepan and heat until the mixture comes to a boil. Add the cranberries and cook for about 5 minutes, until they pop. Stir in the lemon juice.

8. Pour the cranberry sauce over the onion mixture and bring to a simmer. Gently fold in the fried chicken.

9. Stir in the cilantro and scallions and eat immediately.

Tips and Tricks

Canned whole cranberry sauce can be used in a pinch, but this will result in a much sweeter tasting sauce.

Red Harvest Masala Cornish Hens
(M&P, GF)

The delicate combination of spices in this recipe produces a moist, flavorful bird and a sauce that is delicious and richly hued with red grapes. I came up with this recipe on a cold, stormy winter night when I had unexpected houseguests due to a blizzard. I happened to have the ingredients around and found that using smaller Cornish hens speeds up the cooking time. If you allow half a hen per person, you have an elegant, well-presented dish.

Prep Time: 15 minutes | Cook Time: 1½ hours (mostly unattended) | Serves: 4 to 6

Ingredients
For the hens
2 or 3 Cornish hens (about 1 to 1½ pounds each)
1 tablespoon salt
2 tablespoons olive oil
1 cup red seedless grapes, halved
Cilantro to garnish

For the basting and seasoning sauce
2 tablespoons ginger-garlic paste (page 14)
1½ tablespoons balsamic vinegar
⅓ cup red wine (any variety)
1 teaspoon red pepper flakes
2 tablespoons soy sauce
¼ cup coconut milk

Preparation
1. Pre-heat the oven to 350°F.

2. Rub the Cornish hens with the salt and olive oil. Place in a large roasting pan and roast for 30 minutes, until the hens are pale golden and beginning to turn crisp.

3. Meanwhile prepare the basting sauce: Place the ginger-garlic paste, vinegar, red wine, red pepper flakes, soy sauce, and coconut milk in a blender and blend until smooth.

4. Remove the roasting pan from the oven. Spread the hens with the basting sauce and scatter the grapes in the pan. Roast for 1 more hour, brushing the hens as needed with the basting sauce.

5. Garnish with the cilantro and serve.

Brined Turkey with Pomegranate Apricot Glaze
(M&P, GF)

One Thanksgiving someone asked me how I cooked my turkey. I mentioned that I liked to add extra flavors here and there, so she asked me whether I could make a tandoori turkey. This got me thinking, and after a couple of attempts, here is what emerged. Now refined and tested over six Thanksgivings, the recipe is as good as it gets. I prefer an organic free-range bird. These are smaller than most commercial turkeys, so if you have a large gathering, plan accordingly. My method might seem fussy, but it is guaranteed to produce a moist bird that you can present with pride. The brining and covering allows you to cook the bird more quickly, and the orange color from the apricot glaze is perfect for the harvest table.

Prep Time: 20 minutes plus marinating and brining overnight | Cook Time: 4 to 5 hours (depending on the size of the turkey; mostly unattended) | Serves: about 12

Ingredients

For brining the turkey
1 cup kosher salt
⅓ cup garam masala (page 350)
⅓ cup orange juice
⅓ cup tandoori masala (page 349)
3 tablespoons chopped fresh thyme
3 tablespoons chopped fresh rosemary
1 12-pound turkey

For the turkey base
½ cup chicken broth
½ cup white wine
1 stick (½ cup) butter

For the glaze
¾ cup good-quality low-sugar apricot preserves
3 tablespoons pomegranate molasses
⅓ cup fresh pomegranate seeds

Preparation

1. To brine the turkey: Fill a bucket large enough to fit the turkey halfway with water and stir in the kosher salt, garam masala, orange juice, tandoori masala, thyme, and rosemary.

2. Remove the giblets from the turkey. Immerse the turkey in the brine and let sit overnight in the refrigerator.

3. Pre-heat the oven to 300 degrees. (Yes, I do cook the turkey with a lower temperature, but since it is covered it reaches the right degree of heat.)

4. Remove the turkey from the brine and pat dry with paper towels. Neatly seal the turkey, trimming any loose skin, and tying the legs of the bird. Place the turkey in a large roasting pan.

5. Pour the chicken broth and wine around the turkey. Dot with the butter and cover the turkey with foil.

6. Roast the turkey for about 4 hours (approximately 20 minutes per pound).

7. To prepare the apricot glaze, place the preserves and pomegranate molasses in a small saucepan and cook over low heat until melted and smooth. Set aside.

8. After roasting the turkey for 4 hours, remove the foil and brush the turkey well with the apricot glaze. Return to the oven for 15 minutes to let the glaze warm over the turkey and permeate the flesh.

9. Remove from oven and let the turkey rest for 15 minutes. Garnish with the fresh pomegranate seeds before serving.

Spicy Roast Leg of Lamb
(M&P, GF)

Few meats take to marinades and spices the way a good cut of lamb does. This recipe comes from our friend Sabby, who has served it at Christmas parties for almost a decade. Sabby is Indian with an Italian spouse, so this luscious lamb is usually offered alongside penne with marinara sauce. It works!

Prep Time: 10 minutes plus up to 15 hours of marinating time | Cook Time: 4 hours (mostly unattended) | Serves: 6 to 8

Ingredients

2 onions, cut into chunks

10 cloves garlic

1 2-inch piece ginger, peeled

1 tablespoon green cardamom seeds

10 red chilies

10 to 15 black peppercorns

5 green chilies

1 tablespoon salt

2 tablespoons brown sugar

½ cup cider vinegar or balsamic vinegar

1 cup plain yogurt

2 tablespoons cumin seeds

2 tablespoons coriander seeds

1 leg of lamb (about 4 pounds with bone or 2½ pounds boneless)

Chopped cilantro to garnish

Preparation

1. Place the onion, garlic, ginger, cardamom seeds, red chilies, peppercorns, green chilies, salt, brown sugar, vinegar, yogurt, cumin seeds, and coriander seeds in a blender and blend for 5 to 7 minutes into a smooth but slightly grainy texture.

2. Make gashes into the leg of lamb (if on the bone) and smear the mixture on the meat and marinate overnight. If the weather is cool (up to 65 degrees), I do the marinating at room temperature. If the house is heated above this temperature you can leave the meat on a cool patio or in an outside room.

3. Preheat the oven to 400°F. Cover the meat with foil and roast for 3 hours.

4. Remove the foil and and cook for another hour, turning 2 to 3 times. The meat should be crisp and brown outside and tender inside.

5. Cool slightly and then slice and serve.

Tips and Tricks

The leg of lamb can be bone-in or boneless, either way I do not tie the roast and this preparation ensures that the meat is fork tender and quite delectable, but it does not lend itself to neat slicing. I do not trim the meat of too much fat before cooking, but I do not add any extra fat while cooking.

Pineapple and Ginger Spiced Ham
(M&P, GF)

Ham is a holiday meat that works exceptionally well with Indian flavors. I tried many a variation on this recipe and ultimately settled for this version. It looks quite beautiful with its vivid colors, and the meat tastes moist with just the right amount of bite!

Prep Time: 30 minutes | Cook Time: 3 hours (mostly unattended) | Serves: 15

Ingredients

1½ cups cubed fresh pineapple

2 cups pineapple juice

2 tablespoons red cayenne pepper powder

3 tablespoons chaat masala (page 348)

1 cup loosely packed brown sugar

3 tablespoons grated fresh ginger

⅓ cup soy sauce

1 ham (3 to 6 pounds)

Preparation

1. Heat the oven to 350°F.

2. Place the pineapples, pineapple juice, cayenne pepper powder, chaat masala, brown sugar, ginger, and soy sauce in a saucepan and cook for 15 minutes, until the mixture thickens.

3. Place the ham in a roasting pan and pour the pineapple mixture over it. Bake the ham for 3 hours, occasionally spooning the pineapple mixture over it.

4. Turn off the heat and let the ham rest for 20 minutes.

5. Slice the ham and serve with the pineapple sauce spooned over it.

Stuffed Winter Squash with Walnuts and Paneer
(V, GF)

This delicate preparation of acorn squash stuffed with leeks, breadcrumbs, walnuts, and grated paneer, brings the best of autumn flavors together. It makes a delicious Thanksgiving side dish or a nice vegetarian entree for those who prefer to go meatless.

Prep Time: 15 minutes | Cook Time: 45 minutes (mostly unattended) | Serves: 4 to 6

Ingredients

1 large or 2 small acorn or delicata squashes

3 tablespoons ghee

1 teaspoon cumin powder

1 leek, finely chopped

1 cup walnuts or almonds, finely ground

1 teaspoon salt

1 teaspoon sugar

2 tablespoons grated paneer cheese

Preparation

1. Pre-heat the oven to 350°F.

2. Cut the squash(es) in half. Scoop out the seeds and remove the pulpy strands holding the seeds. Spread the cut sides with 1 tablespoon of the ghee.

3. Heat the remaining ghee on medium heat for 30 seconds. Add the cumin powder and leek and cook on low heat, stirring constantly, until the leeks are very soft and beginning to turn brown at the edges. Stir in the walnuts, salt, and sugar and mix well.

4. Gently fill the center of each squash half with the stuffing and bake for 20 minutes. Sprinkle with the cheese and return to the oven to let the cheese melt. Serve hot.

Citrusy Roasted Beets with Toasted Spices
(VE, GF)

Another recipe inspired by the beauty and freshness of the seasonal vegetables at a winter farmers market! I avoid the traditional method of boiling beets in this recipe as I think that roasted beets retain much more flavor. This dish can be served hot or warm depending on your preference. I like to use both red and yellow beets for a wonderful multi-hued effect.

Prep Time: 10 minutes | Cook Time: 45 minutes (mostly unattended) | Serves: 4 to 6

Ingredients
3 medium red beets, washed and greens removed

3 medium yellow beets, washed and greens removed

2 to 3 tablespoons oil

1 teaspoon fennel seeds

1 teaspoon mustard seeds

2 cloves garlic, minced

1 teaspoon ginger paste

½ teaspoon black salt

½ lime

1 orange or Clementine, cut in half

Several grinds black pepper

Cilantro to garnish

Preparation
1. Pre-heat oven to 375°F.

2. Wrap the beets in foil and roast for 35 to 40 minutes. Allow the beets to cool and then peel them and cut into wedges.

3. Heat the oil in a wok or skillet. Add the fennel seeds and mustard seeds and when they begin to crackle add the garlic and ginger paste and sauté lightly until the mixture is fragrant.

4. Stir in the roasted beets and black salt and mix well.

5. Squeeze in the lime juice and orange or Clementine juice and mix well.

6. Stir in the black pepper and garnish with the cilantro and serve.

Tips and Tricks
This recipe can also be made with turnips and/or potatoes.

If desired the dish can be assembled a day ahead and then reheated just before serving.

Mashed Potatoes with Mustard and Chives
(V, GF)

This is my absolute favorite comfort food. As the season fades, winter markets are filled with potatoes and dark greens. The winter garden is also still replete with chives that last until snow falls, so I pick and use them as needed. I like to have this dish with rice and dal—a true winter carbohydrate indulgence.

Prep Time: 10 minutes | Cook Time: 15 minutes | Serves: 4 to 6

Ingredients

6 medium Yukon gold potatoes

2 tablespoons butter

½ cup buttermilk

Salt to taste

1 tablespoon mustard oil or
  ½ tablespoon prepared mustard

2 tablespoons chopped fresh chives

Preparation

1. Cook the potatoes in their skins until soft but not mushy. Peel and quarter the potatoes and place in a mixing bowl.

2. Add the butter and buttermilk. Using a hand beater, whisk the potatoes until smooth, stirring in some salt and the mustard oil or mustard.

3. Finally with a fork, mix in the chives and serve.

Cumin and Chorizo Cornbread Dressing
(M&P)

I can't have a chapter on Indian-style holiday food without including a recipe for holiday dressing, or as some call it, stuffing. I have just one piece of advice for a good dressing: make sure it is flavorful and interesting enough to hold its own beside the other dishes or you will end up with a lot of leftovers. If desired this dressing can be made using my spicy cornbread which will result in a heavier dressing than using pre-made cornbread.

Prep Time: 10 minutes | Cook Time: 20 minutes (using pre-made cornbread)

Ingredients

2 tablespoons oil

1 tablespoon unsalted butter

1 teaspoon cumin seeds

½ cup very finely chopped celery

2 medium white onions, chopped

2 medium Granny Smith apples, cored and chopped

½ cup (about ¼ pound) crumbled chorizo

½ recipe Masala Sunshine Cornbread (page 303) or 3 cups cubed store-bought cornbread

½ cup chicken or vegetable broth

⅓ cup chopped cilantro

2 tablespoons chopped fresh cranberries or pomegranate seeds to garnish

Preparation

1. Place the oil and butter in a heavy-bottomed skillet and heat on medium-low to melt the butter.

2. Add the cumin seeds and when they sizzle promptly add the celery and onions and cook for 3 to 4 minutes, until the onions are softened.

3. Add the apples and cook for about 10 minutes on low heat until the apples are soft.

4. Add the chorizo and cook , stirring, until browned.

5. Crumble in the cornbread and mix with the apple mixture.

6. Stir in the broth and cook until absorbed.

7. Add the cilantro and mix well. Garnish with the cranberries and pomegranate seeds before serving.

Winter — Season of Home, Hearth & Celebration

Winter is the time for comfort, for good food and warmth, for the touch of a friendly hand and for a talk beside the fire: it is the time for home."

—Edith Sitwell

The melody has been played, we have learned and enjoyed its tune. Now it is time for us to gently finish the song. In Indian music it is called *aborohan* (the ending), and for nature this is symbolized with Winter.

The earth too needs its rest and that is what the wintry white season is for. The rustling leaves fall and gradually the trees and branches get bare, waiting for colder, windier days. The final leaves get blown off, leaving the branches ready for the soft white snow. There are few things prettier than the season's first snowfall, promising a few months of quieter days to share and enjoy the comfort of one's home. Simple pleasures like driving along roads amid snow-laden trees or watching the sunset reflected against the bright snow offer me a peaceful comfort. Unlike my native New Yorker children, I still do not relish spending hours outside engaging in snow fights but I love to watch them in action and enjoy helping them build their snowmen. (Last year my daughter very pointedly shaped longer hair on her creation and informed me that she was building a snow woman.)

As the farmer's markets slow down, the surroundings brighten with Winter decorations for the season of celebrations. The last survivor of the markets and the garden tends to be hardy kale, although certain herbs like rosemary and thyme even last through the Winter. These robust herbs provide the depth of flavor so essential for Winter soups and stews. The season also leaves us with roots that are happy and well-nested underground. We discovered this accidentally when we found carrots one year in spring as we were getting the garden ready for the next season. Winter squashes, which keep well for a few months, can also be enjoyed at this time of year. We tend to pick them as late as we can and then savor them through the colder months.

My Winter table actually features more exotic fare than the rest of the year, because I buy things that we cannot grow. Balancing foods is part of the sustainable table. This means supplementing when the months are leaner. I also often bring in vegetables such as cauliflower and green peas from the store, which remind me of the Indian Winter. The Indian Winter is a time of bounty when cooler weather is fodder for colorful fruits, radishes, greens, and an abundance of other vegetables. All manner of stews and hearty lentil dishes grace my table this time of the year.

The Indian Christmas table is bright and plentiful and in the metropolitan Indian cities, the holiday is celebrated by everyone. The streets are decorated with lots of bright lights and the bakeries and other confectionery stores are filled with special holiday items. Christmastime is one of my favorite times to visit India with my family. There is happiness in traveling across the miles to catch up with familiar faces and savor the many Winter treats that await us. At this time harvest festivals are celebrated, such as Lorhi in Punjab and Pongal in Southern India, with their traditional fare of sesame-based desserts and sweet and savory rice and lentil porridges.

Chapter Nine

Draupadi's Cooking Pot:
Rice, Grains & Pasta

In the epic Mahabharata, Lord Krishna gifted Draupadi (the wife of the Pandavas) a cooking pot that would constantly replenish itself until she had finished her meal. Even though I do not have such advantages, I still feel that my rice and grain pot is a magical quick-cooking, ever-ready meal creator.

Indian rice varieties range from the lovely, elegant basmati of the northern highlands to the delicate, fragrant Kalajeera of eastern India, along with several more robust shorter-grained and parboiled rice varieties dotted across the rest of the country. Over the years, we have also included black rice and the occasional red rice on our tables.

There are also risottos made with cracked wheat, semolina, and other processed rice grains. While it's fun to have a dressy side, I don't think we want to spend an entire day in the kitchen creating it! To this end, I have a few practical suggestions and encourage you to explore the boundaries with these recipes. Quinoa is a grain that I have found lends itself well to Indian seasoning and it works well in my household since my kids love it and of course it is full of a great bounty of minerals, fiber, and protein.

The *pulaos* (pilafs) in this book are a great way to add comforting taste and understated elegance to the weeknight table. The key difference between the richer pilafs (ones made with more ghee or oil) and lighter ones in this book is that richer pilafs re-heat better as they retain more natural moisture. Both taste equally good when they are hot and bursting with fresh, fragrant flavors. Much as I like the soft fluffy texture of steamed white rice, it certainly is more healthful to include whole grains in your diet. In this chapter, I strike a compromise between traditional rice pilafs and whole grain rice or non-rice grains that will work well with an Indian meal. I frequently cook unpolished rice such as brown and black rice; these grains do not really need much, so I cook them simply and serve as a side.

In Indian rice and grain parlance, you have: the **pulaos** (pilafs)—lightly seasoned, delicately balanced medleys of rice, fragrant spices, and vegetables or meats cooked to a little beyond al dente perfection; **biryanis**—deeper, heavier casserole masterpieces that essentially layer rice with a spicier gravy and cook together so the flavors meld; and lastly, the **khichris**—softer, risotto-like comfort food. These basic dishes go by different regional names depending on the part of the country we are talking about.

Mushroom and Chickpea Pilaf with Fragrant Spices
(VE, GF)

This is a simple meatless one-dish meal or a side depending on your preference. You can use a variety of mushrooms or just stick to the simple cremini mushroom as I have done here. If you want to add variety and texture, more vegetables can be mixed into the dish. The chickpeas add a deeper texture and convert this dish into a one-dish meal by adding protein into the mix.

Prep Time: 3 to 4 minutes | Cook Time: 40 minutes | Serves: 4

Ingredients
2 tablespoons oil

1½ teaspoons cumin seeds

1 onion, chopped

3 green cardamom pods

3 or 4 cloves

1 (2-inch) cinnamon stick, broken

1 cup thickly sliced button mushrooms

1½ cups white basmati rice

¾ cup cooked chickpeas

1 teaspoon salt

For garnish

Red pepper flakes (optional)

Chopped cilantro

Chopped cashew nuts

Preparation
1. Heat the oil in a pot on medium heat for 30 seconds. Add the cumin seeds and cook for about 30 seconds until they sizzle and become aromatic.

2. Add the onion and cook for 7 to 8 minutes, until they soften and begin to turn golden.

3. Add the cardamom pods, cloves, cinnamon stick, and mushrooms and cook for another minute.

4. Add the basmati rice and chickpeas and mix gently. Add 2¾ cups of water and the salt and cover and simmer for 20 minutes. Keep the rice covered and let it rest for about 10 minutes.

5. Sprinkle with red pepper flakes if desired. Fluff gently and garnish with cilantro and cashew nuts before serving.

Chicken Orzo Pilaf
(M&P)

This recipe is a very flavorful skillet dish made with orzo instead of rice. Adding in a finish of mint and pine nuts gives it a rather Middle Eastern touch. This dish can be very easily made with brown or white rice, depending on your preference of grain.

Prep Time: 10 minutes plus at least 2 hours marinating time | Cook Time: 45 minutes | Serves: 6

Ingredients

For the chicken
½ cup yogurt
2 tomatoes
½ cup chopped cilantro
1 (2-inch) piece ginger
2 cloves garlic
2 green chilies
2 pounds boneless skinless chicken
  (*I use thighs*)

For the pilaf
⅓ cup oil
3 onions, thinly sliced
2 (2-inch) cinnamon sticks, broken
  into smaller pieces
2 or 3 green cardamom pods
3 cloves
1 cup orzo
2½ cups chicken broth
1 teaspoon saffron

For the finish
1 tablespoon oil or butter
1 tablespoon sliced almonds
1 tablespoon pine nuts
1 tablespoon finely chopped fresh
  mint

Preparation

1. To marinate the chicken: Place the yogurt, tomatoes, cilantro, ginger, garlic, and green chilies in a blender and puree. Place the chicken in a bowl and toss with the marinade to coat. Set aside for at least 2 hours.

2. Heat the oil in a large skillet. Add the onions and cook, stirring occasionally, until they soften and turn a golden shade of brown, about 10 minutes. Stir in the cinnamon sticks, cardamom pods, and cloves.

3. Add the chicken with marinade and cook, stirring occasionally, for 6 to 7 minutes, until the mixture is somewhat dry.

4. Stir in the orzo and broth and bring to a simmer and cook for about 6 minutes.

5. Stir in the saffron and turn off the heat. Cover and let this rest for 20 minutes (by now the mixture should be soft and pale brown).

6. For the finish: Heat the oil and stir in the almonds and pine nuts and cook until pale golden. Stir in the mint. Add to the pilaf and serve immediately.

Bulgur or Cracked Wheat Pilaf
(VE)

Bulgur and cracked wheat are much loved in the northern regions of India, particularly as the preferred breakfast grain. Prepared simply as in this recipe, they also work well as a side dish. You could also add beans or lentils to make this a wonderful one-dish meal if you are in a rush.

Prep Time: 10 minutes | Cook Time: 35 minutes (mostly unattended) | Serves: 4 to 6

Ingredients

2 tablespoons oil

1 teaspoon cumin seeds

1 red onion, thinly sliced

1 tomato, chopped

1 teaspoon salt or to taste

¾ cup bulgur or cracked wheat

¾ cup cooked red kidney beans or chickpeas

½ teaspoon red cayenne pepper powder (optional)

1 (3-inch) cinnamon stick, broken

1 lime or lemon, cut in half

1 to 2 tablespoons chopped cilantro

Preparation

1. Heat the oil in a pot on medium heat. Add the cumin seeds and when they begin to sizzle, add the onion and sauté for about 6 minutes, until it wilts and begins to turn gently golden.

2. Add the tomato, salt, and bulgur and mix well. Stir in the red kidney beans, cayenne pepper powder (if using), and the cinnamon stick. Mix in 2 cups of water and gently bring to a simmer.

3. Cover and cook on low heat for about 25 minutes, until the water is absorbed and the bulgur is soft and cooked through.

4. Squeeze in the lime or lemon juice and stir in the cilantro and serve.

Tips and Tricks

This recipe can also be made with quinoa, farro, or any complex grain of your choice.

Saffron Rice Pilaf with Cashew Nuts
(V, GF)

Any recipe that is prefaced with the word *Shahi* is meant to be special, and the Indian name for this rice dish is *Shahi Pulao.* "*Shahi*" originates from the word "*Shah*" (king or nobleman). So what is special about this recipe other than the fact that my family loves it? It is the addition of saffron, which I am sure you will agree is probably as regal as a spice gets!

Prep Time: 5 minutes | Cook Time: 30 minutes | Serves: 4 to 6

Ingredients
2 tablespoons ghee
1 teaspoon cumin seeds
1 cup basmati rice, soaked for 1 hour
2 cups vegetable broth or water
1 teaspoon salt
2 tablespoons chopped cashew nuts
1 teaspoon saffron strands

Preparation
1. Heat the ghee on medium heat for 30 seconds. Add the cumin seeds and when they begin to sizzle, add the rice. Cook, stirring, for 5 to 7 minutes until the rice begins to brown.

2. Slowly stir in the broth or water and salt and bring to a boil. Lower the heat, cover, and simmer for 20 minutes.

3. Add the cashew nuts and saffron, stir and cover. Turn off the heat and let the rice sit for 5 minutes.

Lentil and Quinoa Pilaf
(VE, GF)

This recipe is a riff on the Middle-Eastern recipe called *mujjadara*, a hearty one-dish meal with rice, lentils, and caramelized onions. I like to make it with quinoa and have added a couple of extra spices and garnishes to give this recipe a nice Indian touch. Serve this with a chutney and raita from the condiments chapter and you will have a meal that is hearty, healthy, and very comforting.

Prep Time: 10 minutes | Cook Time: 55 minutes | Serves: 4 to 6

Ingredients

⅓ cup olive oil

4 medium red onions, thinly sliced

1 teaspoon sugar

2 teaspoons freshly grated ginger

2 cloves garlic

4 cups vegetable broth or water

1 cup brown lentils (sabut masur dal)

1 cup white quinoa

½ cup pine nuts or walnuts (optional)

1 teaspoon freshly ground cumin seeds

2 (2-inch) cinnamon sticks

2 bay leaves

1 teaspoon salt or to taste

Plenty of freshly ground black pepper

For the garnish

1 lime, cut in half

2 tablespoons fresh cilantro

Preparation

1. Heat the oil in a pot. Add the onions and cook for 5 minutes. Stir in the sugar and continue cooking, stirring frequently, until the onions turn nicely golden without burning. Remove about one-third of the mixture and set aside.

2. Add the ginger and garlic to the remaining onion mixture. Stir in the broth or water and bring to a simmer.

3. Add the lentils, quinoa, pine nuts or walnuts (if using), cumin, cinnamon sticks, bay leaves, and salt and mix well.

4. Cover and cook the mixture on low heat for 40 minutes.

5. Remove the cover (at this point the grains should be cooked and tender and the water should be absorbed completely). Add some black pepper, squeeze in the lime juice, and stir in the cilantro and serve.

"Surprise the Guests" Pink Chicken Biryani
(M&P, GF)

Biryani is a layered culinary masterpiece that found its way into Indian cooking via Persia, through India's Mughal heritage. I often judge a restaurant by how well it makes a biryani. This recipe takes all of that and simplifies it with the use of one piece of equipment—a rice cooker. It was born on a busy day when I wanted to cook something impressive for some friends who were visiting from India and had some leftover Chicken Tikka in a Tomato Cream Sauce on hand. Why not turn it into a biryani? It was so good that after that I began to serve it to guests regularly. The pink comes from the natural color of the tikka masala sauce, giving a rather pretty appearance and allowing you to skip the saffron if you don't have any on hand.

Prep Time: 10 minutes | Cook Time: 35 to 60 minutes (mostly unattended) plus 20 minutes resting time | Serves: 6

Ingredients

For the biryani

1½ cup basmati rice, rinsed several times

⅓ cup torn fresh mint leaves

2 black cardamom pods

3 bay leaves

1 (2-inch) cinnamon stick, broken

1 recipe Chicken Tikka in a Tomato Cream Sauce (page 235)

1 tablespoon clarified butter

For the finish

⅓ cup oil

2 onions, thinly sliced

⅓ cup raw cashew nuts

¼ cup raisins

¼ cup chopped dried apricots

1 teaspoon saffron strands (optional)

2 tablespoons rosewater (available in Indian or Middle Eastern grocery stores)

Tips and Tricks

Since it is prepared in a rice cooker or a casserole, this recipe can be made well ahead of time and kept warm until ready to serve.

Preparation

Note: This dish can be finished either in a rice cooker or in a casserole in the oven. If using the oven method, pre-heat it to 350°F.

1. Bring the rice to boil with plenty of water and cook for 6 minutes to release the starch and allow the grains to gain some volume (they will still be fairly hard at this point). Drain thoroughly.

2. Line the base of the rice cooker or a casserole dish with half the rice. Scatter in half of the mint, cardamom pods, bay leaves, and cinnamon stick pieces.

3. Add the Chicken Tikka in a Tomato Cream Sauce in a layer on top. Cover with the remaining rice and scatter with the remaining mint and spices. Sprinkle with about ¾ cup of water.

4. If using the rice cooker, cover, turn it on, and let the rice cook for 20 minutes. If using the casserole, cover with foil and bake for 35 minutes. The rice grains should be soft and separate and fluffy.

5. While the biryani is cooking, prepare the finish: Heat the oil in a skillet on medium heat for 1 minute. Add the sliced onions and cook slowly to allow them to soften and gradually turn golden brown, stirring occasionally at the beginning and then constantly in the last few minutes as they get crisp. Carefully, remove the onions with a slotted spoon and drain on paper towels.

6. In the remaining oil, cook the cashew nuts, raisins, and apricots for about 1 minute, until the cashews are a pale golden color and the raisins are puffy.

7. When the biryani is cooked, remove from oven or turn off the rice cooker and let it rest for 20 minutes.

8. Add the clarified butter and then gently stir in the onions and cashew mixture. Stir in the saffron, if using, and sprinkle with rosewater before serving.

Shrimp and Coconut Biryani
(F&S, GF)

This is a Kerala-inspired biryani that uses coconut milk and simpler spices. By adding shrimp to traditional coconut rice, you end up with a dish that is pretty and indulgent. It is traditionally prepared with a short-grain rice rather than basmati rice, but this is entirely up to you.

Prep Time: 5 minutes | Cook Time: 45 minutes plus 10 minutes to rest | Serves: 4

Ingredients

1½ cups short-grain fragrant rice (such as the Sona Masuri or Kalajeera varieties) or basmati rice

1 pound shrimp, shelled and deveined

1 lime, cut in half

1 teaspoon turmeric

1¼ teaspoons salt or to taste

6 tablespoons oil

½ teaspoon black mustard seeds

1 red onion, coarsely chopped

2 teaspoons freshly grated ginger

10 to 12 curry leaves

1 teaspoon white split lentils (urad dal)

1 teaspoon yellow Bengali gram lentils (chana dal)

3 or 4 dried red chilies, broken

½ cup dry-roasted cashews

1 cup coconut milk

½ cup finely chopped cilantro

Preparation

1. In a large pot, bring the rice to boil with plenty of water and cook for about 7 minutes. Drain thoroughly. Set aside.

2. Place the shrimp in a bowl and squeeze the lime juice over them and sprinkle with ½ teaspoon turmeric and salt. Heat 2 tablespoons of oil in a large pot. Add the seasoned shrimp and sear for about 2 minutes on each side. Remove from pot and set aside.

3. Add the remaining 4 tablespoons oil to the pot and heat for 1 minute on medium heat. Add the black mustard seeds and when they begin to crackle add in the red onion and sauté for about 4 to 5 minutes, until softened.

4. Stir in the ginger and curry leaves and cook for 2 to 3 minutes, until the mixture is fragrant.

5. Stir in the white and yellow lentils and cook until they darken.

6. Stir in the red chilies and parboiled rice and mix well. Mix in the cooked shrimp and cashews and gradually stir in the coconut milk and ½ cup water and mix well.

7. Bring the mixture to a simmer, cover and cook for 15 minutes, until the rice is cooked through and the liquid is absorbed.

8. Let the biryani rest for 10 minutes. Fluff the rice, stir in the cilantro and serve with extra lime or lemon if desired.

Rice with Peanuts and Caramelized Onions
(VE, GF)

With its delicate, earthy balance of flavors, this rice adds simple beauty and a soft touch of color to any meal. The light crunch of the peanuts offers a nice contrast to the soft, sweet, golden onions.

Prep Time: 5 minutes | Cook Time: 35 minutes plus 5 minutes resting time | Serves: 4 to 6

Ingredients

4 tablespoons oil

1 large sweet Vidalia onion, thinly sliced

⅓ cup raw unblanched peanuts

1¼ cups white basmati rice, soaked for 30 minutes

½ teaspoon salt

½ teaspoon turmeric

1 (2-inch) cinnamon stick, broken

3 green cardamom pods

1 or 2 black cardamom pods

2 medium carrots, peeled and grated (about ¾ cup)

Preparation

1. Heat the oil in a pot on medium heat for 1 minute. Add the onion and cook for 7 to 8 minutes, stirring slowly, until the onion softens and begins to turn a pale toffee color.

2. Gently stir in the peanuts and cook for a few minutes until they begin to turn a few shades darker.

3. Drain the soaked rice and mix it into the onion mixture. Add the salt and 2½ cups water and bring to a simmer.

4. Stir in the turmeric, cinnamon stick, green and black cardamom pods, and grated carrots.

5. Simmer on low heat for 20 minutes, until the rice is swollen and tender. The rice should be a soft pale yellow color.

6. Increase the heat and dry out any remaining water if needed.

7. Cover and let the rice rest for 5 minutes before serving.

Golden Harvest Red and Green Quinoa
(VE, GF)

I like the sweet tartness of cranberries married with the earthy crunch of walnuts and finished off with the softness of rutabaga or any other winter vegetable of your choice. This dish screams winter from every pore of its delicately balanced being. Enjoy it with your family after a busy day out in the cold. I had originally developed this recipe with Israeli couscous and have switched to quinoa, as I find it a healthier alternative, but for a variation you can make this with cracked wheat or couscous. Luckily for me, quinoa happens to be my daughter's new favorite grain.

Prep Time: 5 minutes | Cook Time: 40 minutes | Serves: 4

Ingredients

2 tablespoons oil

1 onion, finely chopped

3 or 4 bay leaves

1 teaspoon salt

1 teaspoon red cayenne pepper powder

1 cup diced rutabaga or winter squash (such as delicata)

2 cups chicken or vegetable broth

¾ cup white quinoa

½ cup walnuts or sliced almonds

½ cup dried cranberries

¾ cup finely chopped collard greens or kale

2 tablespoons chopped cilantro

Preparation

1. Heat the oil in a pot on medium heat for 30 seconds. Add the onion and bay leaves and sauté for about 3 to 4 minutes, until the onions are wilted and fragrant.

2. Add the salt, cayenne pepper powder, and rutabaga or winter squash. Stir in the broth and bring to a simmer.

3. Stir in the quinoa, nuts, and cranberries. Cover and cook for 28 minutes on medium heat.

4. Turn off the heat and stir in the greens and let rest for 2 to 5 minutes. Remove the cover and fluff the quinoa.

5. Stir in the cilantro and serve immediately.

Pasta with Spice-Infused Ground Lamb and Green Peas
(M&P)

I love the Italian classic Bolognese sauce, and I love the classic Indian dish called *Keema Matar* (ground lamb with green peas). This recipe offers a fusion take on both these dishes, making for an unusual and flavorful pasta dish. It is a wonderful and hearty meal for a winter evening. I like to make this using my stored summer tomatoes. If you wish you can use gluten-free pasta for this recipe.

Prep Time: 10 minutes | Cook Time: 40 minutes | Serves: 4 to 6

Ingredients

For the keema masala sauce

¼ cup oil (preferably olive oil)

1 large white onion (preferably Spanish or sweet vidalia), chopped

1 tablespoon freshly grated ginger

3 cloves garlic, minced

1 (1½-inch) cinnamon stick

2 or 3 green cardamom pods, bruised

3 cloves

¾ pound ground lamb

1 teaspoon turmeric

1 teaspoon salt

4 medium tomatoes (about ¾ pound), cut into a dice

1 teaspoon red cayenne pepper powder

¾ cup frozen peas

2 tablespoons chopped fresh basil

1 tablespoon chopped cilantro

For the pasta

2 cups any pasta of your choice

Salt

1 tablespoon olive oil

Preparation

1. Heat the oil in a pan until medium hot, about 1 to 2 minutes. Stir in the white onion, ginger, and garlic. Add the cinnamon stick, cardamom pods, and cloves and mix well.

2. Add the ground lamb and mix well. Stir in the turmeric and salt and mix well. Cook the lamb for 6 to 7 minutes until it begins to release its juices and starts turning light brown.

3. Add the tomatoes and cayenne pepper powder and continue cooking the mixture for another 10 minutes, until the tomatoes turn nice and saucy.

4. Add the peas and stir well. Add ½ cup of water and simmer for 20 minutes.

5. While the sauce is cooking, mix a large pot of water with the salt and olive oil and bring to a boil. Add the pasta and cook for the amount of time indicated on the box. Drain.

6. Mix the pasta with the sauce and serve immediately.

Spicy Golden Vermicelli with Curry Leaves and Peanuts
(VE)

In this South Indian dish, soft vermicelli is tossed in a heady, tantalizing mixture of ginger, mustard seeds, and curry leaves, with lemon and toasted peanuts thrown in for good measure. This cheers me up anytime of the day. You can use wheat or rice vermicelli or even angel hair pasta or thin noodles.

Prep Time: 5 minutes | Cook Time: 25 minutes | Serves: 4 to 6

Ingredients

1 pound dry short cut vermicelli or angel hair pasta, broken into pieces

4 tablespoons oil

¾ teaspoon cumin seeds

1 teaspoon black mustard seeds

⅛ teaspoon asafetida

10 to 15 curry leaves

2 or 3 shallots or 1 medium onion, chopped

1 tablespoon minced fresh ginger

2 dried red chilies

1 teaspoon red pepper flakes

1 teaspoon salt or to taste

½ teaspoon turmeric

1 large lime, cut in half

½ cup skinless raw peanuts

⅓ cup chopped cilantro

Preparation

1. Cook the vermicelli according to the directions on the package and drain and set aside.

2. Heat 3 tablespoons of oil in a skillet on medium heat for about 1 minute.

3. Add the cumin seeds and mustard seeds and when the seeds crackle (in about 20 seconds) add the asafetida, curry leaves, shallots, and ginger and cook until the shallots turn lightly golden, about 5 to 7 minutes.

4. Stir in the dried red chilies, red pepper flakes, salt, and turmeric.

5. Add the cooked vermicelli and simmer for 1 to 2 minutes. Squeeze in the lime juice.

6. In a separate pan, heat the remaining 1 tablespoon of oil and toast the peanuts until golden. Mix into the vermicelli along with the cilantro. (You should have a fragrant golden glistening mass of thin vermicelli, dotted with specs of bright and dark olive green and golden brown peanuts.) This is best served warm.

Chapter Ten

The Bread Basket:
Flatbreads & Crepes

On the Indian table, bread is as essential as soft, fluffy grains of steamed rice. In most homes, breads are served with the evening meal, and in certain regions of North India, flatbreads are served with all meals. Despite its popularity, naan bread isn't everyday fare in most Indian homes, but enjoyed as the meal and occasion permits. Refined white flour, such as that used for the delicate, fluffy naan breads, is for special occasions. Most Indian flatbreads are unleavened and made with whole grains like millet and whole wheat flours. They are best made fresh and served hot. The good news here is that dough for flatbreads and fried puffed breads can be made ahead and either frozen or stored up to a week in the refrigerator. I have found that doing this actually allows the dough to rest and loosen up, resulting in breads that are light and fluffy in texture.

Indian breads do take a little time and practice to get right, and it took me some trial and error to master and fit them into my everyday routine. On the plus side, some of the more complex stuffed breads can be healthy meals in themselves, thus eliminating the need for complicated accompaniments. In fact, some of these breads are best served simple to allow you to enjoy the balance of their flavors without much competition from other dishes.

Crepes (*dosas*) and pancakes are also a part of the Indian bread basket, especially for those who are avoiding wheat flour. Most Indian crepes and pancakes are gluten free. *Dosas* are great snacks or breakfast dishes, providing a wonderful protein rich and nutritious start to the day. They can be served with chutney or with a drier vegetable if desired.

The Indian "bread" repertoire includes the following: *rotis*, whole-grain pan-cooked flatbreads usually not fried but if desired smeared with some butter or ghee; *parathas*, whole grain flatbreads that are pan cooked and shallow fried with oil or clarified butter depending on your preference; *puris*, deep-fried but surprisingly light breads; and lastly *dosas*, crepe-like pancakes usually made with non-wheat flours.

Rotis—Whole Wheat Flatbreads
(VE)

My first memories of my mother-in-law's North Indian kitchen are watching her knead and roll out these simple whole wheat flatbreads. They require a hot cast-iron skillet and some resting time. These basic flatbreads are popular all around India. I make the dough in bulk and keep it in the refrigerator for up to a week. Cooked rotis can also be frozen and reheated later with great results.

Prep Time: 15 minutes plus 30 minutes to let the dough rest | Cook Time: 50 minutes |
Makes: 10 (6- to 8-inch) *rotis*

Ingredients

2 cups whole wheat flour (atta), plus
   extra flour for rolling

1 teaspoon salt

2 tablespoons oil

Preparation

1. Sift the flour into the bowl of a food processor. Add the salt and 1 tablespoon of the oil and pulse a few times. Gradually add ½ cup of water a little at a time, pulsing to let the dough form a crumbly mass. Run the food processor for about 30 seconds and the dough should roll into a ball.

2. Place the dough on a flat surface and knead well for about 2 minutes, it should form a smooth soft dough. Shape into a ball and coat with the remaining tablespoon of oil. Cover the dough and let it rest for about 30 minutes in a warm place.

3. Break the dough into walnut-size balls. Roll each ball out into a 6- to 7-inch circle on a generously floured surface. (It is fine to use a lot of flour when working with the dough at the beginning. I still use a generous amount of flour and just shake the flour off before placing the bread on the cooking pan.)

6. Heat a flat griddle pan (called a *tawa*). It is important to have a well-heated skillet for the purpose of making Indian breads. Place a dough circle on the pan and cook for 1 to 2 minutes on each side. Remove with a pair or tongs and immediately place on an open fire (your gas stove flame works fine), the bread should puff up and darken. Remove from the fire and serve. Repeat with the remaining dough circles.

Tips and Tricks

An alternate method of cooking these *rotis* that works well if you do not have a gas stove is to use a clean tea towel and press lightly in spots while the bread is on the griddle pan to allow the bread to lightly brown and puff up at spots.

Parathas—Pan-fried Whole Wheat Flatbreads
(VE)

These are a crisper more indulgent variation of the basic *roti* (page 293), but since these are just pan fried, rather than puffed on the open flame, they are actually a little more forgiving. I often like to suggest these as the first Indian flatbread for people to make. For a lighter, fancier variation you can substitute 1 cup of white all-purpose flour for 1 cup of the whole wheat flour, but this is up to you. This recipe uses the basic dough prepared for the *rotis*. I usually make the *parathas* using vegetable oil, but if you want to be more indulgent, you can use ghee or clarified butter for frying, which will result in a crisper *paratha*.

Prep Time: 15 minutes plus 30 minutes to let the dough rest | Cook Time: 60 minutes |
Makes 15 (6-inch) *parathas*

Ingredients

2 cups whole wheat flour (atta), plus extra flour for rolling

1 teaspoon salt

2 tablespoons oil plus oil for pan frying

Preparation

1. Prepare the dough circles as in steps 1 to 5 for the *rotis* (page 293).

2. Heat a flat griddle pan (called a *tawa*) or I have found that a cast iron skillet, such as the lodge skillets also works well. It is important to have a well-heated skillet for the purpose of making Indian breads. Place one of the dough circles on the pan and cook for 1 to 2 minutes on each side.

3. Working carefully, evenly spread the paratha with a teaspoon of oil and flip the paratha, spread the second side with oil and flip again, pressing the paratha down and letting the paratha crisp gently, until it is covered with golden brown circles. Repeat on other side and serve immediately. Repeat with remaining dough circles.

Tips and Tricks

I like to keep the *parathas* in a tortilla warmer to keep warm while others are cooking.

The secret to a good *paratha* is a little bit of patience. The bread needs to be cooked slowly on medium-low heat until well done, and then it needs to be carefully crisped with oil, and this is done by maintaining a hot enough temperature, not by adding loads of extra oil.

Variation: Mint Parathas

To make mint *parathas*, add ¾ cup finely chopped mint to the dough while kneading. (*Both mint and plain parathas are shown in photo.*)

Spicy Potato-Filled Whole Wheat Flatbreads/Parathas
(VE)

This recipe is a variation of the *rotis* (page 293) and *parathas* (page 295). A note on this and all the other pan-fried flatbreads: I use oil for health and practicality, but if you use ghee instead while frying the results will be fragrant, crisp, and quite special.

Prep Time: 15 minutes plus 45 minutes to let the dough rest | Cook Time: 60 minutes |
Makes 12 (7- to 8-inch) flatbreads

Ingredients

For the filling

4 potatoes (Yukon Gold or russet; about 1½ pounds), boiled in their jackets and peeled

¾ teaspoon red cayenne pepper powder

1½ teaspoons cumin-coriander powder (page 353)

1 teaspoon ground fennel seeds

1 teaspoon amchur (dried mango powder) or 2 tablespoons fresh lime or lemon juice

1 teaspoon salt

For the dough

1 recipe *roti* dough (page 293)

Oil for frying

Preparation

1. Place the cooked potatoes in a mixing bowl. Add the cayenne pepper powder, cumin-coriander powder, ground fennel seeds, amchur or lime or lemon juice, and salt. Mash the mixture until smooth and well mixed.

2. Give the prepared roti dough a good kneading to remove all the bubbles and let it rest for about 30 minutes.

3. Gently knead the dough and break into 12 lime-size balls. Roll each ball out on a generously floured surface into a 6-inch diameter circle. Place some potato filling in the middle of a circle and bring the sides of the dough up around the filling and form into a ball. Place the ball seam side down on a greased platter. Continue with the remainder of the dough circles. Let the dough balls rest in the refrigerator for about 15 minutes.

4. Gently roll the filled dough balls out on a floured surface to 6-inch circles being careful not to squeeze out the filling.

5. Heat a griddle or flat pan. It is important to have a well-heated skillet for the purpose of making Indian breads. Place a *paratha* on the hot pan, cook for 2 to 3 minutes, until delicate brown spots appear on the surface, then turn and cook for another minute. Spread some oil on the top of the *paratha* and flip over and fry until crisp. Spread some more oil on top of the *paratha* and flip over and crisp on the other side. Repeat with the remaining dough circles.

6. Serve these hot with a side of vegetables or raita.

Tips and Tricks

Any leftover potato filling can be used as a filling in other recipes such as my short-cut samosas on page 37.

Zucchini, Lemon Thyme and Onion Flatbreads/Parathas
(VE)

Once the zucchini fairy visits for the season, you suddenly find a garden that is filled with this versatile green squash. Instead of complaining, I've discovered fun ways to use up nature's bounty, such as in this flatbread recipe.

Prep Time: 15 minutes plus 2 hours resting time | Cook Time: 60 minutes | Makes: 15 *parathas*

Ingredients

1 large green zucchini

2 tablespoons fresh lemon thyme leaves

2¾ cups whole wheat flour (atta)

2 tablespoons olive oil, plus extra for pan frying the bread

1 teaspoon salt

1 red onion, very finely chopped

Tips and Tricks

This dough, as well as the cooked flatbreads, freezes extremely well.

Preparation

1. Cut the top off the zucchini and cut into wedges. Place in a food processor with the lemon thyme and puree until nice and smooth.

2. Place 2 cups of the wheat flour in a mixing bowl and add 2 tablespoons olive oil and the salt and mix well.

3. Add in the chopped onion and mix well (the dough will be lumpy and dry at this point).

4. Gradually work in the pureed zucchini until you have a dough that is smooth and well mixed. You might need to add a little water to get it to bind but you want a dough that is a little dry since as the dough rests it becomes moister as the zucchini releases some water. Let the dough rest for about 2 hours.

5. Work in the additional whole wheat flour to make the dough pliable and relatively smooth to touch. It should be springy but not sticky at this point.

6. Break-off 15 small lime-size balls of the dough and roll into circles about 6 inches in diameter on a floured surface.

7. As you begin rolling out the first circle, place a skillet or tawa on the fire. It is important to have a well-heated skillet for the purpose of making Indian breads.

8. Place one of the dough circles on the heated skillet and cook for a couple of minutes on each side, the bread should dry out and get evenly coated with little brown spots. Spread on a little oil, spreading evenly with a teaspoon. Turn the bread over and allow to puff up a little. Spread a little oil on the other side and turn over and crisp on that side. Cook till a little crisp on both sides and then remove and place on a plate.

9. Continue cooking all the dough circles in this manner.

Toasted Garlic and Black Pepper Crisps
(V)

This recipe is something like a cross between garlic bread and crostini. With a generous touch of black pepper and cumin, this bread fits in perfectly on the Indian table. They are wonderful with any of the soups and curries featured in this book.

Prep Time: 10 minutes | Cook Time: 25 minutes | Serves: 4

Ingredients

1 large (about 2 pounds) whole wheat or regular baguette
2 tablespoons oil
2 tablespoons salted butter, melted
2 fresh garlic cloves, minced
½ teaspoon cumin powder
Lots of freshly ground black pepper

Preparation

1. Cut the baguettes into rounds about 1 inch thick.

2. Preheat the oven to 375°F.

3. Mix the oil and melted butter with the minced garlic and cumin powder.

4. Brush the bread rounds generously with the butter mixture.

5. Place on a baking tray with the butter mixture up and bake for 7 minutes, until brown and crisp.

6. Sprinkle with lots of freshly ground black pepper and serve.

Masala Sunshine Cornbread for a Crowd
(V)

I developed this cornbread for my lovely cousin Sharmila, who loves "*jhal*" (spicy things). She requested spicy cornbread the last time I made chili, and this recipe was born. This cornbread is also a great accompaniment to the lentils and soups in this book. While a lot of cornbread recipes add fresh corn, I tend to make this recipe during the cooler weather months and add freshly grated carrots instead, giving it a sunny orange-flecked appearance. These flavors are reminiscent of Indian corn flatbreads, making this a good option for the Indian table. If using whole grain cornmeal, you will get a heavy rustic textured cornbread. This recipe can be comfortably halved for a small group.

Prep Time: 10 minutes | Cook Time: 35 minutes plus 15 minutes cooling time (all unattended) |
Makes: 1 10-inch cornbread

Ingredients

1½ cups finely ground or whole grain yellow cornmeal (such as Bob's Red Mill)

¾ cup all-purpose flour

¼ cup granulated brown sugar (grated jaggery if you have it works well too)

1½ teaspoons baking powder

1 teaspoon fine salt

1 tablespoon coarsely ground cumin seeds

1 teaspoon freshly ground black pepper

1½ cups whole milk

¾ cup plain yogurt

2 large eggs

1 stick (½ cup) unsalted butter, melted, plus more for coating the baking dish

2 jalapeno chilies, minced

½ cup grated cheddar

½ cup chopped fresh cilantro

1 medium red onion, chopped

1 cup freshly grated carrots (about 3 to 4 medium)

Preparation

1. Heat the oven to 350°F and arrange a rack in the middle. Coat an 8-inch square baking dish or 10-inch cast-iron skillet with butter and set aside.

2. Place the cornmeal, flour, brown sugar, baking powder, salt, cumin, and black pepper in a large bowl and whisk to combine.

3. Place the milk, yogurt, and eggs in a medium bowl and whisk until the eggs are broken up. Pour the milk mixture into the cornmeal mixture and using a rubber spatula, stir until just incorporated. (Do not overmix.) Stir in the melted butter until just incorporated and no streaks of butter remain.

4. Gently mix in the jalapenos, cheddar, cilantro, onions, and carrots until well incorporated.

5. Pour the mixture into the prepared dish or skillet. Bake until golden brown around the edges and a toothpick inserted into the center comes out clean, about 35 minutes. Do not overcook the cornbread as it will dry out.

6. Remove the dish or skillet to a wire rack and let cool for at least 15 minutes before serving.

Flat Leavened Naan
(V)

It is hard to go wrong with a good naan bread that combines the comfort of fresh baked bread with Indian flavors. Though difficult to replicate the effect of the tandoor or traditional clay oven in which naan is typically cooked, this recipe gets you close with the pizza stone. You can also try using a cast-iron skillet as I have done for the tomato rosemary naan on page 307.

Prep Time: 15 minutes plus 75 minutes for the naan to rise | Cook Time: 25 minutes | Makes: 6

Ingredients

½ cup whole milk

1 teaspoon sugar

1½ tablespoons rapid rise yeast

4 cups all-purpose flour

4 tablespoons oil

2 teaspoons salt

½ cup plain whole-milk yogurt

2 eggs

Pizza stone

Preparation

1. Warm the milk slightly and stir in the sugar and yeast. Set aside for 5 minutes, until the yeast begins to get all frothy.

2. Place the flour in a mixing bowl and add the oil, salt, yogurt, and eggs.

3. Pour the milk mixture over the flour and mix the ingredients to form a soft, smooth dough, adding a little water if needed. Cover loosely and set aside in a warm place until the dough rises and has doubled, usually about 1 hour.

4. Punch down the dough and let it rise for another 15 minutes.

5. Pre-heat the oven to 475°F and place a pizza stone in the center of the oven and heat for at least 30 minutes.

6. Break the dough into 6 lemon-size balls and roll each to an oval of about 5 to 6 inches in length and about ½ inch in thickness. (You can use extra flour for rolling, but shake off the flour after rolling.)

7. Place one of the naan breads on the hot pizza stone and cook for a couple of minutes, it should puff a little at spots. Quickly turn on the other side and cook for a couple of more minutes, the bread should be puffy and well browned and even lightly charred at spots. Repeat with remaining dough disks.

8. If desired, drizzle with a little butter before serving.

Tips and Tricks

Naan bread can also be stuffed with some chopped chicken tikka or mashed potatoes and then rolled out and baked.

Tomato Rosemary Naan
(V)

I used to be a recipe competition junkie! I loved to enter my recipes in competitions and the prizes thrilled me no end. While I don't have the time for competitions anymore, I still love freebies. This recipe (and a few others in this book) won me the joy of free shopping at Whole Foods Market. This naan recipe is laced with the comforting flavors of tomato and rosemary and uses a balance of whole wheat flour. It is finished off on the stovetop in a cast iron skillet. Try this naan with your favorite spread or chutney.

Prep Time: 15 minutes plus 70 minutes for the dough to rise | Cook Time: 25 to 30 minutes | Makes: 4 to 6

Ingredients
1 teaspoon sugar
½ cup lukewarm milk
1½ tablespoons rapid rise yeast
2 cups all-purpose white flour
1 cup whole wheat flour (atta)
1 teaspoon salt
3 medium tomatoes (about ¾ pound), quartered
1 tablespoon fresh rosemary leaves
¼ cup plus 2 tablespoons olive oil
3 tablespoons cream

For topping
1 teaspoon nigella seeds
Extra rosemary leaves
Butter for spreading if desired

Preparation
1. In a small mixing bowl, mix together the sugar and warm milk. Add the yeast and set aside until frothy.

2. Meanwhile, in a large mixing bowl, mix together the white flour, whole wheat flour, and salt.

3. Place the tomatoes, rosemary, ¼ cup olive oil, and the cream in a blender and blend until smooth.

4. The yeast should be nice and frothy by this time. Make a well in the center of the flour mixture and pour in the yeast mixture and mix well. Add the tomato mixture and mix to form a soft dough.

5. Add the 2 tablespoons olive oil and mix to form a smooth round ball. Cover and let the dough rise in a warm place for about 1 hour or until doubled.

6. Break the dough into tennis-ball-size rounds and set aside to rise again for about 10 minutes.

7. Roll out the dough balls into 6-to-7-inch oval-shaped fairly thin flat loaves.

8. Heat a cast iron skillet for 2 minutes on medium heat. Place a naan on the pan, cook for 1 minute and turn and cook until the bread is puffy and golden brown at spots. Repeat with remaining dough.

9. Butter the bread if desired and serve.

Puris—Indian Puffed "Balloon" Bread
(VE)

My first job was on the Lower East Side of New York, which boasts a lot of Indian restaurants on 3rd and 4th Streets. The restaurant scene in this part of town is quite the place for an adventurous eater. I found myself with an addition to my job description: educating my co-workers about the world of Indian food. My supervisor asked if I knew about "balloon bread." I gave him a look of bewilderment. Finally one day when we ordered *puris* at one of the neighborhood restaurants, it clicked. The restaurant served these puffed delicacies much larger than you would normally see at home. This "balloon bread" is known as *luchi* in eastern India and puri in other parts of the country.

Prep Time: 20 minutes | Cook Time: 40 minutes | Makes: about 20 (4-inch) *puris*

Ingredients
½ cup all-purpose flour

1 cup whole wheat flour

1 teaspoon salt

2 tablespoons ghee or oil

Oil for coating and frying

Preparation
1. Sift the two flours into a mixing bowl along with the salt. Mix in the ghee or oil with your hands. Knead into a pliable dough (smooth, not too moist) adding about ¾ cup water as needed.

2. Put some oil in a small bowl, and then put about 2 cups of oil in a medium wok.

3. Shape about 20 walnut-size balls with the dough. Cover with a moist cloth until ready to fry.

4. Heat the oil in the wok. And while it is heating dip one dough ball in the oil in the bowl and roll out into a circle about 5 inches in diameter.

5. Test the oil temperature with a breadcrumb, the crumb should rise immediately to the top. It is extremely important for the oil to be the right temperature to get light textured puffy *puris*.

6. Gently add the dough disk into the oil, it should rise to the surface fairly quickly and puff up. The process takes about 1 minute. Gently turn, cooking the other side for 30 seconds. Remove with a slotted spatula, draining off excess oil on the side of the wok.

7. Repeat this process with all the remaining dough balls. Serve hot.

Dosas—Crispy Lentil and Rice Sourdough Crepes
(VE, GF)

Crepes and pancakes dot the Indian landscape, but South Indian *dosas* have become the best known. It has taken me some time to master these *dosas* because of the temperamental weather we get in the northeastern United States. To get a well-fermented batter you need a fairly hot climate and in most places in Indian this takes about 12 hours. So you do need to plan ahead of time. While I typically serve these with my Potato and Mixed Vegetable Curry (page 159), they are great by themselves with Coconut and Almond Chutney (page 79) and can be filled with almost anything you like if you wish to be creative.

Prep Time: 2 hours (mostly for the dough to settle) | Cook Time: 1 hour | Makes: 10 (8-inch) crepes

Ingredients
1½ cups parboiled idli rice (sold in Indian stores)
¾ cup white split lentils (urad dal)
½ teaspoon fenugreek seeds
½-inch piece ginger, peeled
1½ teaspoons salt
Large onion, cut in half
Oil for cooking

Tips and Tricks
Dosas are usually cooked in a concave-shaped flat pan called a *tawa*, but a well-seasoned cast-iron griddle will also work.

To get the dosa batter to work in winter, start this process earlier, so soak the grains overnight and then allow 36 hours for the dough to ferment.

You can get extra mileage from this batter by saving and refrigerating some to make *oothapams* (page 313) later in the week. When ready to use, it needs to be brought out to come to room temperature before using.

Preparation
1. Soak the rice and lentils separately in plenty of water for at least 24 hours.

2. The next day rinse the rice and place in the blender with about ¾ cup of water, the fenugreek seeds, ginger, and salt and blend until fairly smooth (this will take at least 3 to 4 minutes). Pour into a large mixing bowl.

3. Blend the lentils with ½ cup water in the blender until thick and smooth. Mix with the rice mixture. Place in a large container and set aside in a warm place (I usually keep it in my oven well covered with foil) and let it ferment for about 12 to 18 hours. When the batter is ready, it should be frothy and smell slightly sour, this indicates that it is well fermented.

4. When ready to cook your *dosas*, place a griddle (*tawa*) or cast iron skillet on the fire and let it heat well (test with a drop of water which should sizzle and dance and then evaporate).

5. Add a little oil to the pan and pour in a ladleful of the batter and spread into a circular crepe in outward circles, until the batter is thin and evenly spread.

6. Let the crepe cook on medium heat for about 3 minutes. When you see the crepe turning lightly golden on the bottom, add 1 teaspoon of oil around the edges of the crepe and then lightly try to lift the crepe out of the pan, if it is done it should come out fairly easily. The correct temperature will allow the crepe to crisp without over browning.

7. Place some filling in the center if desired and then fold over. Use the sliced onion to clean the skillet in between cooking each *dosa*. Continue cooking the remaining *dosas* in this manner and serve them hot.

Oothapams—Lentil and Rice Sourdough Pancakes with Vegetables
(VE, GF)

Oothapams are made from leftover *dosa* batter—a residual treat that is as good as the original. I make these with any finely diced seasonal vegetables. My kids get creative and even like their oothapams topped with grated cheese and eggs, so here's another recipe that offers room for a lot of creativity. I usually make these with oil, except when our friend Anju visits. He reminisces about his mother's version made with ghee or clarified butter, so I indulge him. These crepes are best served with Coconut and Almond Chutney (page 79) or Roasted Bell Pepper Chutney (page 71).

Prep Time: 10 minutes (not including making the batter) | Cook Time: 20 to 25 minutes |
Makes: 10 (6-inch) pancakes

Ingredients

2 cups leftover *dosa* batter (page 311)

½ cup very finely chopped mixed vegetables (such as red onions, radishes, carrots, green peas)

1 tablespoon chopped cilantro

Minced green chilies

Oil or clarified butter for cooking

Preparation

1. Heat a *tawa* or cast iron griddle well (test with a drop of water which should sizzle and dance and then evaporate).

2. Pour a ladleful of the batter in the pan and spread. Cover with the lid of a pan (I have found my rice cooker lid works well for this) for 1 minute to set the pancake a little.

3. Sprinkle with some of the vegetables, a little cilantro, and some minced chilies and cover and cook for another 2 minutes.

4. Gently add a teaspoon of oil or butter around the edges of the pancake and remove and turn, the flipped side should be delicately browned. Cook the second side for 1 minute.

5. Continue cooking the remaining pancakes. Allow about 2 or 3 *oothapams* per servings.

Cheelas—Crispy Spiced Lentil Crepes
(VE, GF)

Lentil or lentil-and-rice crepes in different variations are popular across India. These crepes called *cheelas* are adapted from my mother-in-law's recipe. My mother-in-law is up early, usually done with her morning prayers before she is in the kitchen doing what she enjoys the most—cooking and nurturing her family. When she visits us or we visit India, we are greeted in the morning by the enticing scent of these crepes on the griddle. There is not much to making them, outside of a good skillet (cast iron works well) and the patience to wait till they are crisp and golden yellow and easily slide off the skillet.

Prep Time: 20 minutes plus overnight for soaking lentils | Cook Time: 25 to 30 minutes | Makes: 10 medium

Ingredients

1 cup husked yellow split lentils (moong dal)

1-inch piece ginger, peeled

2 green Serrano chilies

1 teaspoon salt or to taste

Oil for greasing the skillet

Preparation

1. Soak the lentils in water for 6 to 8 hours or overnight.

2. Rinse and drain the lentils and place in a blender.

3. Add the ginger, Serrano chilies, salt and about ¾ cup of water and blend to make a smooth fairly thick batter. (It is best to add less water at first and add any more as needed as you are blending so as not to over liquefy the batter.)

4. Heat a cast iron skillet on medium heat (test for heat with a few drops of water; the water should sizzle and dance off the surface of the pan in a ball and evaporate). Reduce heat to medium-low to cook the crepes.

5. Spread a small amount of the batter in the hot skillet in a circular shape to form a 4-inch circle (it is better to start with smaller circles and then move to larger circles, once you are able to control the temperature and crispness of the crepes).

6. Cook undisturbed for 1 to 2 minutes and then spread a little oil (using a teaspoon) around the surface of the skillet under the edges of the crepe, and cook for another minute or so.

7. Gently try to loosen the crepe from the skillet, this should not take much pressure if it is ready and the cooked side should have an even golden color. If you are struggling to free the crepe let the it rest in the skillet for a little longer and then gently ease out of the skillet and flip to the other side. Cook on the opposite side for 1 minute. Clean the skillet well with a cloth or napkin in between cooking each crepe.

8. Serve the crepes folded in half with a serving of any desired condiment.

Chapter Eleven

Sweet Endings: Desserts & Sweet Drinks

My memories of Indian desserts are synonymous with warm fragrant kitchens and images of my mother and grandmother spending hours creating beautiful treats. The delectable Indian fudges and puddings are reward for patience and tender loving care to obtain the right results. Most Indian desserts, such as fudge balls (*ladoos*) and fudge diamonds (*burfees*) are usually made with an assortment of slow-roasted whole grains cooked with clarified butter, nuts, and raisins, or with solidified milk and paneer. They can take almost half a day to prepare. Several of these treats are reserved for holidays and are made in bulk for gift giving, and some of these store well. But they are not always practical for fixing for after a quick everyday meal. But I can't deprive you of the sweetness of Indian desserts. So I culled through collections of essential desserts and reworked and simplified the recipes.

A few cakes and chilled desserts are quite popular in Indian households and find their place here too. Some of these, like my white chocolate truffles, are inspired by recent visits to India, where I saw chefs creating magical desserts with Indian flavors. The dessert section of this book is simple, with a few classic recipes and a few creative recipes using fresh seasonal bounty such as beetroots or blueberries and a generous medley of Indian flavors.

Sometimes synonymous with desserts is a cup of tea, often lightly spiced, something that has morphed into the so-called "chai tea" with many versions ranging from good to excessively sweet varieties. Other drinks for an Indian meal, including alcoholic drinks, tend to be served with appetizers outside the main meal. Most Indians tend to like their main meal with chilled water allowing them to savor the spice flavors without any competition.

Strawberries with Saffron Whipped Cream
(V, GF)

This is a simple, quick way to savor the fresh fruit of the season. Use any fruit of your choice, though I am partial to fresh strawberries as are my children.

Prep Time: 25 minutes plus 1 hour of chilling time | Serves: 6

Ingredients
1½ pounds fresh strawberries
2 cups chilled whipping cream
3 to 4 tablespoons raw brown sugar
1 teaspoon saffron strands

Preparation
1. Wash and hull the strawberries and cut in half. Chill for 1 hour.

2. Whip the cream with the brown sugar and saffron until nice and stiff.

3. Gently place a few strawberries in a bowl and top with the saffron cream and serve immediately.

Watermelon Granita
(VE, GF)

Fresh watermelon is the ultimate cooling solution for the Indian summer. It is eaten as is with some rock salt or pureed and chilled as juice or whipped with yogurt into lassies. I converted this sweet-spicy creation into a pretty, refreshing granita that is beautifully garnished with almonds and optional pink peppercorns.

Prep Time: 15 minutes, plus 4 to 6 hours for chilling | Serves: 6

Ingredients

1 watermelon, seeded and pureed
  (6 cups)

1 teaspoon black salt

Sugar if needed

To garnish

Watermelon liquor (optional)

Slivered almonds

Pink peppercorns (optional)

Preparation

1. Mix the watermelon puree with the black salt and some sugar (if using) and place in a chilling container.

2. Put in the freezer and let chill for about 2 hours or so, until it begins to set. Then remove it from the freezer every half hour to mix and rake the mixture with a fork. At the end of 4 to 6 hours you should have frozen crystals of watermelon (aka granita).

3. To serve, place in serving containers and top with 1 tablespoon of watermelon liquor, if desired, and the sliced almonds. Add the pink peppercorns if using. Enjoy!

Cardamom-Soaked Doughnuts
(V)

Gulab jamuns are the Indian equivalent of doughnuts except that they are mostly milk-based and are served in syrup. They are truly enticing when eaten fresh and warm. This recipe will make about 40 to 45 *gulab jamuns*, but you can half the recipe if desired. At Indian weddings, *gulab jamuns* are usually served a la mode with Indian ice cream.

Prep Time: 2 to 3 hours (mostly to let soak in the syrup) | Cook Time: 45 minutes | Makes: 40 to 45

Ingredients

For the syrup
2 cups sugar
10 green cardamom pods, bruised

For the milk dough balls
1½ cups milk powder (*I have had better results with the variety sold at Indian stores, usually the Deep brand*)
⅔ cup all-purpose flour
¾ teaspoon baking soda
½ cup sour cream
1½ tablespoons ghee or clarified butter
Oil for frying

To garnish
1 tablespoon rosewater
Sliced chopped almonds or pistachios

Preparation

1. For the syrup, place the sugar, cardamom pods, and 3 cups of water in a heavy large pot and boil for 25 to 30 minutes to make a fairly thick syrup (it should be just shy of coating a spoon). Let the syrup stay hot by keeping it on very low heat.

2. Meanwhile in a mixing bowl, mix the milk powder, flour, and baking soda with the sour cream. Keep working the mixture until smooth. Gradually work in the clarified butter to form a relatively smooth dough. It will be rougher in texture than a standard flour dough. Let the dough rest for 10 minutes.

3. Shape the dough into 40 to 45 balls about the size of a grape. You will need to work with moist hands to ensure that the balls are smooth.

4. Heat some oil in a large wok on low to medium heat. Working in batches, fry the balls until they are nice and golden. (They need to be teased around the wok to allow a uniform brown color.) Remove from the wok with a slotted spoon and add them to the syrup as you make them.

5. Once all the balls have been fried and added to the syrup in the pot, remove from the heat and let them soak for 2 hours or longer prior to serving.

6. Before serving, sprinkle with rosewater and garnish with almonds.

Cardamom-Scented Beet Halwa
(V, GF)

In late summer, beets and beet greens are bountiful. The vivid color of beets is truly quite stunning—makes me realize why people use the term beet red to emphasize how much someone is blushing. To capitalize on the natural sweetness, color, and abundance of this vegetable, I decided to make this beet halwa. I bake the beets before cooking them in the dessert to save time and enhance the depth of flavor, since the process of roasting concentrates the natural sugar in the beets.

Prep Time: 5 minutes | Cook Time: 45 minutes | Serves: 6 to 8

Ingredients
6 small to medium beets
2 cups low-fat (2%) milk
3 green cardamom pods
½ cup sugar (*adjust this to your taste*)
2 tablespoons ghee
Toasted coconut to garnish

Preparation
1. Pre-heat the oven to 350°F.

2. Wash the beets, remove the greens, and wrap the beets in foil. Bake for 20 minutes. Open the packet and let cool. Peel the beets and grate them in a food processor.

3. Place the grated beets in a heavy-bottomed pan and pour the milk over them. (The effect of the milk turning pink is quite dramatic.)

4. Add the cardamom pods and cook on medium-low heat, stirring occasionally, until the milk is almost evaporated (you will see the beets in clumps with the thick liquid boiling away around the sides).

5. Stir in the sugar and continue cooking until all the liquid is evaporated.

6. Add the ghee and mix well (the mixture should be a soft, moist but not wet glistening mass). Garnish with the coconut.

Tips and Tricks
I cook the recipe with coarsely grated beets to leave some texture in the dish, but you can grate the beets finer for a completely mashed variation.

You can also add nuts, such as cashews and pistachios, to the halwa.

Variation: Cardamom-Scented Carrot Halwa
Substitute carrots (or a mixture of carrots and beets) for the beets in this recipe.

Cottage Cheese and Chocolate Truffles
(V, GF)

Sandesh is the perfect fresh cheese dessert that originates from Eastern India. It is a mildy sweetened Indian cheesecake that is still difficult to find in sweet shops in the U.S. This recipe for a sweet cheese truffle attempts to improve on perfection.

Prep Time: 10 minutes plus about 2 hours to drain the cheese | Cook Time: 20 minutes |
Makes: 25 to 35 medium truffle balls

Ingredients

2 quarts milk

1 large lemon or lime, cut in half and seeded

⅓ cup sugar

½ teaspoon freshly crushed green cardamom seeds (from about 2 pods)

½ teaspoon freshly ground black pepper (optional)

1 cup coarsely chopped white chocolate

6 tablespoons unsalted butter

¼ cup cream

½ cup coarsely chopped dark chocolate

Preparation

1. Line a large colander with cheesecloth.

2. Pour the milk into a heavy-bottomed pan and bring to a full boil. Squeeze in the lemon or lime juice. The addition of the juice to the boiling milk will curdle the milk and separate it into milk solids and whey (it is important to add the juice only after the milk has reached a full boil).

3. Turn off the heat and pour the contents of the pan into the cheesecloth-lined colander to drain the whey. Gather the resulting cheese in the cheesecloth and hang over the sink to drain for a couple of hours.

4. After a couple of hours, place the cheese in a large wok. Add the sugar and cook on medium-low heat, stirring frequently, until the mixture is drier and soft and separates from the sides of the pot, about 10 minutes.

5. Stir in the crushed cardamom seeds and ground black pepper, if using, and mix well.

6. Stir in the white chocolate, 3 tablespoons of the butter, and the cream and continue cooking until the mixture is well mixed and the chocolate is melted.

7. Cool the mixture until it is thick and cool enough to handle. Shape into walnut-size balls and place on a piece of parchment paper.

8. In the meantime in a separate pan, melt the dark chocolate and remaining 3 tablespoons butter until the mixture is smooth. Cool slightly and then place in a squeezer and drizzle the dark chocolate over the truffle balls in a decorative criss-cross movement.

9. Let the mixture dry and serve the truffles as needed. These balls can be made ahead and stored in the refrigerator for up to a week before using.

Oatmeal Porridge Cooked in Nutty Saffron Milk
(V, GF)

For a treat, try making this recipe instead of your regular breakfast. Most people won't even know they are eating dessert for breakfast. A *phirni* is a traditional milk-based dessert in which the milk is thickened first through slow cooking, and then by the addition of powdered rice. In this recipe oatmeal accomplishes the same effect in a significantly easier manner. I feel that I get the best results in the slow cooker, but this can be made on the stovetop as well. I keep the amount of sugar low, so it can be increased to taste as desired.

Prep Time: 5 minute | Cook Time: 4 hours (in a slow cooker) | Serves: 4

Ingredients
2 quarts half and half

½ cup steel-cut oats

4 or 5 green cardamom pods

¾ cup packed brown sugar or a little more to taste

1 teaspoon saffron strands

Sliced almonds to garnish

Preparation
1. Place the half and half in a slow cooker with the oats and green cardamom pods. Set the slow cooker on high for 4 hours.

2. After 1 hour, stir in the sugar and saffron.

3. After about 2½ hours the mixture will begin to simmer briskly and will have thickened. At this point, begin stirring the mixture every 20 minutes or so to ensure that it does not stick to the container.

4. The finished dessert will have a creamy golden color and a thick rich consistency. Serve in bowls garnished with almonds.

Tips and Tricks
For a different flavor you can make this with ½ cup of ground rice in place of the oats. You can also add in pistachios and raisins if desired.

Raspberry Kulfi Ice Cream with a Blackberry Garnish
(V, GF)

Traditional *kulfi* ice cream in India is not made with cream, but with milk that is cooked down until thick and then frozen. This can be difficult and time-consuming, so I have adapted this recipe using cream and condensed milk to use up the summer raspberries that are so plentiful in season. You get a pretty pink ice cream with a slight texture from the seeds with notes reminiscent of good raspberry jam. It is also difficult to find *kulfi* molds, so I set the dessert in either large ice cube trays or in popsicle molds.

Prep Time: 10 minutes plus about 4 hours for freezing | Cook Time: 20 minutes | Makes: 6 to 8

Ingredients
1 (15-ounce) can condensed milk

¾ cup milk powder

1 cup whole milk or half and half

1 cup heavy cream

2 pounds raspberries, pureed (1½ cups)

1 tablespoon rose water (optional)

½ pound blackberries for garnish

Preparation
1. Mix the condensed milk, milk powder, milk or half and half, and heavy cream in a heavy-bottomed pan. Cook slowly until well mixed together., about 20 minutes.

2. Let the milk mixture cool and then mix in the raspberry puree and rosewater, if using.

3. Carefully place into chilling molds or large ice cube trays and put in the freezer and chill for at least 4 hours until set.

4. To serve, let the mold sit at room temperature for about 15 to 20 minutes and unmold. Serve garnished with blackberries.

Fresh Ginger Apple Chai Cake

The original inspiration for this recipe was a well-spiced fresh ginger cake by David Lebovitz. I loved the use of molasses and spices in the original recipe, but I modified it just a little to use fresh Indian tea spices and chopped apple. A book that talks about exploring seasonal fresh foods in New York is incomplete without an apple-based dessert. This recipe produces a lovely moist cake that tastes even better the next day.

Prep Time: 10 minutes | Cook Time: 60 minutes plus cooling time | Serves: 8

Ingredients

1 cup regular strength molasses

1 cup sugar

1 cup vegetable oil (I use light olive oil)

2 teaspoons baking soda

2 tablespoons freshly grated ginger

2½ cups whole wheat pastry flour

1 (1-inch) cinnamon stick

6 to 8 cloves

½ teaspoon cardamom seeds

¼ teaspoon black peppercorns

2 apples (preferably Granny Smith), peeled, cored, and chopped

2 large eggs

Preparation

1. Grease and flour a round 10-inch springform or bundt cake pan. Pre-heat the oven to 350°F.

2. In a mixing bowl, mix together the molasses, sugar, and oil.

3. Place 1 cup of water in a small saucepan and bring to a boil. When it has just started boiling, stir in the baking soda and remove from heat. Mix the hot water into the molasses mixture. Stir in the ginger.

4. Sift the flour into the bowl of a food processor or mixing bowl. Place the cinnamon stick, cloves, cardamom seeds, and black peppercorns in a spice or coffee grinder and grind until smooth. Stir into the flour. Add the apples to the flour and pulse a few times, until well mixed.

5. Gradually add the molasses mixture and pulse until well mixed (if using a regular mixing bowl, you can use an electric mixer for this purpose).

6. Beat the eggs and add to the batter and mix until thoroughly combined.

7. Pour batter into the prepared pan and bake for about 1 hour, or until a skewer comes out clean.

8. Cool the cake for at least 30 minutes then turn out onto a cooling rack.

Saffron Pistachio Rice Pudding
(V, GF)

Most Indian cookbooks would be incomplete without a rice pudding recipe. My variation lets you make it in a slow cooker with minimal attention and all the indulgence. The dessert does need occasional stirring after the rice is added, but certainly beats nursing it with dedication over the stove for hours. This version is flavored with cardamom and saffron and garnished with pistachio nuts.

Prep/Cook Time: 5 hours in a slow cooker | Serves: 8

Ingredients

2 quarts half and half

6 green cardamom pods

⅓ cup white rice (preferably a short-grain variety)

¾ cup sugar

1 teaspoon saffron strands

⅓ cup shelled, unsalted pistachios

Preparation

1. Place the half and half and cardamom pods in a slow cooker and cook on high, undisturbed, until the half and half begins simmering, about 2 hours.

2. Stir in the rice and continue cooking, stirring every 25 minutes to make sure that it does not stick.

3. After the rice has cooked for about 1½ hours, stir in the sugar (the rice should be fairly soft now).

4. Continue cooking for 1 more hour, stirring every 15 minutes during this period. The mixture will be a soft creamy consistency and will be a very pale caramel color.

5. Turn off the heat and let the mixture rest for ½ hour.

6. Stir in the saffron. Garnish with the pistachios just before serving. The rice pudding can be served hot or cold depending on your preference.

Maple and Yogurt Custard
(V, GF)

I like to make this simple dessert in small ramekins for ease of serving but it can also be prepared in a larger dish. This recipe is very close to a dessert from my childhood called *Misti Doi* (sweet yogurt) that is sweetened with date palm jaggery made from the sap of the date palm tree. The yogurt traditionally sets in earthenware pots overnight. It is difficult to find earthenware pots though, and the setting process may not always work in the cooler months, so I offer this oven-steaming method, which offers very close results and has brought smiles and the flavors of my childhood to my family table.

Prep Time: 10 minutes | Cook Time: 30 to 35 minutes (unattended) | Chill Time: 3 to 4 hours |
Makes: 6 to 8 individual dessert custards

Ingredients

¾ cup maple syrup

1 cups whole milk

½ cup heavy cream

3 cups plain Greek yogurt (can be low-fat)

Clarified butter for greasing

Fruits and chopped pecans for serving (optional)

Preparation

1. Pre-heat the oven to 350°F.

2. Heat the maple syrup in a small saucepan until thickened and reduced by half. Cool slightly.

3. In a mixing bowl, beat the milk, cream, yogurt, and thickened maple syrup until well mixed.

4. Grease six ramekins well with the clarified butter and pour the cream mixture in them until three-quarters filled; or grease a shallow baking dish and pour in all of the mixture. Place in a larger baking dish and fill the dish with about 2 inches of water. Bake for about 30 minutes until set (larger dish will take a longer to cook).

5. Chill the custard for at least 3 to 4 hours before serving. The custard can be lightly garnished with chopped pecans and fruits such as chopped berries if desired. If cooked in the ramekins the custard is usually served in them as opposed to spooning into serving dishes.

Raspberry, Brown Sugar and Sour Cream Crepes
(V)

We do have dessert crepes in India, filled with sweetened coconut or dried fruits and nuts. In fact, there are several variations popular in my grandmother kitchen. This quick-fix variation is inspired by the bounty of our summer garden raspberries and my childhood memories.

Prep Time: 10 minutes | Cook Time: 25 minutes | Makes: 6 to 8 crepes

Ingredients

For the crepes

¾ cup all-purpose flour

2 teaspoons sugar

⅛ teaspoon freshly ground green cardamom seeds (from about 1 pod)

¾ cup milk

½ teaspoon vanilla extract

1 egg

3 tablespoons salted butter, melted

Extra butter or oil for greasing

For the filling

¾ cup sour cream

⅓ cup raw cane sugar or light brown sugar

½ cup raspberries, plus extra for serving

Preparation

1. Sift the flour, sugar, and ground cardamom into a mixing bowl.

2. Place the milk, vanilla, egg, and melted butter in a separate bowl and beat until well mixed.

3. Gradually add the flour mixture to the egg mixture and beat well until smooth and thick.

4. In a separate bowl, mix together the sour cream, cane sugar, and raspberries.

5. Place a griddle or skillet on medium-low heat (I highly recommend a cast iron griddle to ensure smooth and uniform heating). Add about 2 tablespoons butter or oil to the heated skillet and swirl around the surface to coat the pan.

6. Pour a ladleful of the batter into the skillet and spread around the pan like a thin omelet. Gently cook until the crepe is firm and can be removed easily, about 2 to 3 minutes.

7. Spread half of the crepe with about 2 tablespoons of the raspberry mixture and fold over the other half. Place on a serving plate. Garnish with two or three raspberries and serve warm.

8. Continue this process until all the batter and filling are used.

Ginger and Cardamom Shortbread Cookies (V)

These flavorful and crisp shortbread cookies are eggless and fashioned after the Indian shortbread cookies called *nankhaties*. They are my brother's favorite cookies, which is just as well since they travel well and are really very easy to make. If you love tea as much as I do, you will love these cookies with a perfect cup of spiced tea.

Prep Time: 15 minutes (plus 30 minutes cooling time) | Cook Time: 15 minutes |
Makes: 15 to 18 cookies (about 2.5 inches)

Ingredients

1 cup (2 sticks) salted butter plus butter for greasing the tray, room temperature

¾ cup brown sugar (you can use maple sugar for a special treat)

1⅔ cups all-purpose flour

1 tablespoon ground ginger

1½ teaspoons freshly ground cardamom (about 12 green cardamom seeds, peeled and crushed)

½ cup almond meal

½ cup chopped dried cranberries (optional, but fun)

Preparation

1. Pre-heat the oven to 325°F. Grease a large baking sheet and set aside.

2. Place the butter in a mixing bowl and add the brown sugar. Beat well with a hand beater or wooden spoon until creamy.

3. In a separate bowl mix together the all-purpose flour, ground ginger, cardamom powder, and almond meal and stir well.

4. Gradually add the dry mixture to the butter mixture and stir well.

5. Add the cranberries, if using, and mix well. You should get a dry but easily malleable dough.

6. Break off lime-size pieces of dough and roll into balls and flatten slightly and place on the baking tray. Leave about one inch of space between the cookies.

7. Bake in the oven for 12 to 15 minutes. The cookies will be gently browned at the bottom but still fairly pale on top. Turn off the heat and let the cookies cool in the oven. They will turn crisp as they get cooler.

Tips and Tricks

To make a simple variety of fresh almond meal, I grind whole almonds (with their skin on) in the coffee grinder. They are more nutritious this way.

For a variation, you can also use finely ground pistachios.

Saffron, Riesling and Star Anise Poached Peaches
(VE, GF)

I make this with a good fruity up-state New York Riesling and summer peaches when they are in season. It is a very simple treat that tastes wonderful by itself and is decadent perfection with a scoop of ice cream.

Prep Time: 15 minutes | Cook Time: 40 minutes | Serves: 4 to 6

Ingredients
1 bottle sweet Riesling

½ cup brown sugar

3 pounds ripe peaches, peeled and cut into wedges

1 teaspoon saffron strands

3 star anise

Mint leaves for serving

Preparation
1. Place the wine in a large saucepan and stir in the brown sugar. Simmer the mixture until one-third its original volume.

2. Add the peaches and saffron to the wine syrup and simmer for 7 minutes.

3. Add the star anise and simmer for another 3 minutes.

4. Chill and serve garnished with mint.

Peach or Mango Lassi
(V, GF)

My children developed quite an attachment for the tall yellow glasses of the Indian-style yogurt shake called mango lassi. I personally find the versions at most restaurants rather sweet and sometimes lacking the tartness of natural yogurt. So I make this at home and in the peak of summer I love to use ripe and juicy peaches and sprigs of mint for garnish.

Prep Time: 10 minutes plus 1 hour for chilling | Serves: 4 to 6

Ingredients
4 cups plain low-fat yogurt

1 teaspoon salt

2 to 3 tablespoons sugar

4 medium peaches (about 1 pound) or 2 medium fresh mangoes

Sprigs of mint to garnish

Preparation
1. Place the yogurt in a blender with the salt, sugar, and 1 cup of water.

2. Peel the peaches or mangoes and cut into chunks and add to the mixture in the blender.

3. Blend to a smooth shake, adding a little more water if needed (the mixture should not be too thick, but rather have an airy and smooth consistency).

4. Chill for 1 hour.

5. Pour into glasses and garnish with sprigs of mint and serve.

Masala Chai
(V, GF)

I have spent my early formative years in the shadow of two of India's largest tea growing regions—Assam and Darjeeling. The teas of these regions are very different and I am consequently very finicky about my tea. This mixture for Masala Chai is something that I make in large quantities and use as needed. It is especially nice during the cooler months. I do not usually add ginger to this brew, but if desired sliced peeled ginger can be added in. Do not use Darjeeling tea for this simmered chai, it is a delicate tea and looses its gentle flavors and takes on a rather bitter character when boiled.

Prep Time: 5 minutes | Cook Time: 15 minutes | Serves: 4

Ingredients

2 cups whole milk

1½ tablespoons black tea leaves (Assam, Nilgiri, or an English Breakfast Blend)

4 green cardamom pods

1 black cardamom pod (optional)

1 (1½-inch) cinnamon stick

4 to 6 cloves

½ teaspoon whole black peppercorns

Sugar or honey to taste

Preparation

1. Bring the milk and 2 cups of water to a simmer in a heavy-bottomed pot.

2. Once the mixture reaches a simmer stir in the tea.

3. Place the green cardamom pods, black cardamom pod (if using), cloves, and peppercorns in a mortar and pestle and gently bruise the spices.

4. Add this to the tea mixture and boil for about 5 to 7 minutes.

5. Strain the tea and serve with sugar or honey if desired.

Valhalla Morning Ginger Tea
(V, GF)

This tea (named after the town where I live) is what starts my day most mornings of the year. I have a personal preference for Darjeeling tea, and it is important for me to have it brewed just right. Usually I am joined in this ritual of preparing tea by my cat, since most days I start my tea kettle before anyone else is awake, and while the water is boiling I usually get the children's breakfast organized. This tea, however, tastes just as great as a pick me up in the evening and works well with most of the desserts in this chapter.

Prep Time: 10 minutes | Cook Time: 10 minutes (just to boil water) | Serves: 2

Ingredients

2 teaspoons loose leaf tea (Darjeeling or a stronger black tea)

1 tablespoon freshly grated ginger (do not use ginger powder)

Milk (optional to taste)

Sugar or honey to taste

Preparation

1. Bring 2½ cups of water to a boil.

2. In the meantime place the tea leaves and ginger in the infuser basket of a teapot.

3. Pour the boiling water over the tea and ginger and let the tea steep for 3 to 5 minutes.

4. Pour into cups and add milk and sugar to taste.

Chapter Twelve

Masala Dani:
My *Spices & Seasons* Tool Chest

Over time, every cook acquires a personal tool kit or set of signature flavors in the kitchen. This flavor chest is different for all cooks. In my mind's eye, my collection would be stored in a large, well-worn wicker chest, able to accommodate the various shapes of jars and bottles in which I store my spices. My spice collection tends to be too big for any standard set of spice containers, and I also like to reuse mustard or pickle jars since these tend to be of good quality and often have very serviceable lids.

This act of re-cycling goes back to an old tradition that I inherited from my grandmother, and is something I see done in a lot of Indian homes. In her day, a lot of the finer relishes and jams were of English origin, quite different from what she found in her everyday local market. Once she finished the original contents of the jars, she liked to use them for storing other things. Somehow her closet of multi-shaped jars still seemed rather organized. My collection always threatens to overflow my shelves, but it is probably as dear to me as a collection of jewelry is to some other women.

My flavor blocks are a group of essential spice mixtures that I have referred to and used in various recipes in this book and most of these belong to the essential spice starter kit found on page 12. Other items that comprise my tool chest are practical curry pastes, spice pastes, spice blends, and spice rubs. Armed with this selection of quick fixes, you will find yourself saving time and enhancing flavor in your foods.

I often spend an hour on Sundays organizing and replenishing some of the items in my tool chest. This "plan ahead" time can also be taken up with cooking chickpeas, marinating some chicken, and pre-chopping hardy items such as onions, cabbage, and broccoli. A little planning and prep work help me put together a weeknight meal at an even faster pace. I will leave you to decide what works for you and how you will fill and build your tool chest.

Curry

"Do you use curry?" Very few Indian cooks have escaped this question. Unfortunately I have been asked it once too often. It is a baffling and actually strange question since, depending on your point of reference, curry can refer to a blend of spices (a British concoction created to allow the colonial Indian food aficionado an easy blend to by-pass working with an assortment of spices) or a gravy or spicy sauce base.

While the term is not restricted to Indian cooking alone, there is one thing that is true of all variations of a curry—it is a blend of spices, whether wet or dry. In general Indian parlance, it also loosely refers to a sauce-based dish, usually a spiced stew of some sort. Curry leaves are a component of the mixes collectively called *masala*.

Spice blends: To grind or buy?

Most cooks have their preferred selection of spice blends. This segment of the book outlines the common blends present in my pantry. I am often asked whether you should make the blend from fresh spices or buy the spices already ground. The truth is that there are no absolutes. Freshly ground spices do taste fresher and are more flavorful, so it is a good idea to grind more commonly-used spice blends like cumin and coriander yourself, and then buy the more complex spice blends pre-mixed. I provide practical recipes for the common blends used in this book. The reality here is that grinding your own blends is a lot more flavorful and economical, however it does take a little more planning. It really is your choice to decide which option works for you.

Warming spices

Aromatic spices or warming spices are used individually or added whole to foods to add fragrance and depth of flavor in Indian cuisine. Warming spices typically complement other spices, rather than being the sole spice in a dish. Several of these spices are used in cuisines across the world.

Bay leaves (*Laurus nobilis*): There are many varieties of bay leaves, the most common ones being the bay laurel and the Indian bay leaf. The preferred bay leaf for Indian cooking is the latter variety that has a stronger cassia-like smell. The bold smell possibly accounts for the Indian name *tej patta* (bold leaf). It is used almost exclusively in some rice dishes and stews. Bay leaves are edible but are usually removed from food before it is served. In some parts of India, the bay leaf is added to desserts to impart a fragrance that complements the sweet tastes.

Cardamom (*Cardamom*): Cardamom pods are the fruit of the cardamom cassia tree, native to India, Nepal, and Bhutan. Cardamom pods come in green and black varieties. Green cardamom has a thinner delicate skin and a sweet, spicy taste, while black cardamom has a husky outer skin and the seeds have a sharper taste. I tend to use green cardamoms most frequently for the recipes in this book. It is important to note that the black seeds within the pod are what is used. If you extract the seeds for the spice blends, you can still use the green shells to infuse extra flavor into the water you brew for tea. The whole cardamom pods, gently bruised, are used for rice dishes and for deep tasting chicken or other meaty stews. Cardamom is considered the third most expensive spice in the world.

Cinnamon (*Cinnamomum*): This is the bark of the cinnamon tree, a native of South India and the island of Sri Lanka, and has a sweet and mildly spicy taste. In fact, the Indian name for the spice, *darchini*, translates to "standing sugar." Cinnamon is used for both sweet and savory cooking, almost the same way as cardamom. In Indian cuisine, while whole cinnamon sticks are often used, the ground form is not usually used alone the way it is in American cooking to sprinkle over beverages or add to desserts.

Cloves (*Syzygium aromaticum*): Cloves are the dried buds of an evergreen tree in the *myrtaceae* family, native of the Maluku islands of Indonesia. The English name for the clove comes from the Latin word *clavus* (nail). This spice is stronger in taste than some of the others but essentially works well as part of the orchestra in spice blends much like cinnamon. I use cloves in conjunction with other spices to create the gentle finishing effects that make a perfect fragrantly spiced curry. Cloves also have medicinal qualities and are frequently used as a mild antiseptic. Cloves can work well for roasting meats or baking.

Garam masala: The word *garam* means "hot" in Hindi. Garam masala is a spice blend made of aromatic spices such as cinnamon, cardamom, and black peppercorns. It is considered a "warming" spice blend because its ingredients stimulate the blood flow. Nowadays garam masala is popular enough to find its way into most well-stocked grocery stores and Indian-inspired recipes. There is not one garam masala blend because it tends to differ based on the region of India. My favorite recipe for garam masala is on page 350.

Black peppercorns (*Kali Mirch*): Black pepper (*Piper nigrum*) is a flowering vine from the Piperacae family of plants, native to south India. It is cultivated for its fruit which are dried and used as a spice and seasoning. The fruit, known as a peppercorn when dried, is approximately 5 millimeters in diameter and dark red when fully mature. Black pepper is a very common and extremely powerful spice. For all its potency, the peppercorn does not have the same flavor when pre-ground and stored, so I always have a peppermill handy in the kitchen. It helps add a nice burst of heat when the dish calls for it. I find the heat of black peppercorns to be a good complement to other strong flavors such as garlic and fenugreek.

Star anise (*Illicium Verum*): This spice is the fruit of an evergreen tree native to Vietnam. It has a pretty star shape and packs all the flavors of fennel seeds and anise seeds. The star anise is a great spice for decorating and garnishing as well, if you do not always want its anise-like flavor in food. It is popular in the food of certain South Indian cuisines.

Indian Relish or Salad Spice Blend
Chaat Masala
(VE, GF)

Chaat masala is an essential sprinkling spice, originating in North India to sprinkle on the salads called *chaats*. It is, however, very versatile and can be used for various recipes, and is one of my favorite spice blends. This blend is available pre-mixed and sold in stores under the name *chaat masala* but here is my recipe for the mixture.

Prep/Cook Time: 10 minutes | Makes: ½ cup

Ingredients

¼ cup cumin seeds

⅛ cup coriander seeds

2 tablespoons black peppercorns

¼ cup amchur powder

1 tablespoon red cayenne pepper powder

3 tablespoons black salt

Preparation

1. Dry roast the cumin seeds in a small skillet until fragrant and toasty, about 2 minutes. Remove from pan.

2. Add the coriander seeds and black peppercorns to the skillet and dry roast for about 1½ minutes, until they smell fragrant and darken slightly.

3. Grind the spices in a spice mill or coffee grinder until smooth.

4. Stir in the amchur powder, cayenne pepper powder, and black salt.

5. Store in an airtight jar in a cool dry place.

Indian Grilling Spice Blend

Tandoori Masala

(VE, GF)

Tandoori masala is versatile and can be used to cook a variety of foods. Tandoor refers to an Indian clay oven, and this blend was created for grilling and kebabs made at home. High-temperature baking followed by broiling can substitute for tandoori cooking and produces acceptable results.

Prep Time: 5 minutes | Makes: ¾ cup

Ingredients

3 tablespoons coriander seeds

3 tablespoons cumin seeds

4 dried red chilies (optional)

1 teaspoon carom seeds (ajowain)

2 or 3 (2-inch) cinnamon sticks

10 cloves

1½ teaspoons cardamom seeds

2 tablespoons Kashmiri red chili powder

Method of Preparation

1. Place the coriander seeds, cumin seeds, dried red chilies, carom seeds, cinnamon sticks, cloves, and cardamom seeds in a skillet and toast for 2 minutes, until fragrant.

2. Grind the toasted spices to a powder in a spice mill or coffee grinder. Stir in the red chili powder.

3. Store in an airtight jar and use as needed.

Fragrant Spice Blend
Garam Masala
(VE, GF)

Fragrant warm spices such as cloves, cinnamon, and cardamom come together in this all-purpose blend. Like practically everything in Indian cooking, there is no one recipe for *garam masala*—it varies from household to household, and consequently, from chef to chef. For example, I do not add cumin to my *garam masala* mixture, but it is used in several variations of the spice blend.

Prep Time: 5 minutes | Makes: ½ cup

Ingredients
⅓ cup green cardamom seeds

3 or 4 (2-inch) cinnamon sticks

2 or 3 bay leaves

1 or 2 star anise

¼ cup cloves

1 teaspoon black peppercorns

2 teaspoons cumin seeds (optional)

Preparation
1. Place the green cardamom seeds, cinnamon sticks, bay leaves, star anise, cloves, peppercorns, and cumin seeds (if using) in a dry skillet and lightly roast for about 1 to 2 minutes.

2. Grind the toasted spices in a spice mill or coffee grinder and store in an airtight jar in a cool place.

Tips and Tricks
For a compromise, if you do not want to store so many varieties of whole spices, bags of pre-mixed whole garam masala ingredients are sold in spice aisles of Indian stores. They have an assortment of spices, but I think lightly toasted and ground they make an acceptable substitute.

Fenugreek and Black Pepper Rub
Methi Kali Mirch Masala
(VE, GF)

This is a very potent mixture with two of my favorite kitchen spices: fenugreek and black pepper. It makes for a great rub on fish or firm, fleshy vegetables like eggplant.

Prep Time: 5 minutes | Makes: ½ cup

Ingredients
2 tablespoons black peppercorns
1 teaspoon cumin seeds
1 tablespoons coriander seeds
1½ tablespoons dried fenugreek
 leaves
1 tablespoon pink peppercorns
1½ teaspoons salt

Preparation
1. Place the black peppercorns, cumin seeds, coriander seeds, and fenugreek leaves in a small skillet and toast lightly for 2 to 3 minutes, until very lightly roasted and fragrant.

2. Place the mixture in a spice mill or coffee grinder and grind until blended but not too smooth, since this mixture is used as a rub and a little texture is interesting.

3. Coarsely crush the pink peppercorns (these are added for color so you do not want them too smooth) and add to the spice mixture along with the salt.

4. This spice rub can be stored in a jar in a cool dry place for up to a year.

Basic Ginger and Garlic Marinade
Adrak Laisun Masala
(VE, GF)

The following recipe is for a marinade, but it is made from very basic spices that can be added to a curry base for a nice practical all-purpose curry. The core difference between a marinade and a basic spice mix in the Indian kitchen is the use of something acidic in the marinade to tenderize the protein being marinated.

Prep Time: 15 minutes | Makes: ½ cup

Ingredients
1 large piece (about ¼ pound) ginger, peeled and coarsely chopped

20 cloves garlic

3 green chilies

⅓ cup chopped cilantro

2 limes, halved

1 teaspoon salt

Preparation
1. Place the ginger, garlic, chilies, and cilantro in a blender. Squeeze in the lime juice. Add the salt and process until smooth.

2. Store in a jar in the refrigerator for a couple of weeks or freeze in small containers and use as needed.

Cumin-Coriander Powder

Dhaniya Zeera Masala

(VE, GF)

This all-purpose spice blend is an essential combination for Indian cooking. I usually like to keep small amounts of this mix handy or blend it fresh when I'm cooking a lot.

Prep Time: 5 minutes

Ingredients

4 tablespoons cumin seeds
4 tablespoons coriander seeds

Preparation

1. In a heavy-bottomed pan, dry roast the cumin and coriander seeds for 1½ minutes. The spices should smell toasty and darken a little at this point.

2. Grind the roasted spices to a powder in a spice mill or coffee grinder.

3. Store in an airtight jar in a cool dry place. This mixture will keep for about 6 months.

Basic Curry Powder

Kari Powder

(VE, GF)

This all-purpose spice blend can be substituted with a good-quality commercial curry powder.

Prep Time: 5 minutes

Ingredients

2 tablespoons cumin seeds
2 tablespoons coriander seeds
1 teaspoon black peppercorns
1 teaspoon fenugreek seeds
1 (2-inch) cinnamon stick
3 dried red chilies
10 to 15 curry leaves
1 teaspoon turmeric

Preparation

1. In a heavy-bottomed pan, dry roast all the spices except the turmeric on medium heat for about 2 minutes. The spices should smell fragrant and toasty.

2. Mix in the turmeric and grind to a powder in a spice mill or coffee grinder.

3. Store in an airtight jar in a cool dry place.

Magic Trinity Masala
Piyaj Adrak Laisun Masala
(VE, GF)

This is what I call my "magic trinity" mixture: a basic onion, garlic, and ginger starter. I keep this made in bulk and mix it into coconut milk or tomatoes to whip together a quick-fix curry. I store this blend in the freezer in ice cube containers. Each cube is about 1 tablespoon of the mixture.

Prep Time: 10 minutes | Cook Time: 20 minutes | Makes: about 1½ cups

Ingredients
⅓ cup oil

1½ teaspoons cumin seeds

1 medium onion, thinly sliced

½ cup grated fresh ginger

1 whole head garlic (about 20 cloves), peeled and sliced

Preparation
1. Heat the oil in a skillet on medium heat. Add the cumin seeds and when they begin to sizzle stir in the onions and cook for 7 to 8 minutes, until the onions soften and begin to turn a pale toffee color.

2. Add the ginger and garlic and cook for another 5 minutes.

3. Let mixture cool and then grind to a paste in a blender or food processor. Store in the refrigerator or freezer and use as needed.

Basic Tomato Starter
Tamatari Masala
(VE, GF)

I've learned that one should never underestimate the wisdom of any grandmother's kitchen (not just one's own). This recipe was inspired by my Italian friend's Nona. One evening I stopped by their place for dinner and was amazed to have fresh-tasting marinara and pasta dusted with cheese within twenty minutes of my arrival. I learned that they made marinara sauce in large batches. It gave me an idea.

When the season peaks, we are floating in tomatoes. This sauce— what I call my "tomato starter"—is my way of storing garden fresh tomatoes as well as a good way to jumpstart my cooking. It is essentially a curry base and can be used with almost all kinds of spices The recipe here makes enough to last me about a week. I keep this spice free so that it can be adapted to suit the recipe and actually can be eaten with pasta too!

Prep Time: 10 minutes | Cook Time: 40 minutes | Makes: about 5 cups

Ingredients

½ cup oil

5 onions, chopped

⅓ cup freshly grated ginger

20 cloves garlic, minced

20 medium (about 5 pounds) ripe tomatoes, chopped (*I use a food processor*)

1 tablespoon tomato paste (optional)

1½ teaspoons salt

1 teaspoon sugar (optional)

Preparation

1. Heat the oil in a pot on medium heat for about 2 minutes. Add the onions and gently cook for about 15 minutes, stirring frequently, until they begin to turn softly golden at spots.

2. Stir in the ginger and garlic and cook for another 2 to 3 minutes, until the mixture comes together and is turning pale golden.

3. Stir in the tomatoes and tomato paste (if using) and cook, stirring occasionally. The tomatoes will gradually start melting into the onion mixture, continue cooking them slowly until they mix into the onion mixture and the oil begins to surface through the sides, about 12 to 15 minutes.

5. Stir in the salt and sugar and use as needed. This mixture will keep in the refrigerator for about 2 to 3 weeks, or it can be frozen and kept for longer.

Tips and Tricks

For recipes using this starter, see Scrambled Tofu with Colorful Vegetable Medley on page 133, and Chicken Meatballs in a Light Tomato Gravy on page 237.

Tikka Masala Sauce
Tamatar Methi Shorba
(VE, GF)

Heated debates have raged about *tikka masala* and butter sauce (called *makhani*)! Several food writers have made a big deal about the difference between these two. So let me be radical and tell you that *tikka masala* was an attempt to make the traditional butter chicken sound different in England (it is also infamously called England's national dish). There is not a huge difference between the two sauces when done right, but one thing to keep in mind: the fenugreek is as essential to butter sauce as the butter. My Tikka Masala Sauce uses a richer dose of cream and sometimes butter. Here's a baseline recipe without the butter but it can be enriched as you desire (see Tips and Tricks).

Prep Time: 15 minutes | Cook Time: 30 minutes | Makes: enough for 2 curry recipes; about 12 servings

Ingredients
4 tablespoons oil

1 teaspoon cumin seeds

2 onions, chopped

4 cloves garlic, pressed

1 tablespoon crushed fresh ginger

6 medium tomatoes, chopped

1 teaspoon red cayenne pepper powder

1 tablespoon paprika

1½ teaspoons tandoori masala (page 349)

1 tablespoon cumin-coriander powder (see page 353)

½ teaspoon cardamom seeds

2 cloves

1 (2-inch) cinnamon stick

4 tablespoon plain yogurt

3 tablespoons dried fenugreek

2 tablespoons chopped cilantro

1½ cups half and half

Preparation
1. Heat the oil in a pot on medium heat for about 1 minute. Add the cumin seeds and let them sizzle for about 30 seconds. Add the onions and cook on medium-low heat for about 5 minutes, until they begin to soften and turn a pale toffee color.

2. Stir in the garlic and ginger and cook for another minute. Stir in the tomatoes and cook for 6 to 7 minutes, until they soften and begin to release their juices.

3. Stir in the cayenne pepper powder, paprika, tandoori masala, and cumin-coriander powder and continue to cook for 5 more minutes. (The tomatoes should be quite broken down and the oil should seep through the sides of the spices.)

4. Add the cardamom seeds, cloves, and cinnamon stick. Mix well and cook for a couple of minutes. Turn off the heat and cool slightly.

5. Place the tomato mixture in the blender with the yogurt and process until smooth.

6. Pour the mixture back into the cooking pot and mix in the fenugreek and cilantro and simmer for 4 minutes.

7. Gradually stir in the half and half and cook until the mixture is simmering. Simmer for about 7 minutes and then cool and use as needed. This sauce can be stored in the refrigerator for future use as the base for a quick curry.

Tips and Tricks
This sauce can be made richer by adding ⅓ cup of cream. If this sauce is being stored it is best to add the cream when it is being reheated for using in a curry. For a true-tasting butter sauce, stir in a tablespoon of butter to finish. The full spectrum of this sauce can be seen in the recipe for Chicken Tikka in Tomato Cream Sauce on page 235.

Gluten-Free Index

Gluten-Free Index (continued)

Vegan/Vegetarian Index

Vegan

Vegan/Vegetarian Index (continued)

Vegetarian

Recipe Index

Acknowledgements

The process of acknowledgement is a daunting one for me, as I never know where to begin. Do I start with my grandmothers from whom I learned about spices, seasons, and cooking, or should I move to my father, who taught me to dream, or maybe my mother who has always allowed me to make her kitchen mine? To start at the very beginning is never possible, so I will make this a more contained and immediate list.

I want to thank my friends Eric and Helen, who saw this book through its various iterations and rescued it when I almost gave up on it. I want to thank my friend Ken, who accompanied me to so many farmer's markets, even in the height of New York summer and chilly autumn days. I want to thank Chitra and Priti who are always enthusiastic about culinary endeavors. Juliana, my very own photo critic who never forgets to make time for me despite all her life challenges, deserves a very special mention. I thank my brother Khokon for his keen critiques from a non-culinary perspective, as it is always important to think of balance.

I am deeply grateful to Suvir Suran for his support, critique, and help, and of course for graciously taking time to write the foreword for this book. I am grateful to Deborah Madison and Nancie McDermott for taking the time to offer early reviews for the book; to my friend Levana Kirchenbaum for offering review, advice, and support; to Yosef Silver and Stephanie Weaver for their support for this and other projects;

A special thanks to Barbara Gallo Farrel from the *Poughkeepsie Journal* who has been so helpful and supportive of my work, and to my fellow Small Bites blogger Maria Reina, who has been very helpful in making connections with everyone in the local community and farmer's markets. And thanks to Liz Johnson from *Journal News*, who keeps us connected and covered in many delicious ways.

I cannot acknowledge or thank the rest of my family enough. I want to express my gratitude for having them in my life. My cooking skills would not be what they are without my husband Anshul's untiring willingness to try any new creation that I make and his being my built-in source of farm-to-table produce. Produce that I know is organic, sustainable, and local! My children Aadi and Deepta's enthusiasm and excitement about our food and the garden is reward enough for all my time spent cooking for them.

I would like to thank my editor Priti Chitnis Gress for understanding my vision of this book and taking an adventurous step in her willingness to try a new direction with this book, the rest of the Hippocrene team including Colette Laroya for her artistic guidance and production manager Barbara Keane-Pigeon for all the meticulous technical support.

Photo by Aadi Gupta Bhattacharya

About the Author

Rinku Bhattacharya, a native of India, calls Westchester, New York, home. She lives in a small—and somewhat chaotic—home surrounded by a vibrant yard. She is joined in her food capers by her gardener husband, two young children, and a foodie cat. Rinku and her household try to live a sustainable lifestyle. They grow a lot of their produce and source their ingredients locally to connect the bounty of the Hudson Valley with the flavors and traditions of India.

Rinku's practical, sustainable approach to Indian cooking is showcased on her blog, Cooking in Westchester, and her weekly *Lohud* "Spices and Seasons" column. Rinku has also written for the *Journal News*, the *Poughkeepsie Journal*, and other online sites.

Rinku has been teaching recreational home-based cooking classes for the past nine years, instructing students in the essentials of Indian home cooking. She also teaches at local farms, Whole Foods Markets, and other venues on request.

Rinku's debut cookbook, *The Bengali Five Spice Chronicles* (Hippocrene Books, 2012), won the Gourmand Award for the Best Indian Cuisine Cookbook 2013.

Rinku is a financial professional by training and also spends time working with non-profit organizations on financial and infra-structure planning needs.

Also by Rinku Bhattacharya

THE BENGALI FIVE SPICE CHRONICLES

WINNER
OF 2013
GOURMAND AWARD
FOR

BEST INDIAN CUISINE
COOKBOOK IN
USA

ISBN 978-0-7818-1305-1 · $18.95 paperback

"What a seductive book this is, a tantalizing world of flavors waiting to be cooked, tasted, experienced. The recipes alone assure that this will be a well-used and no doubt well-loved book in my kitchen, but the scope of the book is much larger, including a personal and well-told story of Bengali cuisine. I love this book!"

—**Deborah Madison,** author of *Vegetable Literacy* and
The New Vegetarian Cooking for Everyone

"Rinku Bhattacharya has written what could be called the definitive book on Bengali Cooking for the American audience. And, even for those like me who are making a life outside of India and crave the comforting flavors of home."

—**Suvir Saran,** author of *Indian Home Cooking* and
Masala Farm

"Contemporary yet traditional, refined yet candid, exuberant yet sublime, *The Bengali Five Spice Chronicles* is a warm and inviting book of family recipes that convey Rinku Bhattacharya's passion for the flavors and tastes of West Bengal."

—**Ammini Ramachandran,** author of *Grains, Greens,
and Grated Coconuts*

"I am enchanted by the authentic Bengali recipes, sure-fire techniques, and family anecdotes. This is a winning cookbook."

—**Bharti Kirchner,** author of *The Healthy Cuisine of
India* and *Tulip Season*

LIBRARY
NSCC AKERLEY CAMPUS
21 WOODLAWN RD.
DARTMOUTH, NS B2W 2R7 CANADA

Date Due

BRODART, CO. Cat. No. 23-233 Printed in U.S.A.